PARSEGHIAN
AND NOTRE DAME FOOTBALL

PARSEGHIAN
AND NOTRE DAME FOOTBALL

Ara Parseghian
and Tom Pagna

Doubleday and Company, Inc.,
Garden City, New York

ISBN: 0385-06891-3

Doubleday Edition 1973
First Printing, September 1, 1973

First printing, September 1, 1971
Second printing, April 1, 1972

Library of Congress Catalog Card Number: 74-165303

Cover design, art and diagrams by Joseph Schultz.

Photography: South Bend Tribune: pages 75 and 142.
            Jim Hunt: endpapers and pages 11, 20, 21, 29,
            36, 39, 49, 68, 91, 100, 103, 109, 114, 151, 169,
            216, 222, 225, 230, 245, 257, 265, 283,
            288 and 290.
            Notre Dame Sports Information Department:
            jacket and pages 1, 5, 8, 16, 23, 34, 56,
            81, 123, 131, 132, 136, 137, 173, 182, 186,
            190, 194, 198, 201, 206, 209, 214 and 253.

Printed in the United States of America

Dedication

To all those men whose lives, teaching and example
have helped shape my own enthusiasm, ideas and skills.

The dedicated staff of the Akron, Ohio, YMCA
(who helped form my early training habits)
Bill Anderson—grade school coach
Frank "Doc" Wargo—high school coach
Sid Gillman—college coach
George Blackburn—college backfield coach
Paul Brown—professional head coach
Blanton Collier—professional backfield coach
Woody Hayes and John Brickles
(who gave me my first coaching opportunity)
John Reedy, C.S.C.
(for his editorial help)
and finally
to all my staff members and players (past and present)

Contents

Preface

"Why another book on coaching?"

"Does Parseghian think he has that much that is new to tell the coaching fraternity?"

"Is it just a gimmick to produce marginal income?"

Let me deal with that last question first; it's the easiest one to handle.

Considering the amount of time needed by a nonprofessional writer to get his ideas down into a book-length manuscript, he doesn't really need much skill or imagination to dream up a dozen other sources of marginal income which would be far more productive than the slow, painful process of formulating a book for his most critical audience—his fellow coaches.

But the first two questions remain; honesty with my professional peers calls for a candid answer.

First, I have to admit to a selfish motivation. In an activity subject to such pressure and day-to-day crises as are involved in coaching, there is a tendency to leap from a time of intense pressure and preoccupation with *this* team, *this* season, *this* game . . . to a time of complete withdrawal from the concerns of the job—the time needed to catch up with your family, to make sure that you retain some sort of balance in your life, to recharge your personal power plant for the demands that will be made on it as you begin to rebuild for the next season.

Neither of these states of mind makes allowance for the more leisurely reflection on the long-range patterns of your work. Neither is conducive to the "perspective-building" that enables you to see where you have been, what influences have made you the kind of coach you are, what directions are shaping your future in coaching.

I happen to think that this type of reflection and perspective-building is valuable for us as persons and as coaches. Only in this way are we likely to spot serious flaws in the broad patterns of our performance; only in this way are we likely to build on the strong points of our personal skills and characteristics. And, most important, only in this way are we likely to manage the difficult personal challenge of intelligently relating our professional lives to the general values and patterns of our total lives.

This kind of reflection is best achieved through the orderly process of thinking out comprehensive viewpoints—on paper.

So, in a real sense, this book represents part of a personal process of perspective-gaining for me.

That's not a bad reason for writing a book. In itself, though, it would be an insufficient reason for inflicting it on others, for publishing it.

This brings me to the real reason for offering my perspectives to you, the men who share the problems and satisfactions of coaching with me.

It's *not* that there is a great deal in this book that is completely new. If you're interested enough to pick this up, you know our field well enough to recognize that genuinely new approaches do not emerge as completely new systems. (If a complete system were that original, it's not likely that its originator would publish it until he had exhausted the full value from its originality.)

But we all know how football knowledge and understanding grow.

From the time each of us started playing under a serious coach, we were taught basics . . . and many of those basics (polished, refined, adapted) are still the solid foundation of our appreciation of football.

But the process goes on, with all of us. A high school varsity coach develops and sharpens those clumsy skills which we took from our freshman coach. Our college coaches further sharpen precision, timing, understanding of systems and patterns, appreciation of game strategy in differing situations.

For those who go into pro ball, the work on refining, specializing, maintaining consistency of performance continues . . . but building on that knowledge which started with the first coach and accumulated with the instruction, drills and perceptions of each of the other men who worked with us.

The same thing happens as we begin our own coaching patterns. We take what we have learned, try to pass it on to our players, but all the while learning a bit more about techniques, skills, strategy, pedagogy from each of the coaches with whom we work.

Also, from each of the coaches who speak to us in coaching clinics or in the never-ending bull sessions wherever coaches gather. "How do you beat this pass coverage?" "How do you handle a stunting defense?" "What was behind your decision to depart from your basic defense in such a key game?"

From these clinics and bull sessions and collaboration with coaching staffs we don't learn whole new systems. We pick up an insight here, an adaptation there, an improved drill technique from someone else.

But this is the way we learn to stay on top of football thinking, in bits and pieces and suggestions for our own creative imaginations. That's why we keep going to clinics, giving and receiving; that's why we keep talking football endlessly with everyone whose experience and approach might contribute a single new element to our coaching effectiveness.

That's why we keep reading everything that appears by anyone who is living and working with football.

And that's one of the reasons why we write still more books about football.

If this volume leaves each of its coaching readers with just one idea, just one technique, just one insight into strategy—it will be well worth the reader's investment in the price of the book . . . and, far more important, worth the investment of his time.

We all know this is true, even though we might not formulate our study just this way.

But I have still one more reason for writing this book.

We need to communicate with one another in any way we can, because coaching is a lonely, insecure, unappreciated work.

Lonely? We live in crowds. Part of our problem is to try to find ways of extricating ourselves from the time and energy-draining crowds which surround us during the season.

Unappreciated? When we're on, the responses from the crowds and the press give us an appreciation which is enjoyed by few other occupations.

Those responses might satisfy the questions of the reporters who have to do the preseason profiles . . . but they don't represent the reality which all of us experience, whether we are coaching high school, college or pro teams.

We know that those crowds in the stands, even the most knowledgeable fans, are miles away from what we are experiencing as we tense up before each game. We know that the sportswriters who have been covering the game for years, who recognize and report performance accurately, have no real understanding of what is going on inside us as we agonize—aching to transmit our determination into the bodies of our players—to stop a play that is opening our line, that is cutting us to pieces as the minutes drain from the game.

We know that our close friends, who will rejoice or mourn with us in the postgame get-togethers, don't really understand what it's like to spend a few extra minutes in a subdued dressing room after the reporters, the well-wishers and even the players have gone . . . the physical and emotional exhaustion, the "feel" of exultation at having gotten by one that you were afraid of—or the gut-clenching frustration in realizing that you can never, never replay one that you lost.

We know that even our families, our wives, don't *really* appreciate what makes us do it. We try to put it into words but, when we do, it comes out sounding illogical for anybody to stay in such a line of work.

We know the unreasonable expectations of fans, of alumni, of the administrations that hire us. Even when they are good, sensible men, they are caught up in a system which imposes unreasonable demands, which operates on a fickleness that leaves even those coaches with the most successful records subject to secret fears of insecurity. The man might know his job, he might give it all he has—and then be wiped out by a few seasons of bad luck, of injuries to the wrong men, at the wrong time, in the wrong games. We've seen it happen to coaches whose ability we respect. All of us live with that deep-buried fear that it could happen to us.

When we try to talk about why we stay with it, why we go through all the work, worry and stress for the sake of ten or 11 afternoons a year, we can't really explain our lifetime fascination with explosive, hard-hitting physical contact . . . with the contagion of fierce competition, with the addiction to recognition and acclaim when we know that our performance has been good.

Even here, when I try to put this into words, it comes out sounding like a high school sophomore who has found his name in the newspaper write-up for the first time.

But no matter how sophisticated and experienced we are, when we are honest with one another, most of us will admit that some part of that high school sophomore is still inside us. It's not just the name in the newspaper; it's the total experience of being down there on the field—either playing or directing the game—with the crowd contributing to the noise and excitement, but not really being part of IT!

We are! Just the few of us!

I imagine that all truly competitive performers experience the thrill and the isolation of this loneliness—the boxer, the race driver, the track man, probably even the mountain climber.

You don't explain this . . . but from time to time you need to communicate with the few others who share the experience.

And you also need to communicate with those who know all the related dimensions of coaching, from the occasional practices which we all know to be cheap, sordid, degrading to players and coaches alike . . . to the real, almost embarrassing thrill of working with a boy whose fine personal characteristics are combined with extraordinary physical skill (a satisfaction that comes close to that experienced at times by a true teacher . . . or by a father).

Together we know the temptations to use success with a team as a launching pad to jump off into other, more secure careers . . . or to use it for that "marginal income" which is *just* a *little* beyond what is really right and decent. We know the embarrassment of offering sympathy to comrades who are trapped in the maze of mediocre teams, unsuccessful seasons, negative response to recruiting, cruel, biting criticism which tears at them, not only personally, but also through their players, their families.

What I'm really saying, I suppose, is that those of us who really know the experience of coaching simply have to communicate with one another—just because there are so few of us.

XIV

When we talk the game, strategy, drills, personnel, we do look for the new idea, the new insight; but we are also looking for the presence and companionship of others, who do know what it is like.

What I have to offer here is simply an organized, formulated, modified system which I have taken from all the coaches who have trained me, who have worked over me, who have worked with me on my staffs.

There are a few approaches which I think we have developed as our own contribution to today's game . . . at least contributions in emphasis.

While all of us read all the books written on the game, we also know that the knowledge is only one element of success. That knowledge must be channeled through personal traits of determination, ability to work with and inspire people, ability to delegate authority, ability to adapt systems to people, ability to invest immense personal commitment, while stopping short of a soul-destroying fanaticism.

Those personal qualities no one can transmit. We can only understand, appreciate, commiserate.

But knowledge of techniques can be exchanged. I do so with a genuine gratitude for what I have received from others, with a genuine desire to be of any help I can to those of you who are reading these pages.

Ara Parseghian

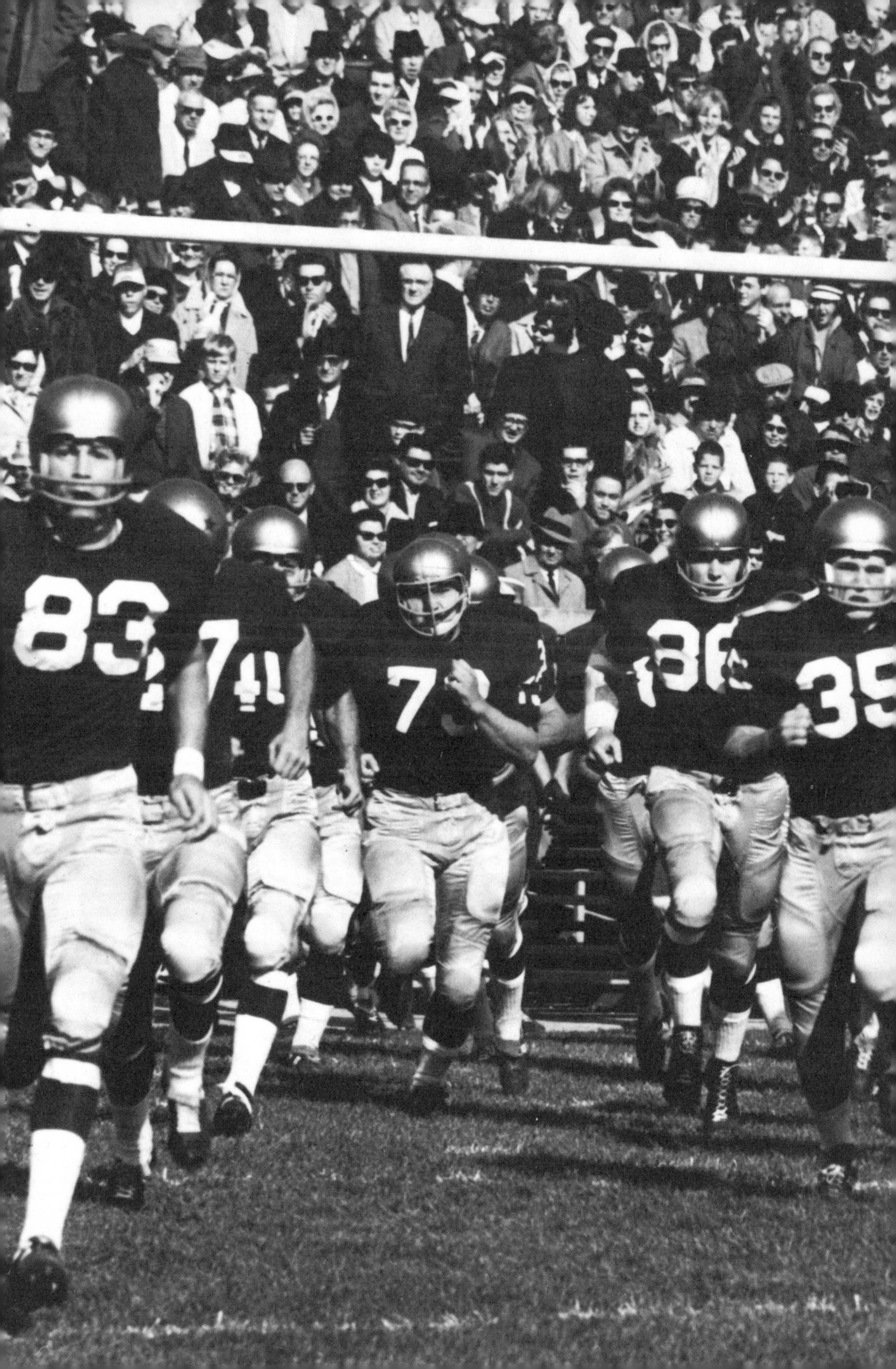

1 Organization and General Philosophy

Staff Selection
Philosophy
  a) Morale
  b) Conditioning—mental, physical, spiritual
  c) Strategy
Theories of Learning
Terminology and Communication
Base Formations and Recognition
Practice Organization
Weekly Schedule
Theory Behind the Practice
Personnel Selection
  a) Defensive Backs
  b) Defensive Linebackers
  c) Down Defensive Linemen
  d) Offensive Linemen
  e) Backs and Receivers
  f) Quarterbacks
The Player's Notebook
Equipment
Trainers
Grades
Films and Officials
Statistical Charts

Organization and General Philosophy

The game of football is essentially a dynamic enterprise, and a very sophisticated one. Progress in the game occurs as a process of evolution. This evolution is usually the product of experience, of trial and error, and of a coaching staff's creativity and great desire to learn and gain command of broader concepts and theories.

There are a number of reasons why this evolutionary process occurs in the game of football and thus gives rise over a period of years to greater sophistication. One obvious reason is the fact that offensive football evolves in response to more sophisticated defensive football, and vice versa.

New offenses or defenses also evolve simply for experimentation purposes. A staff, for example, might add a new offensive dimension or a new defensive look to enable the players to cope with it should they ever be confronted with such an offense or defense during a game.

Related to the evolution of football are the nature and quality of the coaching staff. No man can do the job of coaching a college football team without the invaluable aid of truly dedicated and knowledgeable assistants.

Staff

"Success is certain if loyalty fails not." If a football staff member is loyal he can learn strategy. Age is not so much a barrier, nor is lack of knowledge, but if a staff member is not loyal, he will have no dedication. Loyalty will in itself foster industry, effort, energy and, ultimately, success. Having assembled a staff of knowledgeable assistants who are, above all, loyal, the next item to be concerned about is the philosophy which should permeate that staff and all its endeavors.

Philosophy

In the order of their importance to our staff at Notre Dame, we discuss philosophy in terms of the following: 1) morale, 2) conditioning, and 3) strategy. Here I will briefly develop my thoughts

The Notre Dame Coaching Staff. First row (left to right) Bill Hickey, Tom Pagna, head coach Ara Parseghian, Paul Shoults, Joe Yonto, Wally Moore. Back row (left to right) Mike Stock, John Murphy, Denny Murphy, Brian Boulac, George Kelly and Larry Ballinger.

on each of these three critical components of a philosophy.

1. Morale

It is an accepted fact in football that if two teams are of equal ability in all phases of the game, the team which is characterized by the highest morale will win more often than not. High morale is a state of mind which is rooted in harmony and pride. Great teams develop it for many reasons and in spite of many obstacles. A coach cannot impose morale, but a coach can certainly create and control an atmosphere in which high morale might flourish. Certainly the personality of a team is directly linked to its morale, or to use another word, to its "pride."

To establish the proper atmosphere in which pride develops we try very hard to know our players as men. The effort is sincere and our interaction with them is not in the least formal. We do not sacrifice respect, however, for there is a distinct line which separates teacher from student. If you have a command of what you are teaching, if it is sound, well-planned and current, respect is a normal reaction from any good student. Of critical importance, in creating this atmosphere within which morale or pride, flourishes, are fairness and objectivity in evaluating a player. For football as a competitive sport forces the player into a situation where he is constantly evaluated and compared with others on the same objective plane.

5

Our players know that at least once a day, for no less than an hour's time, we on the staff have discussed each man on our squad. His attitude, physical condition, technique, size, speed, agility, and desire have all been assessed and perhaps sometimes severely criticized in an open atmosphere of discussion. In such evaluations we have one thought in mind: Where can this young man be of greatest help to our team? The young man knows this. He also knows that an evaluation on a particular day is not permanent, it can be changed the next day. Performance counts, and players are not static performers. Improvements are made, injuries force changes, and no one is ever excluded from making a major contribution to the team. The players have faith in the decisions of the staff in exactly the measure of their loyalty. The success of such evaluations depends, of course, upon the competence of the staff which is the foundation of the player's faith and loyalty.

2. Conditioning

There is a phrase coined by one of my assistants which accurately describes the task of coaching: The coach is "a benevolent dictator." Perhaps nowhere else, except in one's own family, is there room for a friendly tyrant. Within the family which is a football team, the player absorbs the knowledge that certain things must be done to achieve success. His faith in the head coach, and all the coaches, assures him that he will not be abused or misused, but he knows he most certainly will be taxed and disciplined, sometimes to the point where he begins to wonder whether it is all worth the effort. Somewhere in his questioning he answers "yes" and he yields to this benevolent dictator, the coach. In so doing he accepts our philosophy that nothing drains one's resources, will to win, energy, dedication, loyalty and morale more than poor conditioning. Further, the player learns that there are three phases of conditioning: mental, physical and spiritual.

Mental conditioning: To be mentally conditioned is to be mentally tough, contact-oriented, with a zeal for the ideal of achieving success. The player knows that there will be minor bumps and bruises which he must "shake off." He knows this is part of the game. Naturally a major injury must be given serious attention; but a young man's ability to recover from minor bumps and injuries is often a reflection of his attitude, desire, and mental toughness.

Physical conditioning: To be conditioned physically to play the game of football is to prepare one's body far in excess of what is actually demanded during a game day. It's like designing a car. Everyone knows that an automobile will operate much more effectively at a speed of 70 miles an hour if it has been designed to achieve 120 miles an hour. The game of football is rugged. It is stance, start, running—running to block, running to tackle, running to score. To do these things well, one must do them often so that they become conditioned reflexes executed smoothly and with minimum effort. Therefore, our practices are geared to running, agility, balance, stance, start and quickness; and these repeated over and over and over again.

"You become what you do." This is the essential underlying principle which dictates the program for physical conditioning of a football team.

The staff, myself, and ultimately the players must, each for himself, decide precisely what he wishes our team to become—champs, second-raters or chumps.

Spiritual conditioning: Spiritual conditioning involves the development of those intangibles which basically cause a young man to want to play football. Though there are many reasons why a youngster may decide to play the game, sooner or later it begins to dawn on him that this competitive sport of "gridiron dominoes" is a means of expressing himself, an opportunity to achieve recognition and success. He sees that the game involves some great lessons for life, lessons concerning values which have become nebulous for many people today. In essence, the young man achieves spiritual conditioning when he comes to the realization that nothing worthwhile can ever be obtained without sacrifice.

He voluntarily submits himself to the harsh judgment of critics. He experiences failure and finds the alternative to quitting: to return with rededication, "to bounce back." He accepts imposed rules in his discipline and in his game conduct, coming to realize that all of life imposes its rules on people who wish to live it well.

Gradually, the successful player discovers value and virtue in work and sweat; he comes to appreciate a special kind of camaraderie which grows out of shared pain and sacrifice, wins and losses, strategies and sorrows. Whether he manages to scramble up the slippery pole to stardom or finds his anonymous satisfaction only in the success of his team, he learns that acceptance of conditions and rules outside himself—and an all-out effort from

7

Pat O'Brien at a fabled Notre Dame Pep Rally renders a stirring portrayal of "Rockne." Spirit and desire to win are intangible qualities that Notre Dame teams regard highly as can be noted by the sea of players' faces in the background.

himself—are the ingredients for his development as a man of worth.

Spiritual conditioning also cannot be imposed, still a coaching staff must work to create a favorable atmosphere. Basic to such an atmosphere is the coach's understanding that all the young men on a team are people first and players second. When I recall all the men who have played for me during my two decades of coaching— every one of whom has been hurt, bled a little and accepted sacrifice—I am reminded that without their sacrifice I could never have achieved any degree of success. This reminder has caused me to feel a reciprocal respect and gratitude.

In my judgment, a coach should feel an obligation to be concerned with the whole person. Our staff, for example, worries about the players' academic life; we are quick to aid them when possible after graduation, and we are proud when they emerge as mature men of keen intellect, full of devotion and courage.

Proper spiritual conditioning, then, is realized or achieved 1) when the coaches and the players reach a state of mutual respect, 2) when they come to the realization that sacrifice is necessary in order to achieve success, and 3) when both coaches and players realize that this sacrifice involves a submission of self to the team.

This spiritual conditioning, unlike physical or mental conditioning, does not deteriorate once it is acquired. When a boy becomes a man, the fiber and sinew and muscle may change, but the gray matter and the inner, deeper commitments involved in spiritual conditioning remain. These three components of conditioning are so closely allied and interrelated that you cannot really deal with them separately. So, if the staff and the head coach establish an atmosphere of high morale, a growth toward this triple conditioning usually follows naturally.

3. Strategy

There are few things more humiliating to a football coach than a realization that he has been outcoached. Not outmanned, not outconditioned, not outhustled or outplayed, but outcoached. This realization requires a considerable sense of humility on his part, but it also can teach him a tremendously valuable lesson in the importance of strategy. When you admit that you have been outcoached you are admitting that your strategy was inferior or that it lacked the range to anticipate all the situations that arose in the particular football game.

To be outcoached is to be incompetent in your profession. You have not remained on top of the changing strategic attacks and defenses. Failures in coaching have many reasons and all of them are painful enough when they lead to a loss. But for a coach to be beaten in his strategy is the most embarrassing loss of all.

Because we realize this, my staff and I work long, long hours to learn— in depth—every aspect of the game of football. Realizing that knowledge knows no owner, we take advantage of every opportunity to gain—and to give —new information at coaches' clinics where both young and older coaches appear, where discussions take place, where exchanges of concepts, tactics, theories and procedures are discussed in open forum. For today, with advanced film and television coverage, no secret lasts beyond its first use. My staff and I try to gain a profound knowledge of strategy, systems, techniques, theory, philosophy and so on. We weigh all sources of information, sorting out what is new and valuable in whatever information comes to our attention. We talk football with others in the profession. We attend clinics, both as teachers and as students. We exchange films. Time permitting, we travel to other schools to view their spring practices. And we reciprocate by inviting others to visit our spring training.

The essential point is that the exchange of ideas, the flow of new currents and trends, must be assimilated if a coach and a team are not to become stagnant or stereotyped.

To avoid stagnation in our general thinking, at our meetings we even encourage (as time permits) the discussion of a wide variety of topics totally unrelated to football.

Having committed ourselves to a command of every aspect of the game, we then face the essential task of conveying to the players our *system*, our *style*, and our *terminology* in an organized fashion. This work of communication is the basic task of the coaching staff. All the study and research were preparation for this. For in a very special way the coach is primarily a teacher, and he must, therefore, use all the aids which any teacher might employ to convey the lesson. Naturally, we make use of visual aids, diagrams, personal notebooks, demonstration films and discussion. But the great principle in coaching, we believe, is to let the player do it himself, as often as is possible. Repetition fosters improvement, as long as the technique is repeated properly, over and over and over again. As we consider ourselves teachers it follows, of course, that we view our players as students, that is, learners.

Theories of Learning

There are two broad theories of learning. In one, the teacher gradually builds up a total picture by teaching the parts of the whole, one at a time. In the other "broad-based" theory, the teacher presents the larger picture first and then fills in the details. While I have witnessed both approaches used in football, I am convinced that the better is that of working from the broadest possible base. Consequently, we literally overwhelm our players with terms, techniques, formations, plays and theories of the broadest possible range.

Thus they are exposed to a broad concept of football and are required to fight their way through a maze, but in the end they better understand the total picture. Eventually, they will even master the specific details as well as the students who started with the details, that is, the part-of-the-whole system. Again, it is our conviction that we must teach far more football strategy than is likely to be required. A study of these two approaches over the years has persuaded me that when a player is exposed from the very beginning to the widest possible base: 1) he can adjust to changes much more easily, 2) he is rarely overcome by the unexpected situation because he has

Our staff meetings give us a chance to discuss and align personnel, set up our practice plans and freely exchange ideas on current trends in football.

been exposed to so many "looks," 3) he probably gains a greater understanding of the system.

The teaching of football from the broadest possible base allows us, the coaches, to be much more versatile in our planning for a particular game; also it causes our opponent greater concern as he must prepare, in a short time, to defend or attack the many looks we have mastered.

Another point recommending the broad-based teaching approach is that, through their exposure to many styles of football, our players begin to teach us. Sooner or later it becomes clear that certain players are geared to certain phases of the game and, within that game, to certain styles. This point, that a particular combination of players dictates the style of offense and defense—through their own strengths and weaknesses—is perhaps the most important factor in a coach's style and strategy.

11

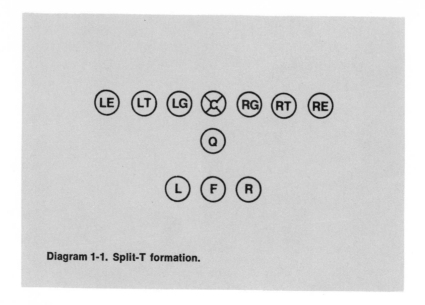

Diagram 1-1. Split-T formation.

Terminology

Building a successful means of communication is a good place to begin your teaching.

Generally we use words instead of numbers. Numbers will serve and many a good system employs them, but words seem to convey or flash a picture more effectively. We reserve numbers for our cadence and blocking patterns so that when a number is spoken in the huddle, it means only a hole to attack or a pattern of blocking for that hole.

This particular system which we use is an outgrowth of the days when football appeared to be a much more symmetrical game; that is, when plays and formations were more balanced and usually an attack was "mirrored" from one side to the other.

As the improvement of defenses and attacks changed, so did the concept of "mirror."

Not as long ago as the day of the single wing, but from the time of the great Oklahoma split-T teams of the early 50's, it was not uncommon to set in a regular full-house formation (see diagram 1-1).

The college game involved more running than the pro play and used two tight ends with a full contingent of backs for greater force, blocking surface and deceptive combinations.

This pattern wasn't new at the time, but in football as in fashions, ideas and approaches become popular, too popular—then decline. As this particular set became fashionable, defensive adjustments centered around it.

Offensively, coaches were reluctant to put men in motion, split ends, or flank their backs, because these moves caused a distortion of their balancing or mirror systems. It is from this style of football that our staff developed our

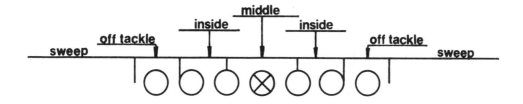

Diagram 1-2. Notre Dame's four areas of rushing attack.

alternative to the numbering system. No longer did we feel that there must be a complete series of plays to hit every hole, with each back being numbered and directed to a hole. "Remember old number 36?" The three back through the six hole.

If you split an end, the six hole expands into a gap. If you motion or flank a back you seem shy a blocker. We evolved a system of terms describing the holes first.

Since you can only run four areas either to the left or right we named them: (1) sweep, (2) off tackle, (3) inside, (4) middle. We taught our players the dimensions of the visual area (see diagram 1-2).

In this way, we reserved numbers and used them to identify our offensive lineman. Actually it is a *dual* system of identification, valuable because words are more effective in conveying instant images, but they are not as practical for cadence. We wanted to be able to identify the area of the right

guard, tackle, end, etc. And we also wanted to use numbers to direct a pattern of blocking (see diagram 1-3).

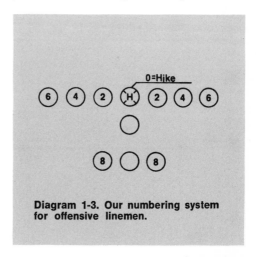

Diagram 1-3. Our numbering system for offensive linemen.

You can bark out the numbers 2, 4, 6, 8 (we substituted the word "hike" for zero). Thus, we needed to convey only (a) which direction, right or left, and (b) whether the number called designated an area of attack or a numbered blocking call.

13

Formation Recognition
(Diagram 1-4)

Offensive View	Defensive View
"Pro" or Strong Rt. — Weak Lt.	Also called Weak Side to SE
"Con" or Weak Rt. — Strong Lt.	Also called Strong Side to TE
"Flank"	
"Wing"	
"East"	
"West"	

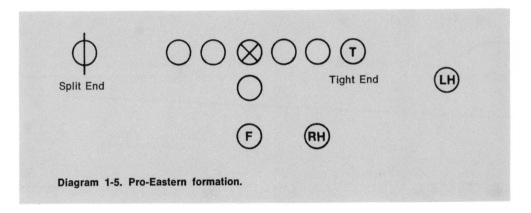

Diagram 1-5. Pro-Eastern formation.

With this as a start, we moved backs up and out, we split ends, we employed motion and developed many "looks," with multiple formations. Though it is true that a game plan can be condensed to just a few formations, greater flexibility allows your defense to be exposed to many looks.

Each formation has a name to the right and a counter name to the left. Examples of the more common formations are shown in diagrams 1-4 and they are identified as each appears in our offense. Our defense, however, while using the same term for each formation, learns to identify it as it faces them.

Words such as "flank" and "wing" or "east" and "west" are simply enlarged to imply a wider alignment. They are called "flanker" or "winger," "eastern" and "western."

When the combination of two formations merges we utilize two words such as: pro-eastern (see diagram 1-5).

This scheme—formations by words; areas or holes by numbers and name—makes play calling clear and efficient.

In the huddle the proper order for a call would be:

(1) Formation
(2) Action
(3) Area or number
(4) Direction
(5) Cadence or Blocking Call

The spoken word would emerge similar to this:

"Flank"—(Formation)
"Belly"—(Action)
"Off tackle"—number (Hole)
"Left"—(Direction)
"Second Sound"—(Cadence)
"Ready . . . Break"

Later this pattern was modified to designate the formation as point of attack at the end of the call.

15

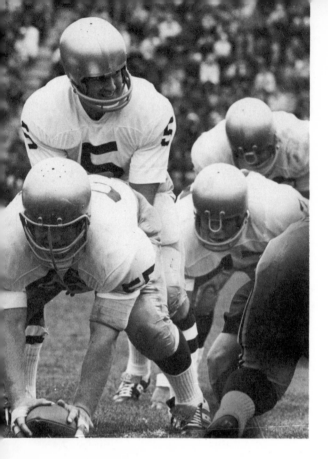

Terry Hanratty with an I backfield looks right and then left before going on with the cadence. He appears to like what he sees.

Cadence

There is no single way to do anything in football; any way that gets the job done can be used. However, we are convinced that the quarterback can best ignite a full team response through a nonrhythm cadence.

The words in our cadence are the commands "Hike," "Two," "Four," "Six," "Eight," etc. These words are sounds also . . . and we leave on sound. The sound comes at the discretion of the quarterback so that no defensive lineman or linebacker can time up a blitz or rush. We coach the quarterback to pause if a linebacker is hedging forward and wait until he settles back. At that precise moment, when he moves back, ignite!

The cadence also involves the much-discussed audible system. Basically there are four types of automatics. These modify a play to:

(1) Change it from one area to another.

(2) Change it from one side to another.

(3) Change it from pass to run or from run to pass.

(4) Direct the most advantageous blocking pattern to the area called.

Within the cadence there must be the flexibility to do all of these. I will discuss this question in the chapter on offense.

16

Practice Organization

In coaching, I can't overemphasize the absolute importance of a well-organized practice session. Each practice day has its own specific goals, as does each week and each season.

In our staff meetings we discuss thoroughly all that will be done on the practice field that particular day. Because the rules now permit platooning, we must plan two parallel practice sessions every day. Our practices progress from individual work to group work to full-team performance and lastly full-team versus full-team.

Daily objectives can best be stated in terms of time. Not all practice sessions are of equal duration; therefore, we lengthen or shorten periods of work according to time available.

Since practice needs constantly change, we never lay out a detailed plan for longer than a day in advance, though the format or routine of practice does remain fairly constant.

In our normal practice sessions we try to include the following: 1. Warm-up and stretch, 2. Sprints and agility drills, 3. Breakdown drills, 4. Kicking game. These four activities are covered in our first 30 minutes of practice. The remainder of the session is divided into blocks of time according to our needs.

Offense	Defense
Run offense	Run defense
Pass offense	Pass defense
Combined full-team	Combined full-team
Goal line and specials	Goal line and specials

A typical breakdown of this daily schedule for a week would be:

Monday: varsity, 45 minutes; remainder of the team, one hour and 45 minutes.

Tuesday: entire team, one hour and 45 minutes.

Wednesday: entire team, one hour and 45 minutes.

Thursday: entire team, one hour and 30 minutes.

Friday: entire team, 45 minutes.

Saturday: game.

Sunday: break a sweat—run a mile.

Theory Underlying Practice Session

Several years ago as offenses became more complicated it became clear that defense had to put greater emphasis on pursuit. That is, the defensive men have to be able to spot the ball carrier as he emerges from the pattern of the play and then pursue him at top speed and proper angle. The defensive player

17

has to explode all his energies in the time between the snap of the ball and the whistle when the ball carrier is tackled. Recognizing this, we decided it would be worthwhile to make a careful study of the actual time of play, the time during which the player must put out his peak effort during a 60-minute football game.

I had our staff run time studies on the average length of a play. We found that normally the shortest play was the straight dive stopped for no gain. It averaged about two seconds. One of the longest plays was a 90-yard kickoff return. We found that the average play, whether defensive pursuit or offensive blocking, took roughly 3.5 seconds. Since we averaged about 80 plays on offense and about the same number on defense (not taking into account time in the huddle and coming up to the line) the total *action* time for an offensive team during a game was found to be about five minutes. This was true also for the defense. We referred to this action time as "the great interval." Thus in a 60-minute football game the actual time during which a football player would be required to put out maximum effort was perhaps five minutes, with each play being roughly 3.5 seconds. So we drilled on this idea and taught that only this period of action—"the great interval"—really counts. This was the time in which "you become what you do." We pounded "the great interval" idea, with a plea to our players to give us on each play three things: 1) effort, 2) execution, 3) endurance.

This concept of the period of maximum effort was incorporated into all of our drills. It is only five minutes, but it has to be spread out over the precise moments of game action. The critical time starts with the snap of the ball and ends with the whistle . . . time spent running onto the field, breaking from the huddle or waving to parents means little or nothing as far as the game is concerned.

While many teams use this idea, it was a realization which evolved within our own group and was not simply picked up from another source. This in itself is unimportant; I mention it only as an example of a coaching point that is invaluable. Large concepts often grow from small ideas.

Therefore, everything in our practices is done with the idea of maximum effort in the minimum time. That is, after all, the way you want to play the game itself. Our drill periods are relatively short, and we rarely use a drill that does not correspond exactly to an action the player will face in the game.

Some years ago one of my younger coaching assistants complained that his drill periods for blocking and technique were simply not long enough and that he needed more time. Several years later that same coach claimed he is the greatest advocate of the simple principle: It is not today's work that finishes the product; it is all of the days' work, repeated over and over and over again.

Thus, our field practice means movement, harassment, running and so on. The boys play under pressure. They must learn to work under pressure. We coach on the move. Except during the first few days, I will not tolerate a mass lecture on the field. A coach will take a boy aside and briefly mention a point to him, but during this time the player will learn more from going through the actions physically than he will by being lectured to. We talk to the boys in the office or in the locker room before or after practice. It is our conviction that our short practice period of one hour and 45 minutes must be completely devoted to doing the job physically. This is our theory of drill interval and practice time.

Under these conditions, single words and phrases become symbols packed with meaning and emotion; they ignite the idea. When we yell "interval" to a boy, the word triggers all the effort described in the previous paragraphs.

Personnel Selection

The recruiting of young college athletes is a subject which deserves a separate book. At best, it is a difficult task that gets ever more involved and sophisticated. And it is one of the least satisfying elements of coaching—when you consider the time invested. Still, coaches work very hard at the task of recruiting because they know it is a necessary lifeline for the future years of any university athletic program.

However, the personnel selection, which I describe here, has to do with personnel allocation within your existing squad.

We work on the premise that "luck follows speed." Therefore, we believe that our defensive unit should be given first choice of the personnel to make sure we will have the fastest defensive team. Consequently, most of our great speed is found in the defensive secondary. This is our area of greatest concern. For it is here that one mistake—or a slight lack of speed—can be most costly. In selecting personnel, therefore, we concentrate on the precise physical and mental demands of the particular position.

Defensive Backs

Speed and a real enthusiasm (a "nose") for contact and tackling are the

19

Linebacker Eric Patton relays defensive signals to his teammates as "Irish" defense prepares for opponent's next play. Spirit, unit pride and a willingness to work together characterize great defensive teams.

requirements of the position. Defensive backs must be tough, agile, proud— able to give complete coverage to a man one on one and to think on the move as they defend a zone. They must be quick of mind and foot. Height is not always a major requirement for backs; very tall men are usually long striders and they may have trouble with a change of direction.

Defensive backs must possess good hands because many times they have to catch "against the ball"—with the force of the throw doubled by their own direction and momentum. Professional coaches have told me that good defensive backs are a rarity even among their personnel. This is certainly true in college football.

Defensive Linebackers

In today's diversified game, the linebacker must have range, speed, size and a love of contact. His position calls for the player to be part lineman and part back; strong enough to ward off the biggest offensive lineman and agile enough to be able to cover quick men on pass plays. Obviously, the more size the linebacker possesses the better he will be able to cope with the lineman, but that size might cost some speed in the pass coverage. For this reason, most of our linebackers are not really big men when measured against the average lineman.

Defensive Linemen

Defensive linemen are usually our biggest men. They are required to squeeze all outside plays in and to stop the progress of inside plays. They must be able to withstand double teaming,

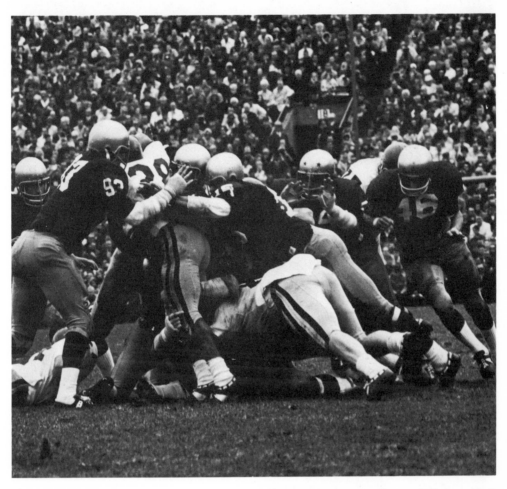

Quick defensive reaction and team pursuit snuff out opponent's attempt for first down. Continuous effort of this kind leads to victory.

to read blockers, to shed people, to fight off trap plays, to read draws and screens. At the same time, they must be fiercely aggressive as pass rushers.

When you select people to play a position, you must keep an open mind and sometimes the image you would like to have will be replaced by the young man who just can't be topped for performance. I'm reminded of the age-old saying in football: "a big man must prove that he cannot play and a little one must prove that he can." Fortunately, for smaller players, this is proven all over the country many times each year.

When the defensive unit finally jells, you should have a group of men who begin to work together, and their work should show the spirit, unit pride, and the wild exhilarating enthusiasm that characterize great defensive teams.

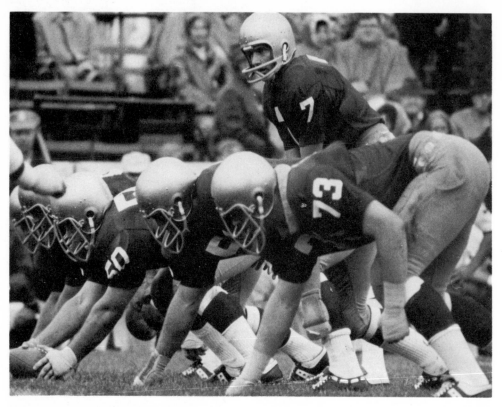

The center projects the ball to insure a maximum neutral zone and the offensive line of Notre Dame awaits ignition through their quarterback's cadence.

Offensive Personnel

Linemen

With the exception of defensive secondary play, offensive blocking is probably the most difficult art to master. Of itself, blocking is unnatural for a really aggressive athlete, because he is not permitted to use his hands on offense. Blocking is uncoil and leverage with quickness for a follow-up. It involves strength, techniques, timing and a great amount of practice. Rarely does a really fine sophomore appear in the offensive line; it usually requires a year of experience and training before a boy can win a starting position as an offensive lineman.

Backs and Receivers

While we have no intention of underrating other positions, we refer to backs and receivers as the "skilled" positions. With backs and receivers we may overlook some blocking inadequacies or size handicap—if they have skills which can be exploited in the backfield or in receiving. If his speed makes a man equally effective at offense and defense, we must then make a judgment as to where he can be of most value to the team.

Joe Theismann executes the proper follow-through after handing off to halfback Denny Allan. Notice that Theismann's eyes are still focused on the handoff area.

Quarterbacks

The quarterback spot is, of course, the key position in your offensive attack. In today's game the quarterback must be first, last and always an athlete. His leadership ability, voice, poise, size, confidence, must be above average. His spirit of competition, loyalty and his dedication to the study and understanding of the game are obvious requirements. But again, first and foremost, he must possess the gifts of an athlete in his coordination, dexterity of foot and hand, and in his general quickness. If your quarterback does not possess these qualities of the natural athlete, yours is likely to be a very long and sad season.

Since modern football is almost equally balanced between the pass and the run, your quarterback must have both these abilities. Coaching such a boy is really a matter of refining his own talents and responses. The better the original "athletic gifts," the better and more refined will be your team leader, the quarterback.

A Point of Reference

It would be difficult indeed to list all of the plans, additions, deletions and changes that actually take place in the team strategy of a season. However, we insist that our players maintain their own base of reference—their own personal notebooks.

Throughout my coaching career I have always believed in the value of a written document as a source for a player to depend upon. The notebook is his record of just about everything he will have to know and do. Naturally, the player builds upon and refines his knowledge of previous years—we trust each year's record will be an improvement on the past. Every boy is entitled to keep all of his four notebooks when he finishes his senior season.

The notebook contains just about every aspect of football my staff and I can organize. It is a private publication, sometimes more interesting and more valuable than a best-selling novel. A typical table of contents is shown on the following page.

TABLE OF CONTENTS

Other Items of Importance

Purchase of Equipment

In the purchasing of equipment we are guided by two principles: 1. Is it the best protective equipment available? 2. Is it the lightest of the most protective equipment?

Each boy uses a pair of practice shoes, with another pair reserved for the games. We use the same helmet for games as for practice sessions. Our pads are annually replenished for the first 33 players of our squad.

The Trainer

The trainer is a very, very important man in our organization. He is essentially responsible for the prevention, evaluation and treatment of all injuries. His training-room manner, cleanliness, organization and rapport show up clearly in the squad's morale.

In addition to the many other areas for which the trainer is responsible, we ask him to maintain the daily weight chart and to insist upon a visible daily record of weigh-ins and weigh-outs.

Academic Grades

At no other time in a young man's career will he ever be so tightly scheduled for time as he is in college

during the fall season when school is in session.

Whether one of your staff members or an interested faculty member monitors your players' academic progress, someone must be on top of the situation at all times. He must be quick to recognize any sign of a player's academic difficulty. We intend that every player we accept at Notre Dame will graduate with a *bona fide* degree in a legitimate discipline. This is our goal and anything less than that goal would be a violation of a player's good faith.

Films and Officials

Funds permitting, we like to get, as early as possible in the season, a film of our squad in action during a scrimmage period. Such films are great teaching aids and an invaluable source of information as we rate the capabilities of our squad. Whenever we do film a scrimmage, we use experienced officials. We try very hard to coach against penalties. Keeping these losses at a minimum is achieved by coaching attention and by exacting game officials when game situations are simulated in scrimmage.

Statistical Charts

One of the last items which we prepare prior to the arrival of our players

25

NOTRE DAME 1965 DEFENSE

Total points allowed	73
Touchdowns allowed	11
Touchdowns passing	8
Touchdowns rushing	2
Field goals allowed	1
Yards rushing allowed	754
Yards passing allowed	1190
Passes completed against ND	106
Passes ND intercepted	18
Fumbles ND caused	26
Fumbles ND recovered	13

1966	Total Yards	Ground Yards	Passing Yards	Passes Interc.	Fumbles Recovered	TD's Running	TD's Passing
Purdue	289	115	174	1	1	1	0
Northwestern	159	40	119	2	1	0	1
Army	157	58	99	5	1	0	0
No. Carolina	230	121	109	1	1	0	0
Oklahoma	158	39	119	3	1	0	0
Navy	64	36	28	4	0	0	0
Pittsburgh	154	113	41	1	1	0	0
Duke	185	83	102	4	2	0	0
Michigan State	284	142	142	3	1	1	0
Southern Cal	72	−12	84	1	0	0	0
TOTALS	1752	735	1017	25	9	2	1

in the fall is a chart which lists the statistics of the previous squads' accomplishments. Here we use all of the statistics which are available. We chart the offense and defense and post it where it is a constant challenge in the locker room. Under this record of past seasons' accomplishments are freshly painted posters awaiting new statistics to record the performance of this season's squad.

These items which we have dis-

1966 OFFENSIVE TEAM RECORD

1966	Total Yards	Rush. Yards	Rush. Att.	Passing Yards	Pass Att.	Compl.	Interc.	Fumbles	Fumbles Lost	TD's	Other
Purdue	453	149	43	304	24	16	1	1	1	4	EP-2
Northwestern	445	200	48	245	25	16	2	4	3	5	EP-3 2Pt-1
Army	408	166	45	242	34	15	3	2	1	5	EP-5
No. Carolina	432	249	35	183	16	9	0	1	1	5	EP-2
Oklahoma	430	273	58	157	25	14	1	4	2	5	EP-5 FG-1
Navy	327	281	64	46	18	4	2	1	0	4	EP-4 FG-1
Pittsburgh	335	213	43	122	19	8	3	2	1	6	EP-2 2Pt-1
Duke	425	278	46	147	16	9	1	1	1	9	EP-8 2Pt-1
Mich. State	219	91	38	128	24	8	1	1	0	1	EP-1 FG-1
So. California	461	206	51	255	31	21	2	5	2	7	EP-6 FG-1
TOTALS	3935	2106	471	1829	232	120	16	22	12	51	EP-38 2Pt-3 FG-4

cussed—the trainer, academic supervision, equipment, officials, slogans, statistics—are precisely geared to unify our squad; they contribute to or diminish morale.

This chapter has presented the general outline of our philosophy and organization. From this point on we wish to show precisely how we teach the theory, technique, strategy of the game, as well as how we create the morale atmosphere which we feel must be present if a team is going to have any kind of success.

2 Defensive Overview

General Concept
Basic 4-4 Alignment
Defensive Objectives
Ten Defensive Musts
Defensive Critical Situations
Five Basic Teaching Areas
Defensive Ends Basic Stance
Technique of Ends
Tackle Stance
Technique of Tackles
Inside Backers Stance and Techniques
Outside Backers Stance and Techniques
Defensive Secondary Stance
Defensive Secondary Technique
The Overall Front as a Base
Example of Strengthening Stress Areas
   (Middle, Inside, Off Tackle, Sweep, Flats & Deep
Setting a Defensive Game Plan)
   a) Prep Team
   b) Other Defensive Phases
   c) Defensive Coordination
Summary

Defensive Overview

The planning of the defense, as noted in chapter one, is our first concern. With a sound defense you are never really out of the football game.

General Concept

Every experienced coach recognizes the need for diversity in defense. This need has produced two schools of thought on defensive football. The first holds that a variety of defenses should be organized around a variety of different appearances and alignments. The second approach builds its variety of defenses, under a disguise, from what seems to be a single look. So, in the first approach you present a number of defensive alignments to the offense; in the second you consistently present a single set which, upon the snap of the ball, breaks into any one of a number of defensive alignments.

Without letting it become totally rigid, I've always favored the second approach—the single look disguising multiple attacks is preferred. With this approach, we build in areas of concentration. Thus, if we are concentrating on run defense, we are obviously building around the effort to shut off the ground game—the sweep, the off-tackle, the inside and middle drives.

When you focus on pass defense, you have to think in terms of both pass rush and pass coverage. Pass rush and coverage must anticipate the roll-out pass, the run-action pass, the pocket pass, screens and draws. So the defense must be able to respond to this diversity of attack.

In each situation, the defense must evaluate and respond. If the QB rolls, the defense must meet strength with strength. The offensive formation determines the defensive alignment (disguised or open). The roll-out demands the response of an outside forcing man who must squeeze, contain and pressure the passer for a rushed throw.

But when you have a man forcing, you have to have another in the flat area on the roll side, still another in the hook area and, of course, a deep man.

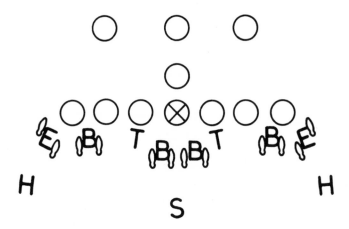

Diagram 2-1. Basic alignment of the Notre Dame 4-4 defense.

Theoretically there are only seven zones to defend, but your seven defenders can be riddled if the passer is given time—and he will probably have enough time if only four men rush, with the other seven covering zones.

This is the game. You have to decide —with this particular team and this particular play—where do you concentrate your effort. Down and distance might help you with the decision, but opposing teams rarely allow you the luxury of predictability.

Obviously, if you invest seven or eight men in a greater rush, you incur a higher risk. This means that coverage is either a form of true man-for-man defense or a combination of more than one form.

Operating as we do from the 4-4-3, we believe that we are in the best position from which an eight-man rush or an eight-man run defense might attack. On the other hand, if a pass should develop, we can limit ourselves to the four-man rush, reserving the seven-man pass defense.

So we work from the premise of meeting strength with strength and we have made our decisions about basic alignment. Then we must go back to the question of personnel choice and the problem of recognition of formations.

From this problem alone, the defense must have a wider range of ability to recognize the formations set by the opposition. Once the defensive players recognize the basic formation coming at them, they must also be aware of possible receivers and the wide range of possibilities in multiple blocking combinations.

Naturally, no set defense can stop

When an opponent runs with the ball away from his body, we try to stress jarring that arm on the tackle. Leroy Keyes unfortunately hung onto the ball pretty well on this particular day.

everything that its opposition can throw against it, but the set defense is the starting point, the base from which we work out the adaptations to meet the particular strengths and weaknesses of each team we meet.

From diagram 2-1, it is clear that in our set defense, the flexibility of the four linebackers is the key to our ability to adapt to the many offenses we must contain during a season. They can give us an eight-man front for rushing or they can give us our seven-man pass coverage. Clearly, the assignment calls for quick, alert minds and exceptional athletic ability.

Defensive Objectives

The fundamental objective of any defense is, of course, to prevent scoring. To achieve this purpose, we stress ten basic rules which every member of the defensive team must bear in mind at all times.

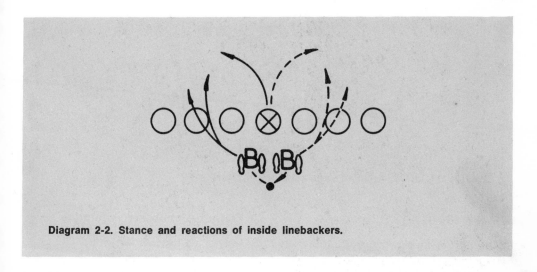

Diagram 2-2. Stance and reactions of inside linebackers.

Your inside leg is back. Depending on the line splits, you will have to vary your position. Your three basic positions are 1) squared on the guard, 2) angled on the guard, and 3) squared in either gap of the guard.

Tackle Techniques and Rules

You must never allow the guard to get through on a direct course to his inside backer. He should never be able to turn you out or hook you in. Read his action: If he pulls away, close . . . expecting a trap while you angle. If he pulls to your side, expect your principal blocker to be on your outside. Shed this man with your near arm or use a shallow spin-out. Never quit. Never allow your legs to be crumpled.

Move on the snap of the ball. If you read a pocket pass, rush but never leave your feet—keep your head up—arms high at the throw—always anticipate that a remaining back may run the draw. As you rush, angle toward the quarterback. Concentrate on the ball. Proximity to the ball is of fundamental importance, for you must not create a natural alley which will permit an escape.

Stance of the Inside Linebackers

Linebackers assume a two-point stance. They are semi-coiled. The inside backers position themselves according to the offensive look. In a balanced line offense, the backers are spaced one and a half yards behind the scrimmage line and in the guard—center gap if the split is normal (see diagram 2-2).

37

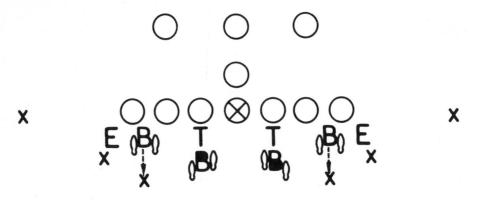

Diagram 2-3. Inside linebackers alternate look of stack.

Inside Linebacker Technique

The inside linebacker is aligned with his feet parallel. His primary responsibility is to wipe off (fill a defensive void) to the flow side through the guard-tackle gap. If the flow is to the other side, he steps forward with the flow and becomes a center linebacker holding for counters or delayed traps (see diagram 2-3). He tries to play the run first and then the pass. A split flow on the part of the offense should cause the linebacker to freeze and then respond.

Outside Linebacker Stance and Positions

1. Align on inside eye of the end, feet parallel.
2. Stacked behind the defensive end.
3. Two or three yards behind the defensive end.
4. "Walk away" to split man.

One of the above positions will be taken depending on the offensive set.

Outside Linebacker Technique

Proper reading of the offense is critical. If the offensive end attacks you aggressively, shed him and remain as nearly parallel to the scrimmage line as possible. Prepare for an inside or outside move to the ball.

If the action of the quarterback is away from you, maintain your inside position on the offensive tight end, and be alert for a throw-back pass.

If the end reveals a pass pattern and the action comes to your side, either cover or rush depending on the defensive call.

If the action is a pocket pass, either rush or cover, according to the defensive call.

Defensive Secondary Stance

The two halfbacks and the safety take positions according to field position and balance. Each staggers his foot toward the greatest area to be covered unless pass coverage dictates otherwise.

38

Notre Dame defensive halfback, Clarence Ellis, readies himself for opponent's next play. Notice the positioning of hands and feet.

Defensive Secondary Techniques

Shout out any formation. Play the pass first. Then go for the run. The halfbacks give support against runs from the outside in; the safety on runs from the inside out.

When the secondary is involved with intricate coverage rather than simple man-on-man or zone defense, disguise your coverage by your stance and alignment—as much as you can while still getting the job done.

Once the ball is in the air all coverage stops; go to the ball and try for the interception at the highest point you can reach.

Bend, don't break; that's the rule for the secondary. It takes many hook passes or down and outs to score, but one bomb can do it.

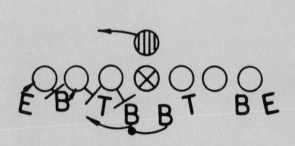

Diagram 2-4. Defensive end-linebacker responsibilities and reaction to offensive tackle blocking down to the inside.

The Total Front As Your Base of Defense

In establishing your defensive plans, you prepare for the offense which that opponent shows most often—it will usually be about 85% of the time. These are their bread-and-butter plays. While some new formation will appear, your basic defense will be against what the opponent has used most often. In my opinion, the defensive game plan should contain an overall defense which can be used as a base and one to which we can revert should confusion hit us.

Though our basic defense (shown in previous diagrams) appears to be a 4-4-3, it may actually become a gapped 8. The tackle must protect his inside backer. The outside backer must cover down if the offensive tackle blocks down to the inside. The end must cover for the outside backer if he is blocked down by the end. The inside backer will flow or fire as the play develops. Diagram 2-4 indicates these responsibilities.

All linebackers are in parallel stance to enhance their lateral movement. The outside backer tries to see a back-field action through the offensive end-tackle-near-back triangle. The inside backer reads the action through the guard-center-quarterback-fullback triangle. The premise is that one man protects the next to construct a solid front. This base defense is designed to cover all problems posed by the offense.

We define the "stress area" as that point in the defense which is being attacked successfully by the opponent. In the running game we have four potential areas of stress; we must be able to defend against the sweep, off-tackle, inside, and middle rush. In the passing game the obvious areas of stress are the short yardage or underneath coverage zone, and the deep coverage areas. In addition there must be stress areas designed to stop the short-yardage or goal-line plays, thus the need for short-yardage defenses or goal-line defenses. To give support to a stress area from the base defense requires, adjustments and—in our operation—disguise.

With a four-linebacker defense, adjustments are confined primarily to the linebackers. If a team can consistently run against your eight-man front, you are already defeated.

If the opponent's talents go into the short throwing game, your stress area changes to that of underneath coverage. This means the defensive four

linebackers cannot all rush, hence, the need for your change and assignment.

In the late stages of a game, where you are protecting a narrow lead, you fight the clock and the long gainer. Your stress area deepens to the deep secondary. This might be the proper time to reduce underneath coverage and go to four deep with the change-up of one of the linebackers. Disguise may not even be called for at this point in a game. Certainly when the opponent is in a position where he must throw, there is no need for disguise. The four deep men simply line up in their deep positions.

The point I make here is simply that your defensive strategy must take into account all of the stress areas and ways to shift or counter strength to them when you are being hurt there. These are: (a) the adjustments by formation, (b) the change-up coverage by disguise, and (c) the knowledge of your opponent's 85% tendency—all these evaluated by your judgment of when to employ them.

The alignment of itself is only preliminary, making men more accessible by position to the stress area. The real support comes from the stunts developing from the alignment and from the new coverage that evolves. This provides a variety of looks for which the offense must prepare.

Examples of strengthening stress areas:

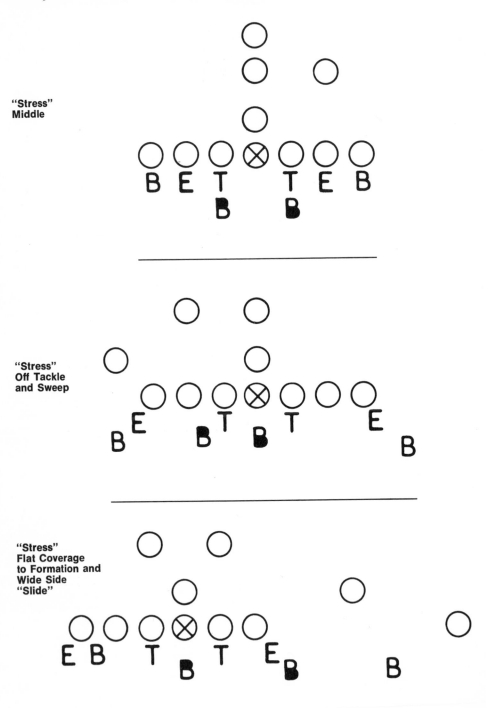

"Stress"
Middle

"Stress"
Off Tackle
and Sweep

"Stress"
Flat Coverage
to Formation and
Wide Side
"Slide"

Outside Linebacker Moves

"X"

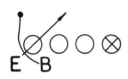

"Backers' Dog"

"Stack" — "Read" & "X"

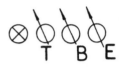

"Squirm" Tight

"Fold"

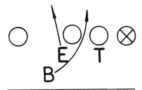

"Pinch" Tight

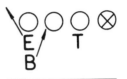

"Backers' Jam"

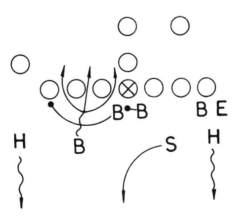

Secondary Moves

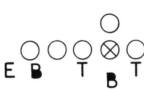

Blitz 2, 4, 6
Rover 4
Man — 4
Invert — 4
Monster — 3

Inside Linebacker Stunts
(Coordinated with Tackles)

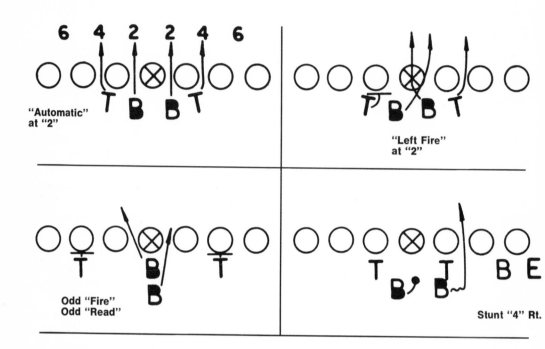

"Automatic" at "2"

"Left Fire" at "2"

Odd "Fire"
Odd "Read"

Stunt "4" Rt.

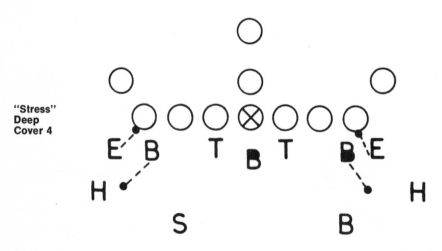

"Stress"
Deep
Cover 4

Setting a Defensive Game Plan

To prepare a defensive game plan, one must have a solid knowledge of the opponent, where his offensive strengths and weaknesses are to be found. Operating from our base defense we begin to set our pattern look, against the formations he has shown. Included in our plan will be a "safe" defense which is to be used when a completely new offensive look is thrown at us. An overriding call from our defensive captain will switch any previously set defense back to the "safe" look.

First, we try to defense the six best running plays a team has shown and the six most frequently used pass plays. Clearly our defensive pattern must be flexible enough to accommodate to any of the regular formations used by the offensive team.

From our scouting charts, film exchange and past year's film, we arrive at the "opponent look." Since we can prepare only two offensive teams and two defensive teams for the game, everyone else is assigned to a "prep" team.

Prep Team

The prep team must prepare us for the opponent. We carefully study the personnel of the opposing team and then try to select prep players who can approximate the roles of the players we will meet in the game. To sharpen responses and recognition we even purchase helmet covers, jerseys and pants in the colors the other team will use.

Clearly the prep team makes a major contribution to the entire team. All our players realize this, and they also know that whenever possible we will dress outstanding preppers for games. Moreover, while a boy may be assigned to a prep team, this is not a final decision. Each day we evaluate personnel, and if a prepper shows more desire and hustle and ability than one of those 44 we are preparing, there will be a change.

This policy generates great competition. A player who is really a competitor never gives up. Some are fully aware that their lack of size or speed will never allow them to be regulars, but they do make a great contribution. Being part of the team means much to them. Many of these men who have worked with us were and are great people. Perhaps not great athletes, in the amount of press coverage they get, but great in everything they do. To our staff and to our team these prep players are the backbone of the effort. They are important; they share equally in all

45

that we do . . . and we are equally fond of them and proud of their achievements both in college and in their lives afterward.

The prep coach draws up on cards the opponent's variety of backfield actions and line blocking combinations. Once we have chosen the men who will represent each individual opponent, this group belongs to a prep coach. They will time up and practice right down to the huddle used by the opponent. They fight to give the "look" of the opponent.

Our practices are lively and competitive because of this great effort put out by the preppers.

The use of words instead of numbers is really a great help here; we call the opponent's plays in terms of our own offense. Since all of our players are exposed to the same terminology, a prepper can move up into the varsity group already knowing the terminology of the calls.

Other Phases of Defense

We are particularly concerned with all aspects of the kicking game. For the defense this means:

1. Kickoff rush and coverage.
2. Punt rush, block, return.
3. Field-goal rush and coverage.
4. Extra-point rush and coverage.

Also included in the week's preparation are: goal-line defenses, prevention defenses, and short-yardage defenses.

Defensive Coordination

We believe we must prepare at least three members of the starting defensive team as defensive signal callers. Our defensive signal caller is the counterpart of the offensive quarterback. His knowledge of the opponent, of our defense, of the total game of football must be greater than that of the other members of the defensive squad. Since the defensive signal caller must be able to read a pass as well as a run, we think that the linebackers are best qualified.

The caller will have a master-call defense, based on down and distance, field position, formation and tendency. We spend time with the callers to sharpen this judgment. Within the limits of that master call there is some leeway for secondary calls between an outside linebacker and an end, or an inside linebacker and a tackle. In other words we have a major defensive signal called for a particular situation, but within that major defensive set there can be minor defensive adjustments between combinations of players. A "safe" call reverses everything back to our "safe" defense.

We find that a player of experience

will often have the true feel of the game in progress. Between the training you give him during the week, and any helpful information you can send in to him, and his own feel for the game the defensive signal caller should be able to direct an intelligent game.

Offense is action, and defense is reaction. The defense reacts to a situation with a calculated guess about what sort of play will develop. The defensive team reacts to the offensive formation; it reacts to the action of the play. While coaches say that football is a guessing game, I want the guesses to be educated ones—educated along the lines which we have developed. In the last team meeting before our pregame general meeting, the defensive signal callers and quarterbacks are able to call every defense or play; they are also able to tell us the why, the when and the where . . . of their decisions.

In all this preparation, we have worked for good physical condition, high morale, and sound strategy. If we have been able to instill this training to a higher degree than the opposition coaches, victory is easily attained.

Defense in Summary

If you have made proper selection of personnel, know that they can do the things you ask of them; align them in a strategically sound formation; allow them adjustments of spacing; give them diversified coverage to stress areas; implement stunts (inside linebacker moves), games (end and linebacker moves); blitzes (deep back moves); dogs (outside backer moves) —then you have fashioned a good defensive unit.

Here I want to speak of one of the intangible factors which every coach tries to build into his defensive unit—pride. I've come to appreciate this attribute as I have witnessed in the past a lesser group of men possessing unit pride who were able to overcome singly proud opponents. Pride is something we discuss and talk about with the boys constantly. We think about it. We attempt to add class and polish to foster pride. Our players have a kickoff alignment, a defensive huddle alignment, and a time-out alignment. And in everything that they do we stress unit pride.

The necessity of pride is an already accepted point of coaching and I do not wish to spend time attempting to define it in detail. However, I merely want to point out that it is an ingredient which makes a great team of one which, lacking pride, might only be mediocre. However, being aware of the necessity of pride is not sufficient.

47

We adopt slogans and successful mottos. They are not just "coined phrases." They are the ideas and thoughts that our team lives with. We purchase the best equipment money can buy, try never to be less than first-class in our travel, lodging, meals, medical treatment and overall procedure. We stress promptness to our players by being prompt ourselves. We regard them as men; yell at them, praise them and laugh with them, and sometimes, frankly, cry with them. Every day that we work they know that much planning, effort and time has been spent in preparation. We attempt to be a proud staff in what we do, knowing that how we act will affect everything that our players do by way of reaction.

We constantly criticize unwarranted penalties, and we praise fumbles caused, fumbles recovered, blocked kicks and passes intercepted. Symbols are painted on defensive players' helmets to recognize their achievements. To the casual observer such actions may appear corny or unimportant. Truly though, it is a need to "achieve" that governs most players and in this light nothing is unimportant, corny or trivial.

Notre Dame herself has a certain mysterious pride about her. Our players recognize it and if it could be explained then it obviously would not be mysterious. Our players "feel deeply" about giving their very best effort. This is extremely important.

Pride, coupled with the pressures constantly exerted by the coaching staff on the players while they are on the practice field, provides our team with the best possible preparation for a game. We exert both physical and mental pressure upon them in the practice sessions simply because that is exactly the atmosphere in which they must play on Saturday.

3 Defensive Drills

Defensive Front Four Drills
   a) Read and Destroy Drill
   b) Two-Man Sled Drill
   c) Pocket Pass Rush Points
   d) Tackles-Blast-Read-Spinout-Rush
Defensive End Drills
   a) Hazard Drill
   b) Read Near Block, Flank Back, Switch, Action Away
Linebacker Drills
   a) Hit and Deliver Blow
   b) Foot Dexterity
   c) Shed Drill
   d) "Peek-a-Boo" Drill
   e) Coverage—Man and Zone
   f) Positions
   g) Playing Option with End
   h) Courses to Action
Deep Secondary Drills
   a) Hash—Man Coverage Drill
   b) Interception Drill
   c) Tip Drill
   d) Angle Tip Drill
   e) Eye Drill
   f) Combat Drill
   g) Hash—Zone Drill
   h) Wave Drill
   i) Pass Defense Principles
Summary
   a) Full Team Drill

Defensive Drills

Defensive Front-Four Drills

Our drills are designed so that a player does during the drill period precisely what he must do during the game.

Read-And-Destroy Drills

The drill progresses from one-on-one to two-on-one and, finally, to three-on-one situations. We teach the defensive man to find the "drive" or principal blocker. In a three-on-one situation, the defensive man is taught to recognize patterns of blocks, traps, double teams, draw techniques, and so on. As with all defensive drills, we drive home the point that the action determines the reaction; the defensive man must react to the offensive action. In the simple diagram (3-1) below, we show the basic one-on-one, two-on-one and three-on-one drills for the defensive tackle.

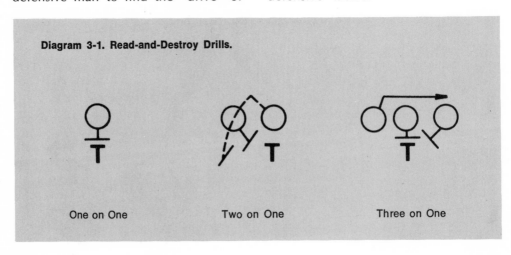

Diagram 3-1. Read-and-Destroy Drills.

One on One   Two on One   Three on One

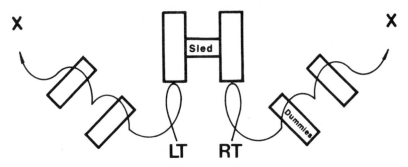

Diagram 3-2. Two-Man Sled Drill.

Two-Man Sled Drill

In the above diagram (3-2) the two-man sled drill for the left and right tackle is shown. To the right and left of the sled, two dummies are stretched out. The ball carrier is designated X.

The tackle moves on the snap of the ball. With legs back, he uncoils a forearm blow. He then spins or glides laterally, picking up his feet as he avoids the dummies and drives in for the tackle. This drill is designed to teach (a) lateral pursuit and (b) the ability to avoid obstacles in pursuing a ball carrier to the outside.

Tackle-Coaching Points

Pocket-Pass Rush

Fight to keep your feet. Force the quarterback to unload the ball quickly.

1. Decide as early as possible whether a pocket pass is developing, when it does, square up and go directly for the quarterback, putting *constant pressure* on him. Stay in your proper lane. Never get caught inside.

2. When rushing the passer, try to keep blockers away from your body by using your forearm and hand in front of you. Get your hands up high over your head as you reach for the quarterback. In this way, you might obstruct his vision or block the pass.

3. NOTE: We usually have one tackle designated to watch for the draw and the center screen. This assignment is determined week by week.

Additional Information

1. When only the tackle and guard are on your side, with the end split out, you should move in closer to the offensive guard. Align the top of your head with the outside ear of guard.

2. On a slide call from linebacker, square up.

Tackles must be dedicated, mean, vicious . . . outstanding team members.

Defensive tackles—Make contact with guard, must never be blocked out by the guard, must never be hooked by the guard . . . reads the head of the guard.

Tactics

Diagrammed below are the four basic moves of the defensive tackle.

Blast 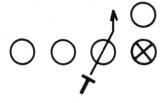 Basic: Move on snap of ball. Keep guard from blocking inside linebacker. Play the guard's head on the move.	**Spear and Spin Out** 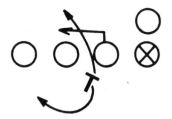 Pulling guard and tackle blocking down: If offensive tackle gets head in front, spring off; if head is behind, use arm for leverage and go to ball.
Read and Close 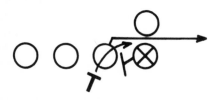 Pulling guard crosses center: Close down hard and try to pick off ball carrier.	**Square Up Rush** 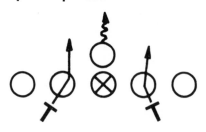 Pocket Pass: Drive through blocker. Stay in your alley. Pressure quarterback —favor outside.

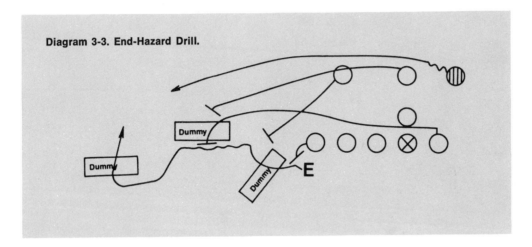

Diagram 3-3. End-Hazard Drill.

Defensive-End Drills

Our defensive ends work on all the drills used by the tackles except for the spin-out and those designed to teach how to read one-on-one, two-on-one, and three-on-one.

With the ends, we use an end block to replace the one-on-one, an end and flanker to replace the two-on-one, and an end, nearback and guard for the three-on-one block. The end concentrates on setting to his point, proper form, ability to shed with inside arm, and on skill in keeping his legs free. He learns to work laterally, squeezing from the outside in.

His greatest effort must be in learning to avoid being cut down by a blocker who is throwing to his out-side; at the same time he still must pressure and fight through all blockers.

End-Hazard Drill

In the hazard drill (diagram 3-3) the end (1) avoids a hook (2) sheds guard or nearback and (3) sheds next blocker. All these evasions are tough in themselves and become even harder when executed over dummies strewn along the way.

The end must also be taught to read pattern blocks—when the offensive end blocks down or when he is flanked close or when he is flanked wide. Our drills throw all these looks against the defensive end.

55

Bob Kuechenberg rushes from his defensive
end position trying to force a high throw and
still not leave his feet prematurely.

Alignment	Defensive End Play	Coaching Points
Base Unflanked or Wide Flanker		Know when you are out-flanked and how wide the flanker is. Drive off inside leg as step #1, step #2 on outside leg, step #3 with inside leg up.
Three Step, Inside Leg and Arm Up		Come to point with inside knee and arm forward. Crouch to ward off blocker. Stagger outside leg. Protect it. Inside arm hit.
Read Thru End to NB Keying His Course		The nearback's course will key his intention. React after coming to point.
Close Flank Up to 3 Yds.		Endangered by flank up to 3 yards, end moves to leverage point. (Normal when there is no nearback.)

57

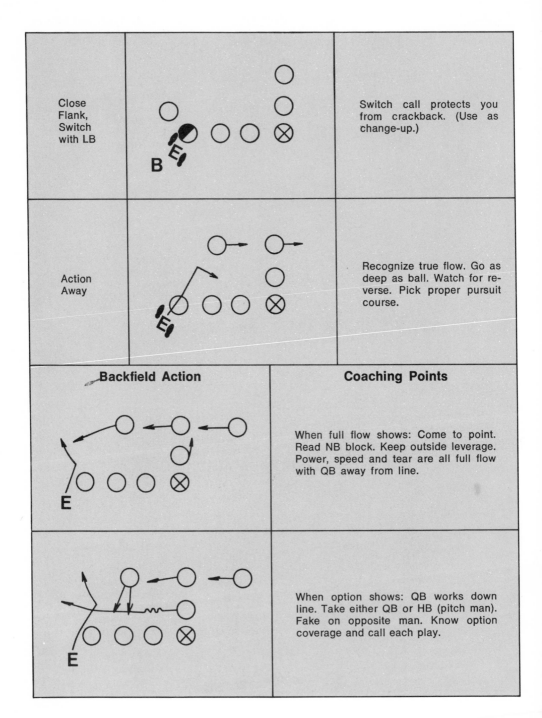

Close Flank, Switch with LB

Switch call protects you from crackback. (Use as change-up.)

Action Away

Recognize true flow. Go as deep as ball. Watch for reverse. Pick proper pursuit course.

Backfield Action

Coaching Points

When full flow shows: Come to point. Read NB block. Keep outside leverage. Power, speed and tear are all full flow with QB away from line.

When option shows: QB works down line. Take either QB or HB (pitch man). Fake on opposite man. Know option coverage and call each play.

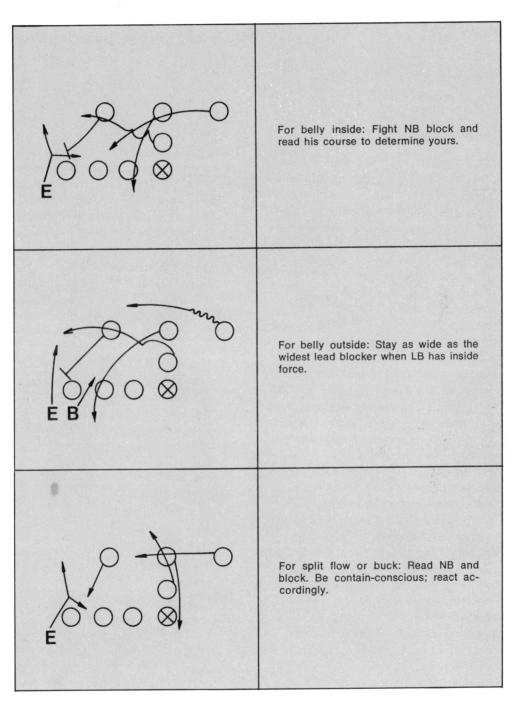

For belly inside: Fight NB block and read his course to determine yours.

For belly outside: Stay as wide as the widest lead blocker when LB has inside force.

For split flow or buck: Read NB and block. Be contain-conscious; react accordingly.

Linebackers

The nature of the linebackers' duties demands that personnel selection be given most serious consideration. Ideally, this position should be filled by a man who possesses the abilities of both a defensive back and a lineman. These positions constitute the very heart of the defense.

Size, strength, quickness, durability, awareness, and a desire for contact — these are the qualities needed by the linebacker. Size is possibly a luxury, but it is important against both the run game and the pass game. Strength is a must in the ability to ward off the running block, make the hit, and prevent that extra yard after contact. Quickness is a common requisite today even though in the past we were able to hide those who lacked it in nonstrategic positions. Since the linebacker is not protected in every defensive alignment, quickness is vital to his rushing defense as it is to his passing defense. We expect linebackers to make the greatest number of defensive stops and thus durability is essential. Blocking angles against him vary so greatly that he must be able to withstand a great deal of physical abuse.

The most important knowledge for sound defensive football is a constant awareness of what the opponent must gain in order to maintain possession. The linebacker, controlling the defense, must realize down and distance, field position, and opposition tendency. In addition to his physical qualities, he must possess mental alertness.

In training the linebacker, we start with the stance. His stance will depend on alignment, keys, etc. We first ask the player to assume a comfortable "hit" position — weight equally distributed on the balls of the feet, knees flexed, arms bent and not rigid, shoulders parallel with the line of scrimmage. Positioning of feet in a stagger stance varies with individuals as well as with what is expected of him in a particular assignment. The parallel stance is the one most desired for outside backers in our system.

Linebacker Drills

1. Hit - Deliver Blow.
2. Foot Dexterity.
3. Shed Drill.
4. Peek-a-Boo.
5. Zone and Man Coverage Drill.

Hitting—Delivering A Blow

The two-hand shiver (or blow) and the lift (to halt momentum of blocker) are the two main tactics used by the linebacker to break down the offensive block. Overstriding in the per-

formance of either will result in a defensive breakdown. We spend much time initially on the swinging bag (see illustration above) in an effort to develop proper technique. Use of this apparatus permits a close check by the coach. He can work with more than one man at a time and with multiple "shots."

In working the shiver, when the set command is given both individuals assume the comfortable hit position with feet pumping. We want their arms to "snap" with the elbows locked. The coach checks to make sure that neither is overstepping or reaching for the dummy; it is the snap of the arms that neutralizes the block.

In teaching the lift, we work to synchronize arm and leg movement in order to meet the oncoming swinging dummy. We have the linebackers alternate blows and they generally take eight to ten rapid shots. Again, we watch for the overstepping or windup with the forearm.

Foot Dexterity

Since the linebacker is always working in heavy traffic and on cluttered ground, we work over bags to simulate this condition. The standing dummy is put on its side and three round trips are made (see diagram 3-4). On the first, we will clear the dummy and gather into hitting stance, avoiding a jumping motion and keeping our shoulders parallel to the line of scrimmage. We aim to improve body control in a good hit position while pumping the legs between each dummy. After going through this drill in each direction, we go to sprint action. At this time we merely sprint over the dummies, keeping eyes and shoulders upfield. On the third trip, we line up at the top end of the first dummy, facing the coach. Move quickly forward in a good hit position, a quick lateral step to the base, and then backpedal to the top. This action is repeated in each lane. Eyes and should-

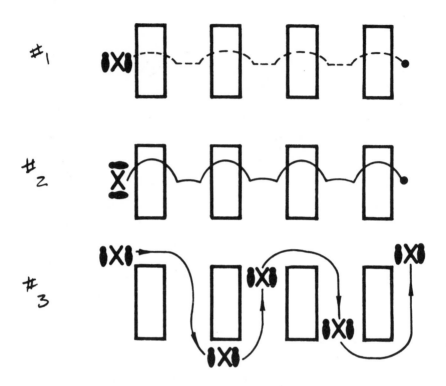

Diagram 3-4. Foot Dexterity Drills.

ers upfield in all cases and working for quickness.

Shed Drill

In our shed drill (diagram 3-5) the defensive backer faces a line of blockers coming to alternate sides and sheds their block by use of forearms. He is attacked by a vertical line of blockers, and must work past them to tackle the ball carrier.

Since our linebackers make a high proportion of the tackles, form-tackling drills are important. To develop hitting ability, we use a drill in which linebackers drive forearms into a sled from a down stance.

In this drill look for the linebacker to shed blocks, one from each side, and then meet the ball carrier in the hole. Again, we are working for the good hit position, square shoulders, explosion, and putting the nose on the ball carrier at the line.

Diagram 3-5. Shed Drill.

X — Ball Carrier
B — Blocker
D — Defender

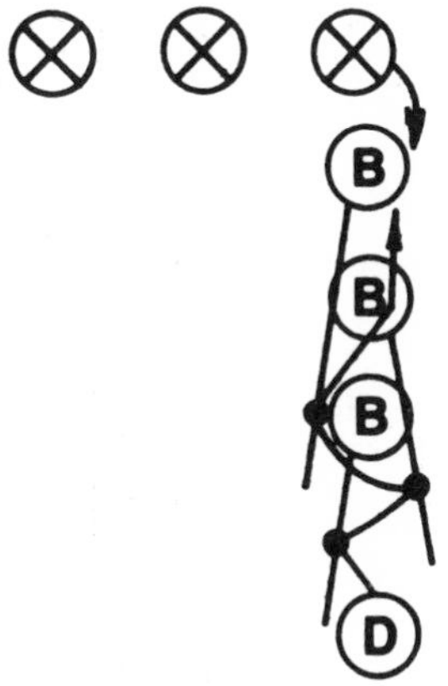

Diagram 3-6. "Peek-a-Boo" Drill.

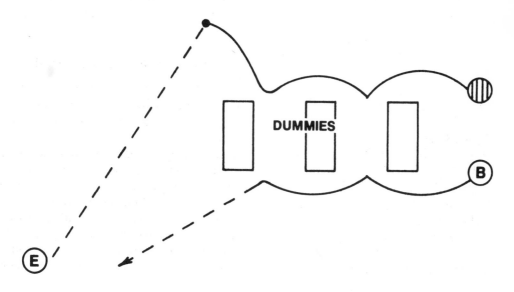

DUMMIES

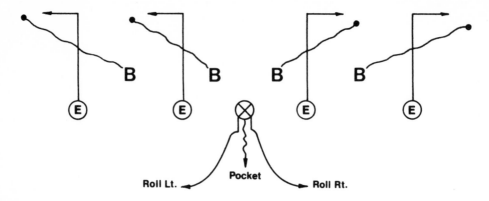

Roll Lt.   Pocket   Roll Rt.

Diagram 3-7. Linebacker's Underneath Expansion Zone Coverage.

"Peek-a-Boo"

Our "peek-a-boo" drill (diagram 3-6) emphasizes proper leverage on the ball carrier from inside out.

The broken line indicates a backer reading and reacting to the halfback pass. The backers are constantly reminded not to overrun the ball but rather to stay to its backside.

All of our pass defense assignments involving the linebackers will be found in the following chapter. The daily work of our backers is split into three parts. First, they work as a group, with the coaching emphasis on the technique of the individual man. Then they work with the forcing unit, the front four, on support-and-fill functions. Finally they work on pass defense with the secondary.

The linebacker, as the heart of the defense, must radiate leadership. Like the offensive quarterback, he is responsible for the clutch play and he must demonstrate toughness and awareness to gain the confidence of his unit. His performance will give an anchor to the pride of a defensive unit in destroying an offensive strategy. Stopping the opposition short of a score is not maximum performance. The goal is to attain good field position for the offense . . . and to work for the ultimate satisfaction: scoring with the defense.

Linebackers' Pass-Defense Drill

The two drills (diagram 3-7) we employ in the linebackers' underneath expansion zone coverage are as shown above.

The backers read the pocket, roll right or left, expand back to underneath coverage, maintain proximity, move to ball when it's in flight.

We use the same drill with a clock on them and ask them to play "man" up to four seconds. A whistle tells them when the four seconds are up.

Defensive End and Outside Linebacker vs. the Option
(Dotted line is switch position — end and linebacker switch assignments)

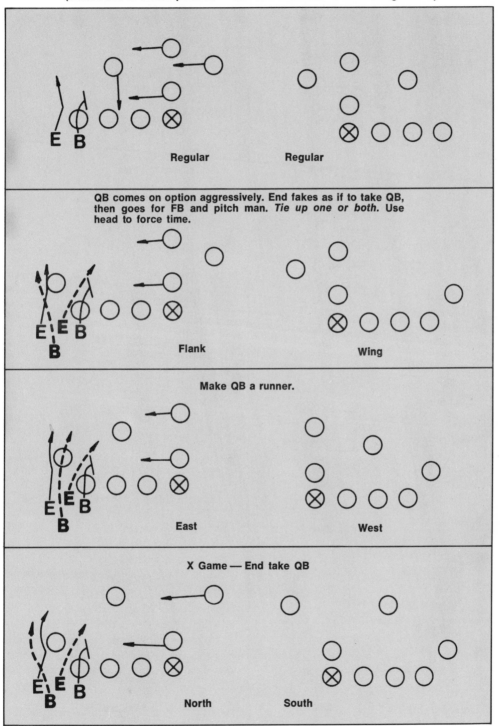

Regular   **Regular**

QB comes on option aggressively. End fakes as if to take QB, then goes for FB and pitch man. *Tie up one or both.* Use head to force time.

Flank   **Wing**

Make QB a runner.

East   **West**

X Game — End take QB

North   **South**

Defensive End and Outside Linebacker vs. the Option
(Dotted line is switch position — end and linebacker switch assignments)

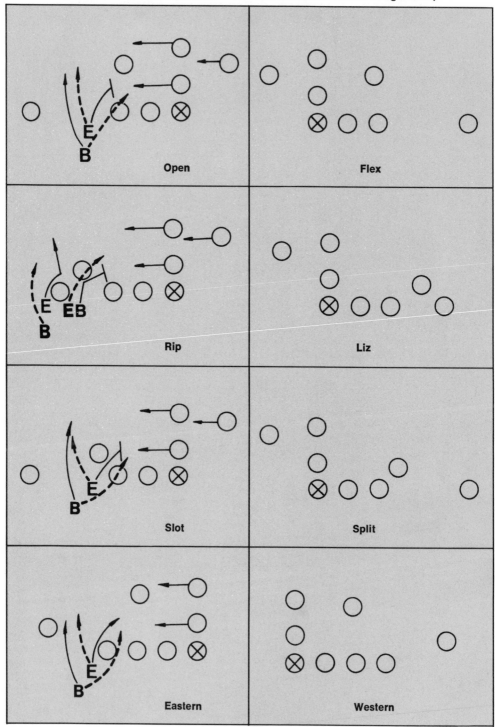

Belly Action

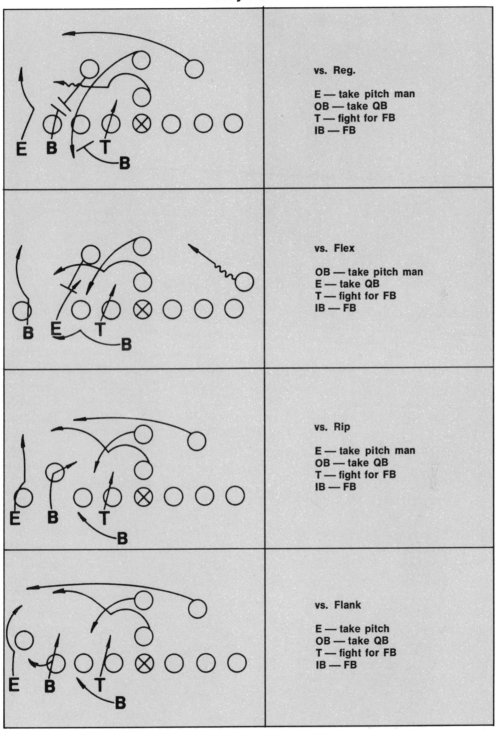

vs. Reg.

E — take pitch man
OB — take QB
T — fight for FB
IB — FB

vs. Flex

OB — take pitch man
E — take QB
T — fight for FB
IB — FB

vs. Rip

E — take pitch man
OB — take QB
T — fight for FB
IB — FB

vs. Flank

E — take pitch
OB — take QB
T — fight for FB
IB — FB

Notre Dame defensive back, Clarence Ellis, brings this outside running play to a quick halt. Speed and quick reactions are great assets in defensive secondary play.

Defensive Secondary Drills

1. Rope Maze and Reaction.
2. Form Tackle.
3. Catching Àgainst Force of Throw.
4. Open Field Tackle.
5. True Man Coverage.
6. Three-Deep Zone Drill vs. Ten Receivers.
7. Two-Deep, Half-Field Coverage vs. Many Receivers.
8. Interception Line and Tip Drill.
9. Sideways, Backwards, and Forward Running Drills.

These are the various forms of drills which we use for the deep backs. Though we don't run the same ones every day, our rotation process assures that we cover every phase of defense for the deep backs.

Field position, of course, dictates how tight we play a man. The closer the offense gets to your goal line, the tighter the defense must play its men.

Man-Coverage Drill

For drill purposes, we work for three different areas: with hash marks to the right, with hash marks to the left and in the middle between the hash marks (diagram 3-8). We start coverage with a backward shuffle step. The relative speed of our player and the opponent helps dictate how tightly we can play. Our defensive secondary is trained to watch the belt and stay with their men. When the receiver's hands move for the ball, our men then play the ball. Until that time, they play the man. It is absolutely necessary that we get a good rush on the passer to help our covering men. Unless we have fine speed and agility in our defensive backs, we are better off using more zone than man coverage. Of course, we have to mix up our coverage if we are going to stop our opponent.

68

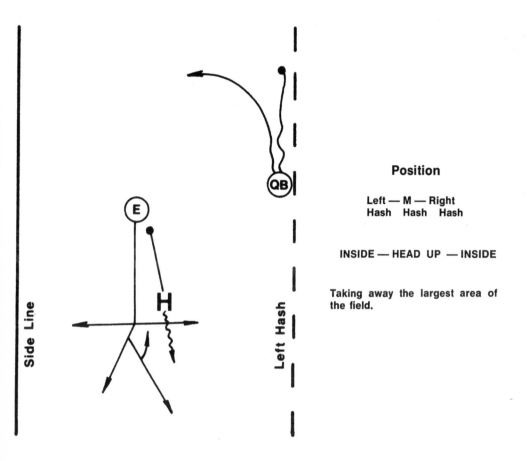

Position

Left — M — Right
Hash Hash Hash

INSIDE — HEAD UP — INSIDE

Taking away the largest area of
the field.

Diagram 3-8. Man-Coverage Drill.

Our defensive back will cover the
receiver using the techniques we
talked about earlier. The receiver can
run any cut staying between the hash
mark and sideline. Of course, the ball
must be thrown at the proper time,
and not held too long by the quarterback. The longer the quarterback
holds the ball, the more difficult it is
for the back to cover the receiver.

69

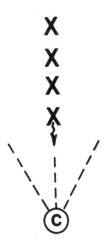

Interception Drill

Coach throws ball high and low, to the right and to the left.

Tip Drill

Both players start forward. First player reacts to the ball and tips it. Second player intercepts. Call out your word for interception.

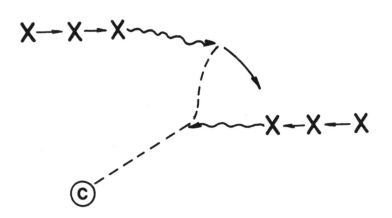

Angle-Tip Drill

Player starts toward coach, reacts to the flight of the ball and tips it to second player moving in opposite direction. Lines keep rotating.

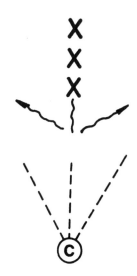

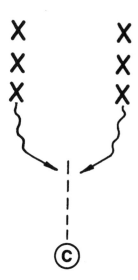

e Drill

ach looks right or left. Player
es back in that direction for ball.

Combat Drill

Players react to ball and fight hard
for the interception.

Hash-Mark Drill

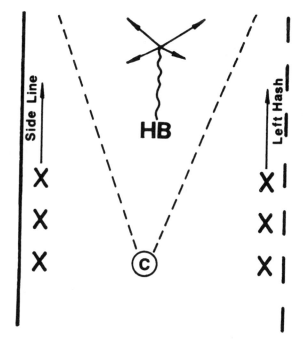

Diagram 3-9. Wave Drill.

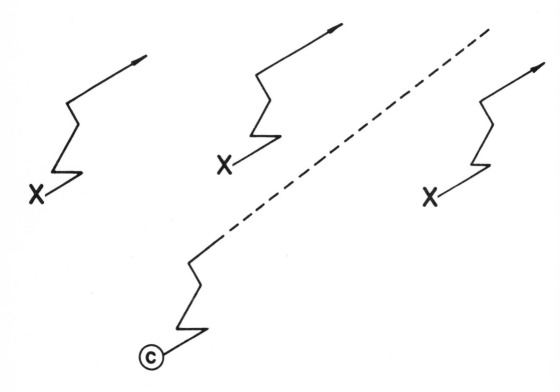

Coach runs with ball toward three players; one intercepts and the other two become blockers.

The drill above (diagram 3-9) is used to increase interception distance. It also teaches the defensive back to watch the quarterback, and to follow the ball (as he should when playing zone coverage). For this training, we want the ball to be thrown at least 35 yards.

Basic Pass-Defense Principles

1. Be in a good fundamental football stance so you can move quickly.
2. Maintain field balance and use the side lines. Never be closer than eight yards to the side lines.
3. Know your proper coverage.
4. Know the down and distance in order to anticipate the pass.
5. Take your proper keys to determine your area of coverage.
6. Get to your area as quickly as possible.
7. Always play the ball and not the man.
8. Be aggressive in playing the ball; fight for it.
9. Go through the receiver for the ball.
10. Don't worry about the short hook passes. Yield the short ones, but never allow the long one. Bend, don't break.
11. Unload full force on any opponent who catches the ball.
12. Try to intercept. If you can't, make sure that you knock the ball to the ground.
13. Once the ball is in the air, all defensive men should converge on it.
14. Be ready to block if the ball is intercepted.
15. The closer you are to your own goal, the closer you play receivers.

Summary

One of the most effective defensive drills we use to teach tackling is that in which we set our front four, our four linebackers, and then our three deep men as separate units against a full offensive team. Of course, the offense has the advantage because it is playing against only four linemen and a three-deep secondary at one time. In another instance, the full offense will go against four linebackers and a three-deep secondary. In still another instance, we pit the four linemen and four backers against the full offensive team. Naturally, the offense is confined to running only a handful of formations and plays. These drills are used for three purposes — none of which is to punish or stack matters against the defense.

1. Such a drill forces the line and the linebackers into making realistic open-field tackles. It is considered a top drill by players and the staff, and through it our defensive unit gains considerable self-confidence. Further, the offensive backs have larger openings to run against. Thus, they experience a sense of "trouble" running and

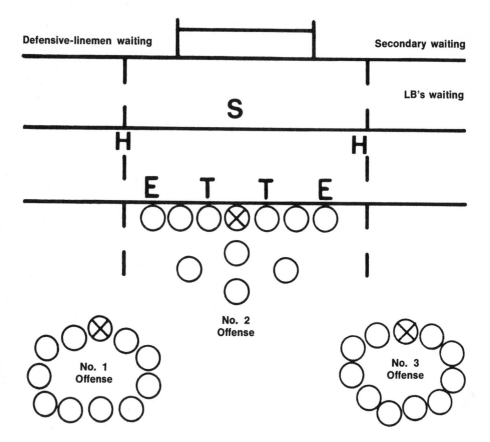

Diagram 3-10. Full Unit Offensive vs. Partial Defense Drill.

breaking free to daylight. We combine different units of our defensive group after each play. We also run at least three offensive units. This allows everyone to have an opportunity to block, run and tackle.

2. This drill allows our staff to evaluate all of our personnel. When time and funds permit we use numbered jerseys and film the action.

3. With three groups on offense and a comparable number on defense, you can run a 20-minute rough drill and evaluate players quickly under circumstances which are extremely competitive. Our staff is assigned to watch specific positions and each member is thus able to evaluate individual performances.

I favor this full-offensive-unit-versus-partial-defense drill because it is real football, not merely an exercise. Diagram (3-10) shows our overall organization of the drill described above.

Pass Defense

Pass Defense

It is impossible to win a football game without a sound pass defense. At Notre Dame we employ every type of pass defense. We play zone, man-to-man, and some free safety. I feel you cannot confine yourself to only one type of coverage throughout a game. You must vary your pass coverage to control your opponent's passing game. However, as with most colleges, we probably play more zone than any other type of coverage. We make more interceptions during a season when we are using zone coverage. Basically, we play a four-three zone.

We strive to educate our players to understand an overall concept of the pass defense we use. In addition to a specific defense, pass defenders must be schooled in fundamental principles and terms which allow for defensive deployment to compensate for: (1) motion; (2) formation; (3) the wide side of the field with strength and (4) the short side of the field with strength.

Terms

Field position: Our players must understand precisely which areas of the field constitute points of vulnerability in terms of pass defense. An area may be vulnerable by reason of people (strength formation) or because of the actual area itself (wide side). It may be vulnerable by both reasons. Field position also refers to where an opponent possesses the ball—on their side of the 50-yard line or on ours. With all this information, down and distance must also be considered. We play "tight" when an opponent has short yardage to make and loosely when he needs longer yardage. The distance played between a receiver and our secondary and linebackers is governed by down and distance, the yard line, and the territory—all these elements determine "field position."

Field balance: This phrase refers to deployment of defenders in a ratio which will balance the offensive formation. On occasion the offensive team

Diagram 4-1. Zone Coverage Assignments.

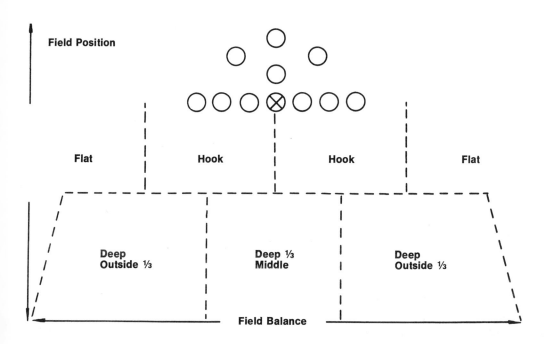

puts the defense in a difficult position by crowding a strength formation to the short side of the field. Now the defense is faced with a choice of defending against the strength of that formation or of maintaining adequate coverage to the wide side.

The balance we seek involves *lateral* alignment to more or less match or mirror the offensive formation. I say "more or less" because the ground left uncovered is vital. Usually we will take away the largest area the offensive player has by aligning our players to his inside—particularly when the side line is near us. If it is not, we may be forced to go head up.

When we zone, the three deep men will deploy in a way which will balance the offensive alignment and field position. Our coaching on this point allows our deep three access to the middle of their zone while not allowing a receiver to penetrate deeper than themselves. For our zone coverage assignments see diagram 4-1.

Although zone coverage is common, I believe that all coverages have both weaknesses and strengths. It is imperative that our players realize and digest this point thoroughly. When they realize this, they will not panic when an opponent completes passes designed to exploit the weakness of the particular coverage they are using. This leads to the importance of change-up coverages, which can reduce an opponent's passing success to a minimum.

Zone Concept

Roughly speaking, the width of the field is divided into thirds, each 17½ yards wide. In a zone defense a player covers an area, not a man. Therefore, a defensive man best defends his zone by covering the center of that zone and then reacting to the ball.

To play a full zone covering the seven vulnerable areas indicated in diagram 4-1, you must use seven people. The deep three occupy the center of their one-third of the field, (a 17½ yard area). They have to cover approximately eight yards to their right or left laterally; they play as deep as the deepest receiver.

The underneath coverage (flat and hook zones) is the responsibility of the linebackers and/or the ends. These zones are confined to a vertical depth of from ten to 15 yards. As indicated in the diagram, the underneath zones are divided into four equal parts, each about 13 yards wide. Since the underneath coverage men already occupy, by their bodies, about one yard of the area they only have to cover approximately six yards, laterally, right and left.

Zone Theory

Normally speaking, zones will be occupied by seven people; two for the hook areas, two for the flats, and three deep when the pocket pass is shown. On roll-out passes, most teams will rush one of the seven zone men. Usually the one who rushes is the man away from the roll side who occupies a flat, or it might be an interior backer who then brings the flat defender into his vacated area. This is a form of underneath coverage rotation.

Obviously run-action passing, when well executed, prevents immediate backpedaling of the linebackers to the center of their zones. One defender pushed to the boundary of his zone rather than staying in its center creates a seam or wide breach which can be exploited by the opposition.

Underneath Hook and Flat Areas

If you call for a player to get to the "hook" area, he must understand that this area is determined by field balance and position.

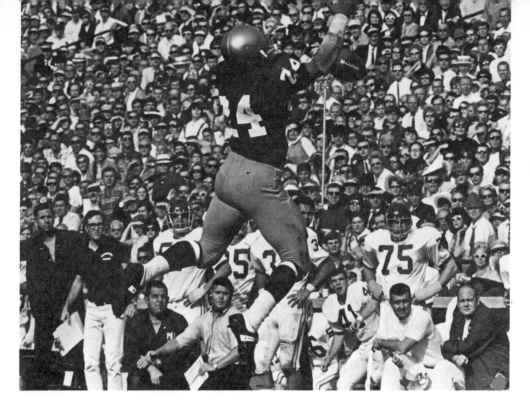

Linebacker Larry Schumacher shows how to get to the ball at its highest possible point as he intercepts this Northwestern pass.

A good defender must expand to the center of this zone as quickly as possible and react to the ball in flight from that position. Good reaction depends on innate speed, and skill in regarding the quarterback's eyes, feet, and off throwing arm. Using peripheral vision, the defender must learn to be aware of men near him; often he must defend in front of a man who is just beyond his underneath coverage. The guiding principle is this: The underneath coverage man must not "play" a man but be aware of him. He must learn to play the zone regardless of how many men are in his area, and he then reacts to the football when it is in flight.

Young, green players find hook zones and flat areas nebulous and hazy borders. They find it difficult to grasp the concept of team play and the equidistant relationship of the four underneath defenders.

When we first teach the principle of zone and area, we align ten offensive men across the field spaced at equal intervals and tell them to hook or run a "sharp out" at ten or 15 yards. Only four defenders are at work against them, but they soon gain confidence that they are able to cover any number when the pattern and distance relationship is preserved . . . and when they learn to react to the ball. The deep pattern is not their concern.

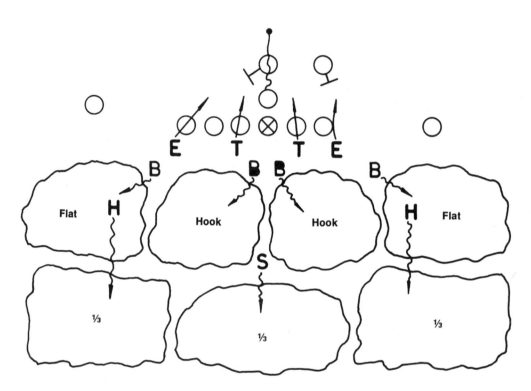

Diagram 4-2. Three-deep zone coverage vs. pocket pass.

Deep Secondary Coverage Zone

Sound secondary zone coverage is achieved in various ways. We have used four men deep, three men deep, and two men deep. However, the alignment shown still requires three major areas of coverage.

Using three deep, if the ball goes to the direct pocket, the easiest full zone coverage is as shown in diagram 4-2.

You can evolve into this pattern from four deep by moving an inside safety man to the flat area or the predetermined strong side when the pocket shows. Then he can also move back to the middle deep if an away roll-out shows (see diagram 4-3).

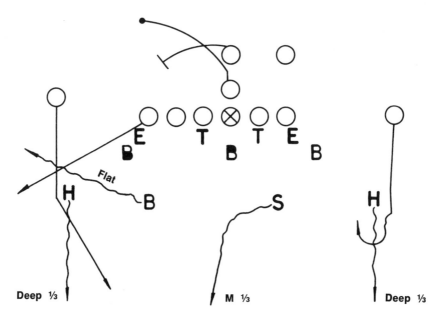

Diagram 4-3. Invert to three-deep vs. roll-out.

Teams which use this invert will act on the basis of the strength of forma- tion and/or the wide side of the field if pocket shows (see diagram 4-4).

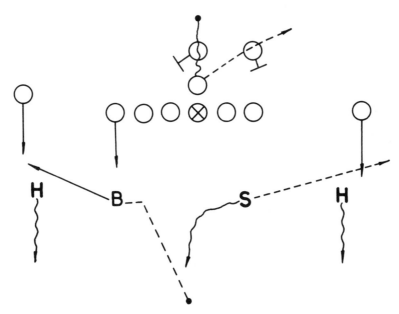

Diagram 4-4. Invert to three-deep vs. pocket pass.

A similar method of arriving at a three-deep zone coverage is a "revolve" or, rotation (diagram 4-5). This avoids the necessity of a foot race by the backside of the invert to the deep middle third. Here again, the move is directed to a strong side or to a formation when the pocket shows, but it develops automatically against a roll-out action in which the ball favors a distinct side.

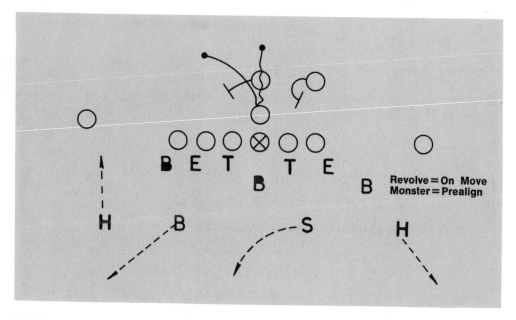

Diagram 4-5. Rotating to three-deep zone coverage.

Both the invert and the rotation are, therefore, on the move adjustments which become a three deep. Most monster teams (those using a rover back) declare three deep immediately and align the monster (or rover) to formation, personnel, or to the wide side of the field.

In our basic alignment we choose to start out balanced with a three deep secondary and then we react from that alignment.

Prerotation

When using a rotation or set alignment to react to a roll-out pass, it is usually acceptable to give up coverage of the flat away from the roll-out side. (See diagram 4-6.)

Diagram 4-6. Rotation vs. roll-out.

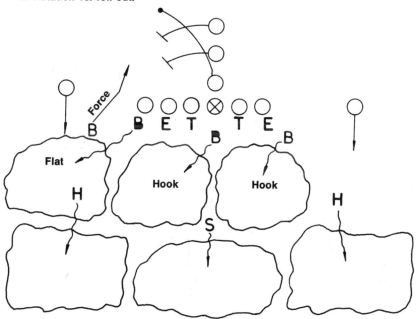

In some defensive alignments which are unbalanced by the monster or in a prerotation, there is a calculated risk. The risk involved is that you choose to strengthen your rush by gambling against an improbable pass across field to the vacated flat.

If a defense remains balanced, the coverage can be full with fewer people rushing. A stronger rush to the point of attack will require defensive secondary adjustments. Offensive formations are important here because close formations allow more adjustments. On the other hand, wide splits lengthen the area of coverage, and increase time and error margins.

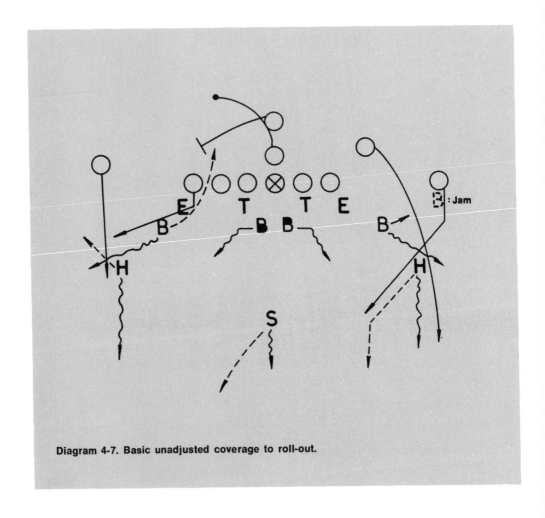

Diagram 4-7. Basic unadjusted coverage to roll-out.

The above defense confines the rush by placing maximum coverage in the zone areas. A change-up on this, which would allow more rush, is determined by (1) formation, (2) field position, (3) down and distance, (4) your personnel and that of the opposition. (See diagram 4-8.)

86

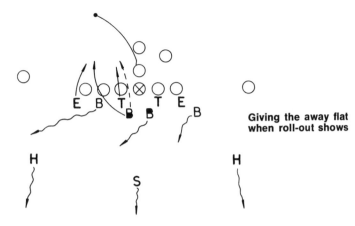

Giving the away flat
when roll-out shows

Diagram 4-8. A change-up emphasizing the rush.

A closer formation (diagram 4-9) is more easily adjusted to from the viewpoint of time and area, and it more easily allows a maximum force with frontside rush of the pass. Admittedly, this weakens the backside coverage, but the offensive quarterback is now pressured to pull up and make a quicker throw.

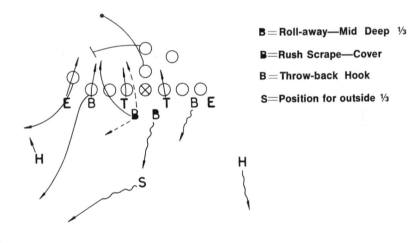

B = Roll-away—Mid Deep ⅓

B = Rush Scrape—Cover

B = Throw-back Hook

S = Position for outside ⅓

Diagram 4-9.

Again, on the basis of down and distance, the inside left backer on a roll-out to his side can either rush or defend a zone defender in the hook area. This, then, calls for line and linebacker stunts, and it raises the need for true man coverage.

87

Man-Coverage Concept

Here we are talking about strict man-for-man coverage. The defenders will follow wherever their receivers go. The eligible receivers are:

1. Split end.
2. Tight end.
3. Left half.
4. Right half.
5. Fullback.
6. Quarterback.

Therefore, full man coverage would use six defenders. However, defensive ends can usually pick up the flaring FB.

Also, the QB is not usually covered.

Thus, this coverage would normally use only four men and allow a seven-man rush.

Man-Coverage Theory

Defenders playing up tight on the two ends and two halfbacks can cover them tightly for four seconds. Meanwhile, the rush should reach the quarterback. The idea of man coverage is to keep the defender in front of you and to deny him the widest portion of the field. Diagram 4-10 below demonstrates this.

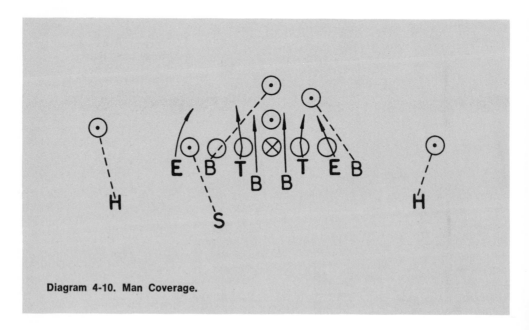

Diagram 4-10. Man Coverage.

Free Safety Coverage

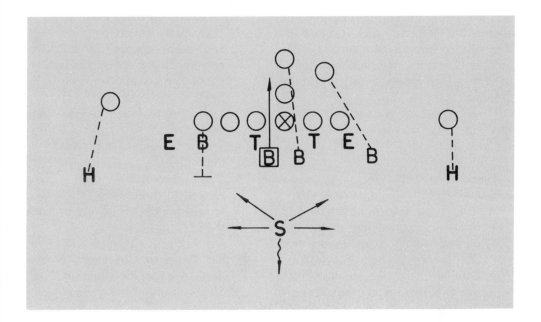

Principles of Free Safety Defense:

1. Man coverage. All coverage people play outside shoulder; angle in.
2. Force or funnel receivers to inside.
3. Play your man tight. Safety will help on any deep pattern.
4. Safety man—key on the QB and ball. Play 12 yards deep.
5. Linebacker—can rush passer or plug great receiver.

This defense is used primarily to take away the out patterns. It is also very useful against any deep pattern because you have one man playing and reacting to the ball. Of course, the 10-15 yard in pattern will be hard to stop. Effectiveness depends on the particular abilities of your defensive backs and linebackers.

89

Summary of Our Pass Defense

Though we seldom use four deep, we do include it in our spring practice and in the early fall practice just for the sake of overall exposure. Fundamentally, though, we think in terms of three-deep zone as our primary defense.

Then coverage is adapted on a week-to-week basis with these considerations in mind.

Three-Deep Coverage:

1. Full zone and full zone jam—seven men used in coverage.
2. Minimum zone—five men employed in pass coverage and two linebackers playing run action.
3. One-half coverage in which we use only two men deep with nine playing the run. One halfback to the action side becomes an underneath man.

Four-Deep Coverage: (Involves one linebacker in deep alignment.)

1. True man—covers six men.
2. Spot man—covers four quick receivers with two linebackers spotting receivers from the backfield.
3. True invert—four deep to three deep.
4. True rotation—four deep to three deep.
5. True prerotation—four deep moved to three deep in response to alignment, tendency, or wide side.

Other Types of Coverage: (Formulated to a specific situation.)

1. Single-double-free safety.
2. Prevent.
3. Goal line and short yardage.

5 Offensive Overview

Establish Formation Concept
Base Formation Identification
The Complete Huddle Call—Word Terminology
Areas of Attack—Dual System
Backfield Actions
   a) Two Back
   b) Three Back
Splits and Cadence
Line Symbols and Terms
Line Stance
Backs Stance
Types of Line Blocks
A Total Line Blocking Scheme
A Single Play Blocked Four Ways
Recognition of Defensive Fronts

Offensive Overview

In creating a system of offense, we want to start with a total concept and then work down to each of its component parts.

Based on the facts of team skills and the maneuverability of our linemen, we establish our formations. The basic formations will not change much —just enough to force each week's opponent to make adjustments in his defense.

When we think of personnel alignment, we must face the questions: Are we a two-back offense? A two-and-a-half-back offense through the use of motion and close formations? A three-back offense?

We choose to use the best of these three, but we think in terms of a running back (our best runner), a fullback (our best blocker and runner), a flanker back (our best receiver and runner). With the ends we use the same kind of judgment. Our tight end is our best blocker and receiver; our split end is our best receiver.

The entire inner line is the best combination we can put together to do the job.

In determining formation, we think of (1) one wide receiver to one side (three back); (2) a wide receiver to each side (two back); (3) two quick receivers to the same side (two-and-one-half backs); (4) two wide receivers to the same side. Of course, there are many other possibilities, but this combination will serve as a base (see diagrams 5-1 through 5-4).

Each backfield action is designed to hit either the middle, the inside, the off-tackle, or the sweep area in a particular way. Naturally, no two hits should be the same because this would be a duplication of effort. Our running plays are built with three theories in mind:

1. Speed—we must get there quickly. This is primary. If necessary, sacrifice some other effect but achieve speed.
2. Power—we must get there with maximum blocking force and leverage.
3. Finesse—we should get there with deception and options.

Some plays depend on all three, on two, or on one of these qualities. Each has its place and we build our attack with all three in mind.

When you talk of offensive systems and identify formation alignment, blocking assignments, backfield ac-

tions, areas to run, and ignition to get there, this is your total offense. The structure and variety of attack will be dealt with specifically in the following chapters. The passing game fits into the general patterns of offense.

Diagram 5-1.

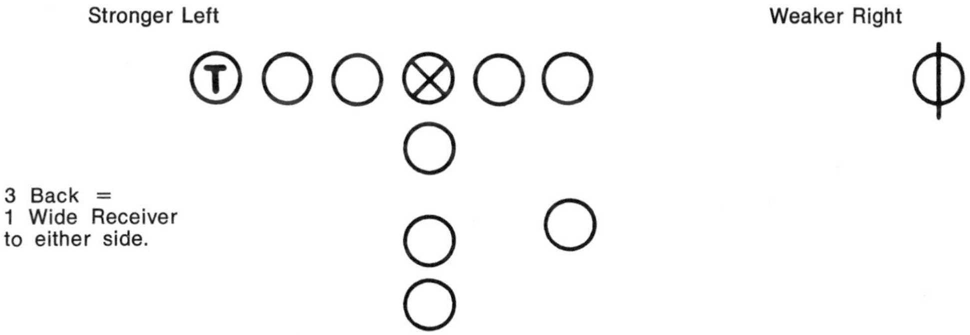

Stronger Left

Weaker Right

3 Back =
1 Wide Receiver
to either side.

Diagram 5-2.

Weak Left

Strong Right

2 Back =
1 Split Receiver
to both sides.

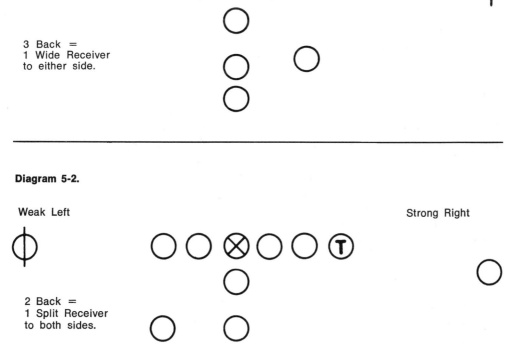

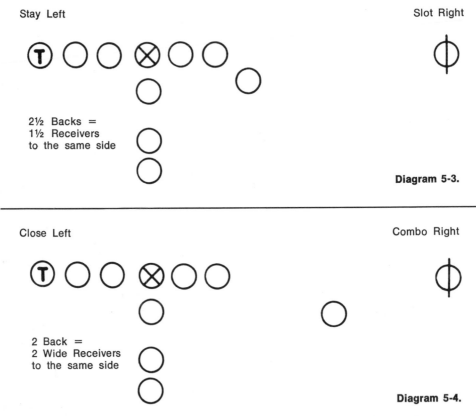

Stay Left

Slot Right

2½ Backs =
1½ Receivers
to the same side

Diagram 5-3.

Close Left

Combo Right

2 Back =
2 Wide Receivers
to the same side

Diagram 5-4.

In calling the offensive formations, we give instructions to the split end and the tight end for direction and tell the backs whether it is two back, two-and-one-half or three. We also designate the point of attack. All this is done with a single word and a direction.

In order to limit words and spark ideas, we label formations as we have indicated in diagrams (5-1 through 5-4); we also affix a word which designates the backside of that same formation. This allows complete flexibility in calling for an attack on each area of a particular set, right and left.

96

Weak Left   Strong Right

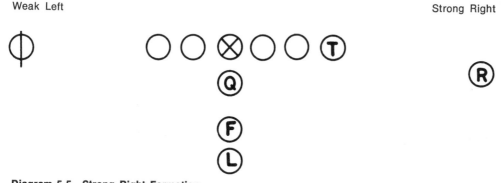

Diagram 5-5. Strong Right Formation.

For example, consider the formation we have designated Strong Right in diagram 5-5 above. Since Strong Right means tight end-flanker back to the right, the backside of the formation is weak. Obviously, it is two back because it involves a flanker.

If the quarterback calls a play "Dive, Left, Strong," the strong side would be left where the tight end lines up and weak would be to the right where the split end lines up. (Remember that we call the direction of the play and the formation at the point of attack.) The backside of the formation falls into place.

If we desire a tight end and flanker to the right side, but desire to run left to the split end side, we merely call, "Dive, Left, Weak." In this way,

we have called the play (the Dive), the side (Left), and how the formation should be established (Weak or Strong).

The terms *Weaker* and *Stronger* are used in the same way but they designate three backs in the backfield by the additional "er" on the formation call.

Slot has a backside known as *Stay* (two-and-a-half backs).

Combo has a backside known as *Close* (two backs).

In this manner, we can efficiently set a formation to the wide side or short side of the field and attack the frontside or backside of this formation using very few words for direction.

Backs in the backfield are not usually concerned with formation unless

97

they are flanked out or slotted or in combo. Where they position themselves in the backfield is decided by the backfield action which is called. It may require them to be in the I or power-I, in the divided back set, in the fullback-halfback set, in the double wing, in motion, etc. This is determined by the backfield action and the area designated for attack . . . which is the next sequence of the call.

A complete call might be: "Speed, Sweep, Right, Strong on the first sound. Ready! Break!" It tells the team these things:

1. The backfield action is Speed (this formation is set forth in greater detail in a future chapter).
2. The area of attack is Sweep or the number-eight area.
3. The direction is Right.
4. The formation is strong right, that is, the tight end and right half flank to the right, putting the split end to the left (the weak side).

Obviously, only two backs are deep in the backfield. Also, obviously, the backs must know what alignments are required by each backfield action, such as Speed. While every backfield action is given a descriptive word and only one word, this is not quite true of the four areas we attack because these require two identifications: word and number, for cadence purposes, as we noted earlier. The spoken word refers to the areas as right or left, inside, off-tackle and sweep. Middle is simply middle. These areas of attack and the corresponding numbers are indicated in diagram 5-6. Here in this figure we have numbered our men on the line. You will recall that the purpose of these numbers is to permit either direct calling of blocking codes in the huddle, that is, precalled, or to allow for audibilizing by the quarterback at the line of scrimmage.

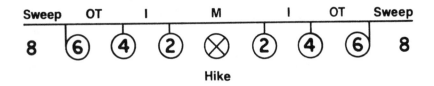

Diagram 5-6. Offensive areas of attack.

Diagram 5-7.

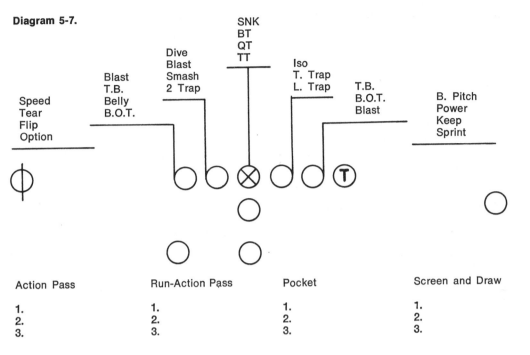

Action Pass	Run-Action Pass	Pocket	Screen and Draw
1.	1.	1.	1.
2.	2.	2.	2.
3.	3.	3.	3.

The coordinated numbering of these areas is as follows:

Hike: The *middle* area between half the space occupied by one guard to half the space occupied by the other guard, with the center in between.

2 and 4: The *inside* area between half the space occupied by a guard to one half the space occupied by his neighboring tackle.

6: The *off-tackle* area between one half the space occupied by a tackle to the outside shoulder of his neighboring end.

8: The *sweep* area outside the end.

The dual system is useful in calling cadence, but it also allows us to call blocking patterns and audibilize holes (which will be discussed later).

We then set up the basic formations to be used and construct a picture graph of our base attack from each formation. Under the cover sheet of this picture graph is the passing game which proceeds from the same set.

Our passes are designated:

1. Action or sprint-out pass.
2. Run-Action or ball-faking action pass.
3. Pocket or dropback.
4. Draws and screens.

All these are identified with abbreviated words or terms that are quickly learned by our players. Diagram 5-7 indicates typical mosaic: above the action and below the four pass categories.

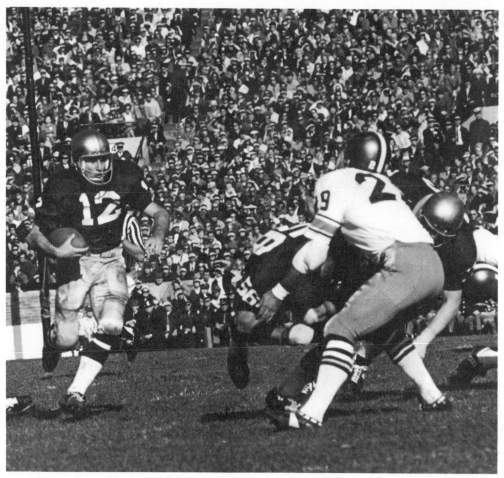

Ed Gulyas rambles for good yardage behind the blocking of guard, Larry DiNardo. The backfield action on this play is simply called "speed sweep right."

Our players now know their alignment in a given formation, the plays that can be run to each side of the formation, and they need only be schooled in "a line-blocking scheme" and "backfield actions."

The Backfield

Every backfield action which can be numbered can also be described by a word. Our scouts, too, use these words. Because line-blocking techniques and schemes of blocking are more difficult, I will describe backfield actions first. This way you can recognize the sequence of the action and how it attacks various holes. You will also see how words allow the backs to understand whether a play calls for a three-back or a two-back offense.

2 Back
Backfield Actions

M—Middle, I—Inside, OT—Off Tackle, S—Sweep

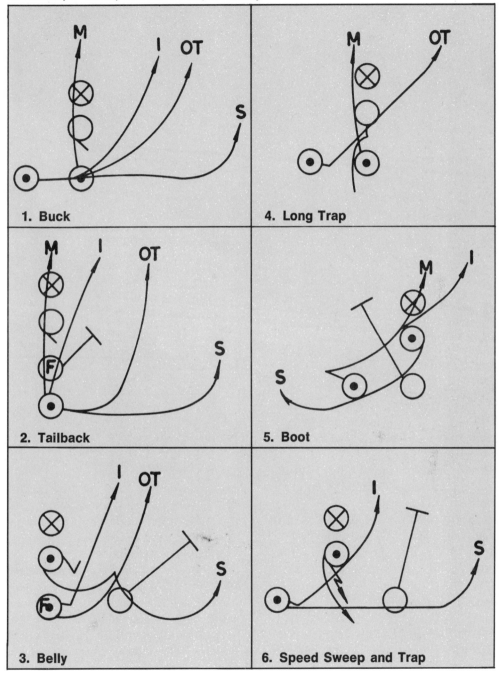

1. Buck

2. Tailback

3. Belly

4. Long Trap

5. Boot

6. Speed Sweep and Trap

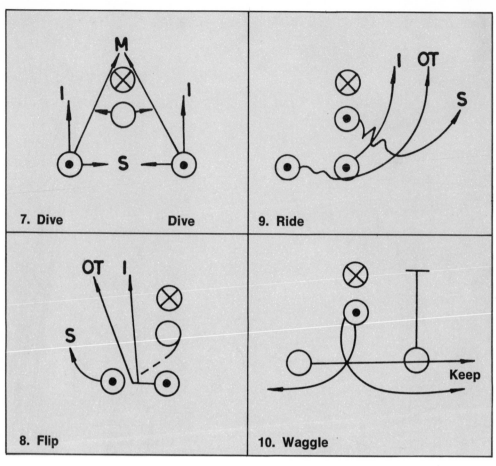

7. Dive   Dive

9. Ride

8. Flip

10. Waggle   Keep

(These diagrams, numbered 1 through 10, are described in the following notes.)

1. From two-back backfield action we have the buck action. The fullback goes to the backside of the halfback flow. If fullback carries, it is a middle play. If he fakes and the halfback carries, it is a buck inside, or buck off tackle, or a buck sweep depending on where the attack goes. The key word is *buck*. The word tells the backfield their formation.

2. This action is simply called "tailback middle" or "in" or "off tackle" or "sweep." It calls for a tailback, so the backs must go into an I formation. The key word is "tailback."

3. "Belly" is a fullback action so the fullback always aligns at the fullback spot; the remaining back always goes to the call side or "belly" just as he aligns opposite on "buck." We have belly at middle, inside, off tackle and sweep. Numerically, in cadence, it goes, "belly, hike, two, four, six or

Basic Stance and Splits

We have a basic stance and system of splits with alterations determined by formation and backside action. The diagram below and the accompanying table show the basic stance and splits.

G's optional

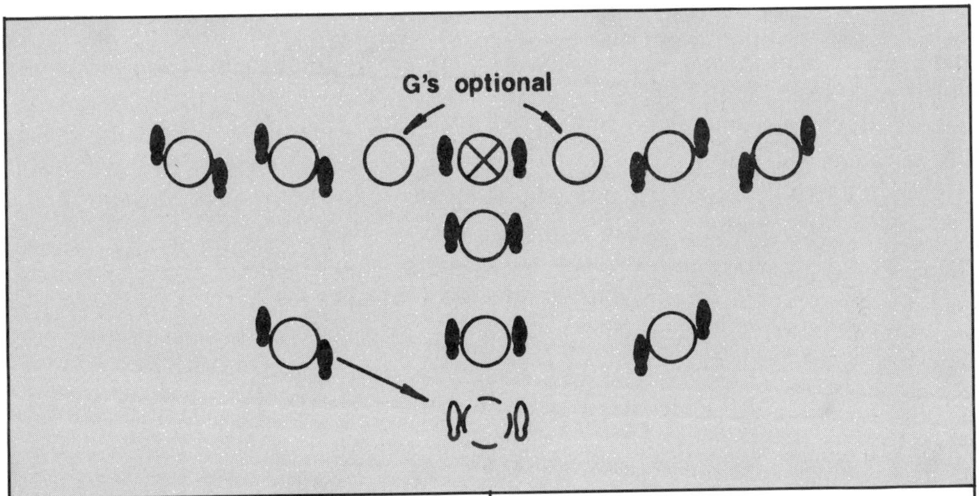

Stance	Splits
C—Feet Parallel.	
G—Optional—Toe and heel stagger.	Foot to foot—to four feet.
T—Inside leg back. Inside hand down. Toe and heel stagger.	Foot to foot—to four feet.
SE TE—Inside leg back. Inside hand down. FLK	TE—start at four yards. Move in or out according to play.
LH—Right leg back. Right hand down.	Hand at three and a half, feet at four and a half. Directly behind tackle.
RH—Left leg back. Left hand down.	Hand at three and a half, feet at four and a half. Directly behind tackle.
FB—Feet parallel. Either hand down.	Hand at three and a half, feet at four and a half. Directly behind quarterback.
TB—Two-point stance. Hands on knees.	Six inches to one foot, behind fullback
QB—Feet parallel.	

4FT.   3FT.   3FT.   3FT.   3FT.   4FT.

Base Split

We split according to blocking schemes, the play and the defense. Backs widen out according to the play called, the defensive alignment and the coverage we face.

Our linemen, contrary to our general theory of teaching, must master individual blocks and know basic techniques before attempting to block more complex situations. We use terms and symbols to communicate the technique we want and the meaning of the written rule they will eventually follow. These symbols are shown below:

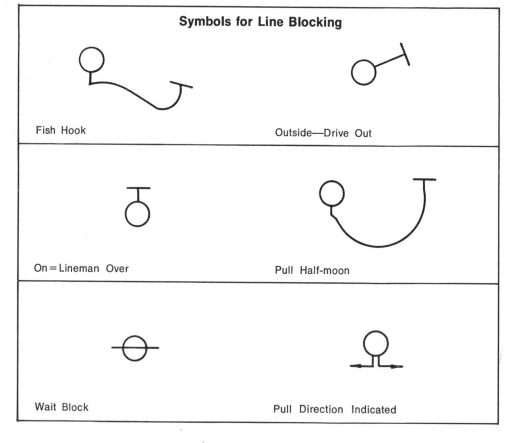

Symbols for Line Blocking

Fish Hook

Outside—Drive Out

On = Lineman Over

Pull Half-moon

Wait Block

Pull Direction Indicated

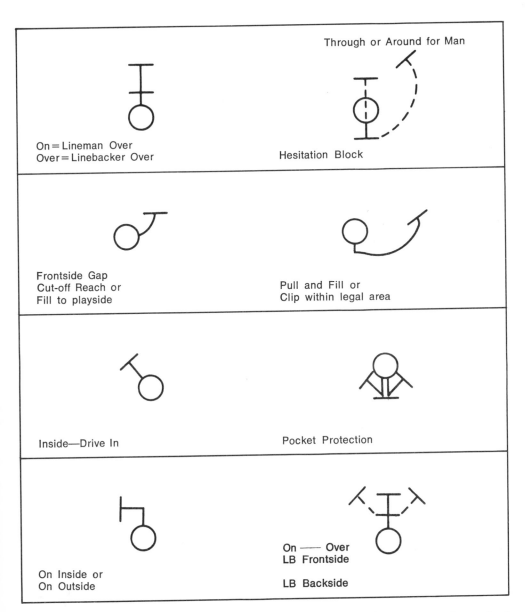

On = Lineman Over
Over = Linebacker Over

Through or Around for Man

Hesitation Block

Frontside Gap
Cut-off Reach or
Fill to playside

Pull and Fill or
Clip within legal area

Inside—Drive In

Pocket Protection

On Inside or
On Outside

On ——— Over
LB Frontside

LB Backside

All our offensive players are exposed to various defensive fronts from the first day of practice so that they will recognize defensive fronts and block effectively.

Since stance becomes an important part of all that we do, as does proper splitting for particular plays, we stress stance and start, hitting out and blocking technique.

Stance—Linemen

A. Center
1. Feet—absolutely parallel and wide as the shoulders or slightly wider.
2. Head—raised slightly from a position parallel to the ground.
3. Tail—slightly higher than the head.
4. Knees turned out.
5. Moderate weight forward.
6. Head up in stance and eyes open.
7. Keep back flat as ball is snapped.
8. Heels—raised slightly, about one to two inches.
9. Relationship of ball to center's head: ball pointing slightly up in front is ahead of the center, not under him.
9. Exchange: lift ball with stiff wrist. Palm down, quarter turn of the ball. Ball hits quarterback's upper hand. (Never turn wrist down.) Lower forearm will contact inner thigh.
10. No weight on the hand holding the ball.
11. Important—the snap of the ball and the entire body movement forward are one motion.
12. Elbow will be outside thigh.

13. Center is responsible for quarterback hand position and pressure.
14. Center is responsible for checking team alignment.
15. Don't snap ball too early. Better to "feel" that the line is moving before snap. When you are away from point of attack, make sure you are on, or slightly behind, count. At the point of attack, try to be right on count.

Stance—Guards, Tackles, Ends

1. Feet — armpit width pointing straight upfield, staggered, heel to toe, weight on the balls of the feet. Let heels come up naturally—don't flex backs of legs—adjust to the physical size of the opponent and the play called.
2. Head—slightly raised—enough to see belt-high of man you're blocking. Look out of the tops of your eyes—don't flex muscles in back of neck.
3. Shoulders—parallel to the ground. Should be ahead of legs.
4. Hips and back—straight, not twisted. Back parallel with the ground, same height as shoulders and flat.
5. Knees—in line with insides of feet and ankles. Bend knees enough to

Split receiver Tom Gatewood readies for quick acceleration off the line of scrimmage as he looks in to see the snap of the ball.

flatten the back to create power-producing angles. The drive-leg knee must bend a little more than lead-leg knee to level the hips.

6. Arms—the up arm is bent at the elbow and the forearm rests on the knee, parallel to the ground. Hand, loose-fisted. The down hand reaches out from the shoulder to a point even with the tip of the head-gear and on a line just inside the rear foot. Fingers make a five-point cupped bridge. The length of reach can vary according to the forward weight needed to execute a particular assignment.

109

Guards—Special Instructions

1. Right- or left-hand stance.
2. Down hand reaches slightly ahead of shoulder.
3. Vary weight distribution without revealing the direction of your move.
4. When pulling or using pocket protection, the heel of the forward foot will touch the ground because of weight redistribution.
5. Line up on the rear tip of the ball.

Tackles—Special Instruction

1. Inside hand down—Inside foot back. The toe of the back foot should be level with the heel of the front foot.
2. When pulling or using pocket protection, the heel of the front foot will touch the ground because of weight redistribution.
3. Line up on the rear tip of the ball.

Ends—Special Instructions

1. Inside hand down. Inside foot back. Toe of the back foot should be level with heel of the front foot.
2. Line up on rear tip of ball.

Stance—Quarterback

1. Knees flexed. Feet parallel and spread about 12-18 inches.

2. From the hips stand tall, weight favoring toes with head up. Always look to both sides before calling play.
3. Right hand in to accept ball, wrist deep, fingers well spread, palm pushed down. Left hand joins right at thumb, spread fingers.
4. Important to have hands and arms ride in under the center to receive ball.
5. Be careful never to tip off play. (Eyes are a giveaway.)
6. Correct angle bend in quarterback arm. Elbows flexed.

Stance—Backs

A. *Halfbacks*

1. Feet—Inside leg back at shoulder width. Inside hand down. Stagger —toe of back foot level with heel of front foot.
2. Head—Level. See the defensive alignment. Don't give away play.
3. Back—Parallel to ground.
4. Heels—Up foot, heel down. Back foot, heel raised.
5. Hand—cupped.
6. Weight distribution—Varies according to play. Don't reveal direction of flow.

B. *Fullbacks*

1. Feet parallel (right or left hand down). Always the same.

2. Weight—Don't reveal direction of flow.
3. Head—See the defensive alignment.
4. Back—Parallel to ground.

C. *Tailback*
1. Feet parallel.
2. Hands on knees.
3. Two-point stance.
4. Six inches from fullback's heels or adjusted to the play.
5. Head and shoulders square.
6. Weight evenly distributed.

Line Blocking

Consider the fact that you want different angles of blocking; different combinations of blocks and disguised patterns; it becomes necessary to teach all linemen all the techniques of blocking.

We categorize line blocking for the player and try to teach each of them the best time and place at which to use a particular block. In his daily drill period or team time-up each lineman must have the opportunity to use all these blocking patterns.

Head-On Block

Theory

This block, a direct blast or blow-off block, is used at the point of attack when you have the option of taking the defender in either direction. It is the block all linemen must first master, since all other types build off this move.

Technique

1. Fire out on the cadence.
2. Lunge off the front foot and step with the rear foot.
3. Keep back flat and shoulders wide, parallel to defender.
4. Aim forehead at defender's numerals. Your head is always up.
5. Gather for explosion. Uncoil with timing and balance.
6. Hit out when contact is made. Use a lifting action for leverage.
7. Keep knees bent, but legs under the body at all times.
8. Battle the defender for yardage. Avoid stalemate. Dig with your legs.
9. Maintain your time interval. Maximum effort for full interval of action.

The Post Block

Theory

We will use this block when an inside man can expect help from an outside blocker.

Technique

1. Fire out on the count.

2. Lunge off leg away from man you are posting.
3. Jab your near foot to the middle of your man.
4. Gather for explosion. Timing is critical.
5. As soon as you feel drive-man's blow, swing your tail toward him and try to get a 45-degree lateral movement.
6. Never let him split you or get lower than you are.
7. If he angles, you must block him alone.
8. Maintain your time interval. Maximum effort for full interval.

The Shoulder Block

Theory
This block is used when you have an angle on the defender at the point of attack.

Technique
1. Maintain proper line split.
2. Lunge off leg away from defender.
3. Follow-up step with nearest foot.
4. Attempt to keep shoulders parallel as you thrust your near foot to defender's far foot.
5. Try to make contact on man's hip first, hitting with forearm and shoulder together.

6. Use head as front leverage.
7. Use lifting-driving action with legs for lateral movement.
8. Maintain your time interval. Maximum effort for full interval.

Drive Block

Theory
To be used by an outside man with inside help or post.

Technique
1. Hit out with the count.
2. Lunge off with the away foot, jab with near foot.
3. Uncoil body, aim at hip while delivering forearm and shoulder blow.
4. Maintain angle of leverage, never allow seam to be split.
5. You must achieve lateral movement.
6. Maintain time interval. Maximum effort for full interval.

Coaching Point
When faced with angles or stacks you must adjust on the move. Don't waste your effort.

Cut-Off Block
Theory
This block is used by linemen on

the backside of a play to stop pursuit or penetration.

Technique

1. Hit out with the count.
2. Shoot beyond the man with your head and arms beyond his inside leg.
3. Head up. Elbows stiff. Hands to the ground.
4. Stay parallel to ground. Never go to your knees.
5. Gather your legs. Scramble quickly on the move. Get your head up field.
6. Maintain time interval. Maximum effort for the full interval.

Cross-Shoulder Block

Theory

This is used when blocking to the inside and when it is necessary to stop penetration. When your block is coordinated with another man inside, this should not be used.

Technique

1. Maintain proper line split.
2. Hit out with count.
3. Step with near foot.
4. Anticipate area of opponent's charge.

5. Aim head in front.
6. Explode outside shoulder and forearm into defender's side.
7. Drive opponent laterally using choppy, digging steps.
8. If he spins out, reverse body block, staying on all fours and crabbing him.
9. Maintain time interval. Maximum effort for full interval.

Scramble Hook

Theory

This block is used to stop a defender from pursuing to the outside of a play.

Technique

1. Hit out with count.
2. Thrust off of both legs.
3. Ram head to outside of defender's hip.
4. Thrust arms so that they straddle your man's outside leg.
5. Head up. Gather legs. Never go to your knees. Work on all fours.
6. Fight to get your head upfield.
7. It is important that you make initial contact and maintain the momentum.
8. Maintain time interval. Maximum effort for full interval.

113

Dan Novakov shows proper form for centers with head slightly raised, feet parallel, knees turned out, and ball in a raised position just ahead of Dan, not under him.

Pull and Fill

Theory
This block is used to fill an area vacated by a pulling lineman.

Technique
1. Pull on the count.
2. Thrust off your outside leg while stepping down the line with inside leg.
3. Snap your inside elbow back as you twist your body to step down the line.
4. Try to get your head on your pulling lineman's tail to prevent large seam.
5. If another man seals the area, continue to pull up and through it. Know the legal clipping zone.
6. Maintain time interval. Maximum effort for full interval.

Coaching Point
If only filling a gap to your inside, use cutoff technique.

Short Trap

Theory
A close proximity trap.

Technique
1. Pull with count.
2. Thrust off drive leg, parallel to line with lead leg.
3. Twist your head in. Thrust shoulders in the direction of the pull by snapping elbow back.
4. Do all this while raising up.
5. Work into the line for an inside-out approach, body under control.

6. Blast with lifting motion, head inside or downfield of your man. Hit with your right when trapping right, with your left when trapping left.
7. Maintain time interval. Maximum effort for full interval.

Coaching Point

If man stays in the tight area, log him in. If he penetrates deep, wildly, let him go. Get up and through the hole as an extra blocker.

Long Trap

Same as short-trap technique.

Hit-Out Pass Protection

Theory

Used to simulate a running play when we want to use a run-action pass.

Technique

1. Hit out with count.
2. Use head on blocking technique.
3. Knock man loose in order to recoil.
4. Don't overextend.
5. Make contact and recover.
6. Stay in front of the defender.
7. If you are losing your man, throw on him with a cross-body block.
8. If possible stay off your knees.

9. Maintain time interval. Maximum effort for full interval.

Pocket Protection

Theory

To be used with pocket passes, draws, or screen techniques.

Technique

1. Set up with count.
2. Push back off your down hand and forward leg. Don't rock.
3. Assume an inside set position, giving defender an easier lane to the outside.
4. Drop outside foot back at about 30-degree angle. Arms down. Get as low as possible. Knees bent. Back flat. Head up.
5. Let your man come to you. Don't lunge.
6. When he is on your toes, deliver a snapping uncoil upwards—never out. Use a lifting motion.
7. Recover—stay in front of him as long as possible.
8. If he insists on coming inside, throw your head across his chest and drive him into pile.
9. If you are losing deep to outside, as last resort throw a cross-body block.
10. Maintain a prideful interval. Maximum effort for full interval.

Putting It Together

In our teaching we try to work on all the blocks daily through repetitious drillwork aimed at mastery. When the player understands the theory of when to use a particular block and has mastered the technique of executing it, his next step is to incorporate it into a live blocking scheme.

To begin, we try to teach four or five ways to block each area of sweep, off-tackle, inside and middle. Our players know the area we are running and recognize that it has priority. Depending on the attack area called, "2" blocking will be a sweep block or an off-tackle block or an inside block or a middle-trap block.

The players then do not have to master more than about four ways to attack an area—but they must know the *area* of attack first. The various "2" blocking assignments are as shown in the following diagrams.

2 Blocking, Middle

2 Blocking, Inside

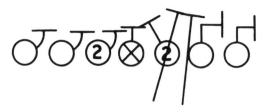

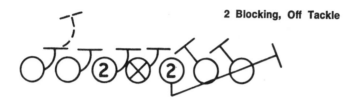

2 Blocking, Off Tackle

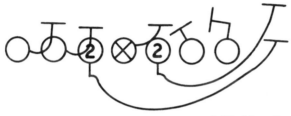

2 Blocking, Sweep

(In Chapter VII, "Refining the System," you will find extensions of block concepts and applications.)

In the past we used a "4" block in all areas, a "6" in all areas, an "8" in all areas.

This allows for great flexibility and different looks in attacking a particular hole area. The aspect of this system we really like is the fact that there is no key even if the quarterback always uses the same calls in his cadence. We can also precall plays with a precalled block.

Having established the line-blocking code we simply add the backfield ac-

tion, formation and direction and we have established the complete play-calling system.

Using formations, we build isolated plays which fit each formation attack. A formation cover sheet (already shown) will lay out all the areas of action which can be used. This cover sheet will be followed by individual play sheets which give the theory and rule of a particular play. Though they are taught as isolated plays they are related to area blocking, run action, action and pocket passes. An example of a play sheet for an individual play in a notebook is shown next.

117

4 Ways to Block Buck Trap

Patterns	Assignments

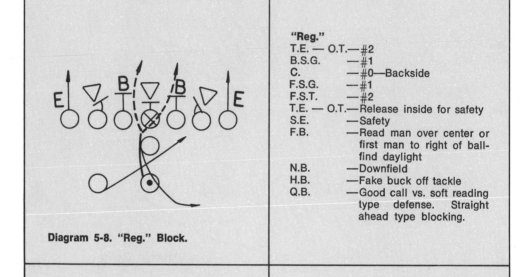

"Reg."

T.E. — O.T.	—#2	
B.S.G.	—#1	
C.	—#0—Backside	
F.S.G.	—#1	
F.S.T.	—#2	
T.E. — O.T.	—Release inside for safety	
S.E.	—Safety	
F.B.	—Read man over center or first man to right of ball—find daylight	
N.B.	—Downfield	
H.B.	—Fake buck off tackle	
Q.B.	—Good call vs. soft reading type defense. Straight ahead type blocking.	

Diagram 5-8. "Reg." Block.

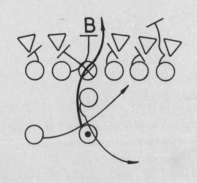

"Hike"

B.S.T.	— Cut-off
B.S.G.	— Short trap up & through LB
C.	— Post over—backside
F.S.G.	— Inside—over—outside
F.S.T.	— Over—outside.
F.S.E.	— Safety
F.B.	— Cut for daylight off trap on LB
N.B.	— Same
H.B.	— Same
Q.B.	— You are directing the B.S. guard to the LB

Diagram 5-9. "Hike" Block.

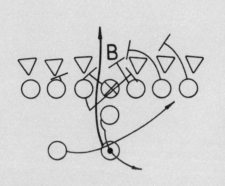

"2"
B.S.T. — Cut-off
B.S.G. — Short trap first man on line to outside of ball
C. — Backside
F.S.G. — Inside on M.G. or LB
F.S.T. — Inside LB
F.S.E. — Safety
F.B. — Read odd or even—pick daylight
N.B. — Same
H.B. — Same
Q.B. — You are directing the F.S. guard and tackle to the LB

Diagram 5-10. "2" Block.

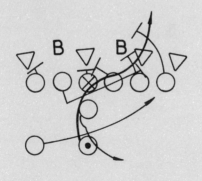

"Go"
B.S.T. — Cut-off
B.S.G. — Short trap on line
C. — Over, backside
F.S.G. — Inside—influence and block out
F.S.T. — Inside LB
F.S.E. — Safety
F.B. — Read odd or even—pick daylight
N.B. — Same
H.B. — Same
Q.B. — You are directing the F.S. tackle to the inside LB

Diagram 5-11. "Go" Block.

The numbers used in the assignment refer to blocking patterns. For example, in the first diagram (5-8) you see "Tight End, outside tackle, # 2," indicating that he is to block the number 2 defensive man.

Naturally, recognition of defenses becomes an important factor and more will be said of this in the chapter dealing with "Training the Quarterback."

The number of variations possible in defensive fronts is so great that you can't train your team to respond to each. For this reason we train just what our opponent has been using in recent games.

The next set of diagrams illustrates some of the more common alignments and our terminology for each.

Fronts

Split 4-4	Oklahoma 5-2
Switch	
ᴮE ᴛ B B ᴛ Bᴇ	E T ᴮ M ᴮ T E
○ ○○⊗○○○	○ ○○⊗○○○
4-3	Eagle 5-2
Switch	Switch
	B
ᴮE T B T BE	E T M T B E
○ ○○⊗○○○	○ ○○⊗○○○
6-1	Tackle Stack 5-2
	B B
ET G ᴮ G T E	E ᴛ M ᴛ E
○ ○○⊗○○○	○ ○○⊗○○○

120

Stack 6-2   Wide Tackle 6-2

```
        B            B
    E T G   G       T E
 O    O O ⊗ O O O
```

Gap Stack 5-2 Left

```
            B       B
    E T     M   T     E
 O    O O ⊗ O O
```

Guard Stack 5-2

```
        B       B
    E   G   G     T E
 O    O O ⊗ O O O
```

Gap Stack 5-2 Right

```
          B   B
    E T       M     T E
 O    O O ⊗ O O O
```

Gap 7 or 8

```
    E T G G T B E
 O    O O ⊗ O O O
```

Guard Stack 4-4

```
    B     B     B     B
     E     T     T     E
 O    O O ⊗ O O O
```

Goal Line 6-5

```
          B   S
    E T   G G     T E
 O    O O ⊗ O O O
```

Tackle Stack 5-3

```
 Eagle 5-3        B     B
    E B T     M     T     E
 O  ◌  O O ⊗ O O O
```

It is not my intention in this chapter to actually give specific plays, but merely to indicate a base blocking scheme and a pattern of backfield actions. I have already mentioned that the many methods used by a coach to formulate a blocking scheme and backfield action constitute his system. We incorporate more than one method for greater flexibility. The basic necessity is to have a means of total communication which is meaningful, practical, and as simple as possible. In subsequent chapters some development of specific plays in a sequence will be shown, along with principles governing audibles.

121

6 Offensive Drills And Theory

Lineman — Daily Work and Drills
Backfield — Drills and Theory
Receiving the Ball
Full Team Time-up
Prep Fronts and Stunts
The Passing Element
Halfback Routes
Flank and Spilt-End Routes
R/A Pass, Action Pass, Pocket Pass
Theory vs. Man Coverage
Theory vs. Zone Coverage
Combined Cuts
Stress Areas of Coaching

Offensive Drills and Theory

Each workday has a period for break-down drills. During this time the offensive linemen hit the seven-man sled working as a total line unit to hit-out from stance, to uncoil a blow, to follow through for a full-time interval. They also alternate shoulders and hit out with a lunge technique on the two-man sled using a six-point, four-point, and then a three-point stance.

All linemen block dummies set along boards which the men must straddle. All possible angles of approach are used. There is a segment of time in which they block live men head on, in stacks, in gap stacks, in short traps and long traps.

After the drill period there is a line breakdown period in which they work as a total unit against a total defensive look. Here they must use their pattern blocks and their complete recognition and understanding of the play concept. Here, also, they practice pocket-protection and screen technique, followed by hit-out protection for run-action plays. These are daily maneuvers done for mastery of stance, start, technique and execution. Agility or conditioning drills are separate matters and a separate period is devoted to them. This total practice period is given to blocking plays and adjusting to stunts.

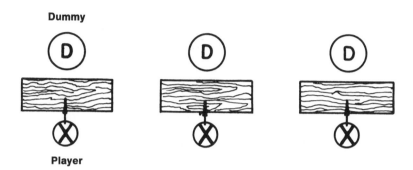

Dummy

Player

1. Explosion Lunge-Step Drill

This drill focuses on starting from a stance, determining the *drive foot*, and exaggerating the *lunge step* with the other foot. This is done with block-ing boards, ten inches in width, placed horizontally in front of a dummy. The player drives, lunge steps, *fits* into the hitting position on the dummy and drives it.

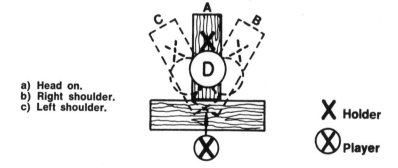

a) Head on.
b) Right shoulder.
c) Left shoulder.

X Holder

⊗ Player

2. Step-Fit-Drive Drill

This second portion is a continuation of the drill above. Add another board in an inverted-T arrangement and allow the blocker to drive the dummy along the vertical board with a holder offering resistance. The angle is changed to include all directions.

127

3. Two-Man Sled Drill

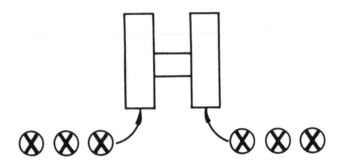

In this two-man sled drill, three techniques are used.

a. Six-point stance, five hits, then roll-out and scramble up.

b. Three-point, lunge hit to belly slammer, scramble up.

c. Three-point, hit and drive for interval of four seconds.

4. Seven-Man Sled

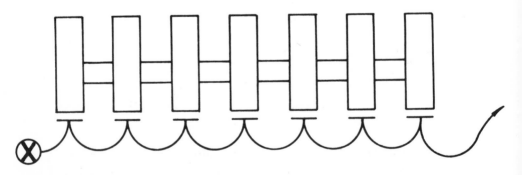

a. Hit and slide drill: Player hits, slides to the next, hitting each dummy in the line.

b. Full line hit and drive.

5. **Guards Pulling Drills**

6. **Pass-Protection Circle Drill**

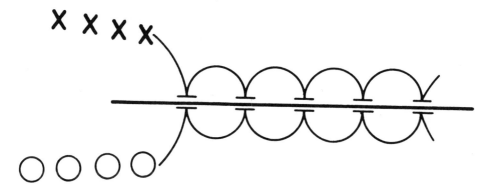

Players hit down the line (from hash to hash—never cross feet).

7. **"Chuck" Them and "Chop"**
   (Pocket Pass Protection)

8. **Hit and Shadow**

(taking away a side)

9. Downfield Blocking Release

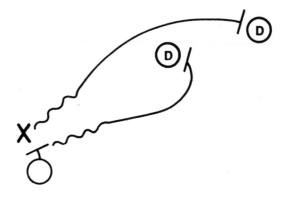

10. Breakdown Drill

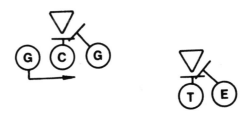

   a. Center and guards.
   b. Tackles and tight ends — work
      double team.

11. Full Line. Block all.
Opponent sets and stunts.

#20 Bob Gladieux illustrates a sweep left with ball carried properly, expecting inside out pursuit. A gifted runner, Bob is cutting off of his inside leg, something that normally we try not to do. In the case of a talented performer, correcting this would be "overcoaching." Gladieux scored on this play.

Backfield Drills and Theory

Offensive backs are a special breed. They usually enjoy running with the football, catching it, and naturally they exult in scoring. They are rarely good blockers, because they are not primarily responsible for blocking. It is for this reason that we drill them daily on this particular function.

Every practice day during my time at Notre Dame has included some kind of back-blocking drill. Backs must be as much—even more—concerned with stance and start than any other player on the field. Too easily, they can give a "key" by stance or foul up timing through improper footwork. Our daily drills call for backs to block ends out, block ends in, throw beyond ends to sprint the quarterback outside, go through the line and block backers, provide pocket-pass protection. These they do every day from an up stance (as an I-back) or from down stances in the halfback position.

Joe Theismann shows an excellent frontal shot of carrying the ball. Notice the webbing of fingers over the frontal point of the ball, the rear point well into the body, the outside perimeter protected with the forearm, the inside perimeter close to the body, and the off hand ready to ward off or insure safety of the ball.

The worst offense a runner can commit is a fumble. One can forgive a missed block or a blown assignment but a fumble is one of the things which destroy a good offensive drive and may ultimately demoralize a team. Therefore, we incorporate in all our practice sessions extensive work on ball-carrying techniques . . . our "anti-fumble" drills.

We simply cannot shout at a boy "damn you, don't fumble." He must understand the essential point: running with the ball is unnatural, falling with the ball is even more unnatural.

Hence, the player must run with awareness of the ball, know how to protect it, know that 90% of the pursuit is from the inside out—thus he carries the ball in his outside arm. He must be instructed and drilled so that

the entire oval of the ball is confined —the forward point sealed by the webbing of his hand, the backpoint high up and sealed in the crevice of his armpit. The front perimeter should be protected by his outer forearm, the back perimeter by his body or side. Violation of this last rule is one of the most frequent causes of fumbles. A boy will allow his arm to get away from his body as he pumps it or hits with it. He may even reach out unconsciously as he falls to the ground. This knowledge of proper carrying, coupled with awareness of the ball, must be drilled. I know, of course, they will still fumble occasionally, but I like to think that our work on antifumble drills makes those occasions much rarer.

Diagram 6-1. Ball-carrying drill.

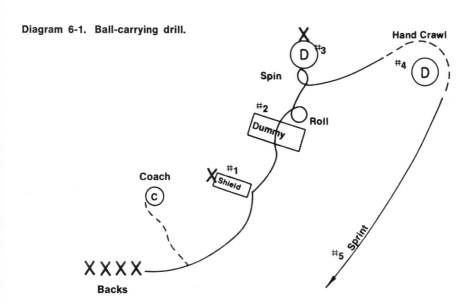

Aside from blocking and antifumble drills the backs incorporate a running drill which uses four major factors in ball carrying. They first receive a pitchout "badly thrown" to cause them to concentrate on fielding the ball; then they get it into their proper arm (right when going right, left when going left). They must then shed a blow with the off arm, immediately follow this by a roll or fall over a dummy, scramble up and run at another held dummy, deliver a blow and spin off. After the spin off, they sprint to the tight corner and work around a point with their off hand on the ground. They then sprint back. The drill is illustrated in diagram 6-1. We usually do this each day of practice. To the right one day and to the left the next day to minimize the time necessary to set up the drill.

This drill—the catch, the ward off of #1, the roll over #2, the spin off of #3 and the balancing of #4 ending with a sprint—incorporates many of the running skills and movements a back must perfect.

133

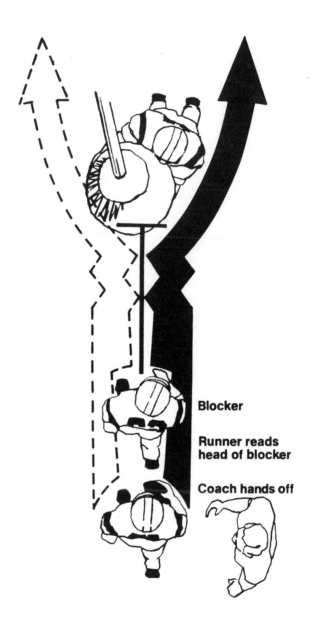

Blocker

Runner reads head of blocker

Coach hands off

Sometimes, if we need work on option running, we merely lead a man on a dummy and let the back cut off as he reads the head of the blocker.

Another option running drill has the back run to the dummy. At the last moment, we move the dummy right or left making the runner cut on reflex.

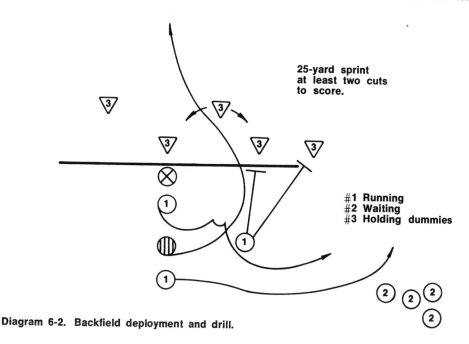

25-yard sprint
at least two cuts
to score.

#1 Running
#2 Waiting
#3 Holding dummies

Diagram 6-2. Backfield deployment and drill.

After their drill period is over and before they join the line for full-team time-up, our backs run! They line up on a quarterback and a center about 25 yards from the goal line. We usually run three sets of backs. Here they work on timing and running. The ball carrier must sprint across the goal line any time he is given the ball. He must switch course at least twice.

The remaining men of that backfield must carry out fakes or block dummies for a full four-second interval. They time new plays first and then go back and retime all the old.

They are told to run, and really run. Immediately after one group goes off, the next group is up. The third group holds the dummies twice and then they move up to run.

Dummies are carefully spaced for blocking purposes. In this way, a back carries from his drill period the timing of all his blocks. We don't work with passes during this phase; we devote it entirely to stance, start, timing ball reception, running, cutting, scoring. It is a rehearsal of a 25-yard gainer — over and over and over again. This tunes the back to spurts of effort similar to those of the game itself!

Each group repeats each play, first to one side then to the opposite. The deployment of backfield squads is shown above (diagram 6-2).

135

Nick Eddy typifies what we like in "traffic" running with his body lean, high leg action, and bunched shoulder position. His head is still in a position to see daylight.

Receiving the Handoff

There are many ways to receive the handoff, but in my opinion the most adaptable, the safest and the one allowing maximum faking opportunity is that in which the receiver has his inside arm up. The other arm is down at his waist with the palm up.

We tell the quarterback to lay the ball in flat, forward of his own vision, not behind it. Not only should the ball go in flat, but it should be as nearly horizontal as possible. It should go in with a slight force and cause a light thud on contact in the belly area. Immediately, the ball carrier feels for a point of the ball with the webbing of his fingers and eases it to that side.

If the ball is being ridden, the faker never clamps, but runs through the ball until he feels himself beyond the quarterback's arm extension. He then snaps over as naturally as he can and drives at least five yards beyond the scrimmage line.

We are extremely demanding and precise with the backs for these first three steps of their play. These depend on and establish timing in that they are always the same and they always take place at the same depth.

Quarterback Joe Theismann properly executes this handoff with fullback Bill Barz. Notice how Joe's eyes are focused on the contact area.

When a bad handoff comes and causes a fumble, we look first to the quarterback. "Did you handoff in front of your vision or behind?" "Did you lay it in flat and horizontal with a slight thud?"

If he says yes to both of these, we can turn and blast the ball carrier, "Your fault!" This handoff maneuver must be rehearsed daily to become smooth. Sometimes a very short back or a very tall one will cause timing or handoff difficulties. This just illustrates why we are so careful; it is a delicate

thing whenever they are exchanging the ball!

Frankly, I get upset—and I want to show it—when we fumble a center exchange or a handoff exchange. I'll shout at players and at my staff to emphasize that dissatisfaction. I have to convey the absolute importance of a particular point and make them work at it under pressure.

They've already recognized that no malice is involved—or they wouldn't be there.

137

Full-Team Time-up

When we arrive at the point of calling for a full-team offensive time-up, it involves two elements. (1) The running game stressed and complemented with a few passes. (2) The passing game stressed and complemented with a few runs.

Here we do not time on dummies, but rather against our prep players. While not full force, the uncoils are real enough, the interval is maintained, but this is understood to be for controlled timing. Not completely passive; forceful enough to the point of getting a true picture. The players get the idea.

If we are working on our running game against a team that employs one particular defense, with all its veers and stunts, that is what our prep defense will use.

From scouting reports and film, we make up a huge card on this defense. We allow the prep defensive coach to call defenses on a down-and-distance basis.

At this time we can no longer run three teams; limited numbers and time permit only two. The third unit of offense now runs against our defense. The third unit of defense now becomes the offensive opponent.

Because our scheme is built on repetition, we huddle the two offensive units and run at the prep alternately. We run two plays on the left hash, two in the middle, and two on the right hash. The second unit repeats the call (a learning procedure built in for the second group). The defensive prep will run every "game" or stunt twice.

Within a span of 20 or 25 minutes, we can run all of our middle, inside, off-tackle and sweep plays.

As soon as a play is completed by the first unit, I want the second unit breaking the huddle. That is how fast it must go. I mentioned that this forces the prep squad to hustle, and I also said that it forces the staff to "coach" on the run. This is all deliberate, however; here we are working for maximum exposure and repetition.

An example of the defensive card used by the defensive prep players would be:

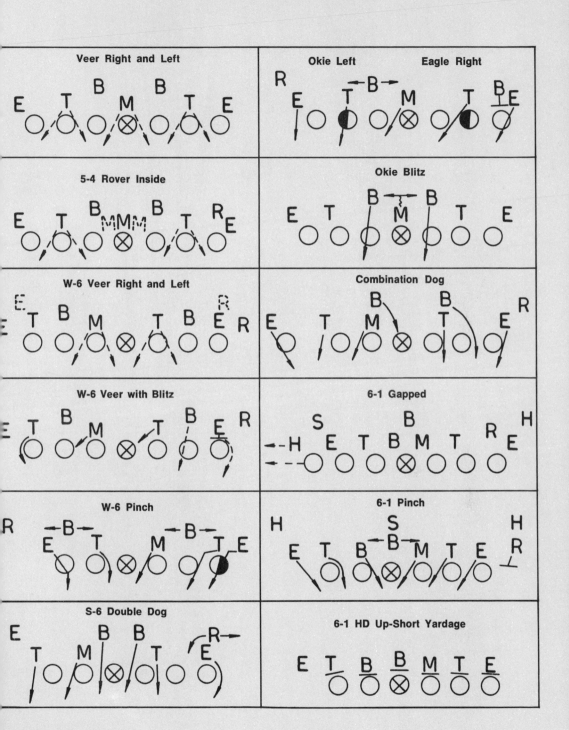

Veer Right and Left

Okie Left   Eagle Right

5-4 Rover Inside

Okie Blitz

W-6 Veer Right and Left

Combination Dog

W-6 Veer with Blitz

6-1 Gapped

W-6 Pinch

6-1 Pinch

S-6 Double Dog

6-1 HD Up-Short Yardage

When the time is right and we have developed far enough in our understanding, we call for a "live" all-out scrimmage. Of course, while all this work is going on in the offensive practice area, the same thing is being done on defense. Of necessity, I must be aware of what is happening with both and give my time to each as needed. If I am more worried about one aspect of our game against a particular opponent, I'll spend most of my time on it. From experience, I really don't see much merit in trying to work offense and defense at the same time. Platoon football allows the luxury of separation and concentration.

I don't concern myself about any division within the team. I have seen a separate pride and spirit emerge in the defense, with a completely equal but different spirit in the offense. This is as it should be, I think.

When game day arrives, we are not separate units, but two unified forces with a single goal. We can thank our staff, past captains, and the great common sense of our players for that!

The Passing Element

Specific thoughts and schemes concerning the passing game have evolved a long way within the past ten to 15 years. While I have devoted a chapter to "The Passing Game" and will deal with it separately, it is necessary that I explain here how it is built into our practice sessions.

We classify our passes into three basic categories. 1. The run-action pass coupled with all our running plays. 2. The action pass, no faking of handoffs but involving a true roll-out or sprint. 3. Pocket passing coupled, of course, with draws and screens.

Our belief in the need for three separate passing schemes is rooted in the recognition that each scheme attacks a defense in distinctly different ways and thus forces different types of coverage. Clearly, if a defense has to prepare for only one of these passing schemes it can deal with it more effectively or efficiently. Beyond forcing the opponent to prepare defensive measures for all three phases of pass offense, this approach also allows us to judge which pattern our players handle best.

Of course, we develop patterns that best attack both man coverage and zone even when we know that the zone is likely to be used against us. Defensive disguising has forced a new development in passing offense; that is, the need to develop passing cut patterns which will be effective against both the

140

zone and man coverage. These developments in defensive pass coverage also require that our receivers learn to examine defensive reactions on the move and understand the principles of adjustment while they are on the move. The danger is the loss of communication between receiver and passer if too much freedom is granted. We don't want a free-lance operation —"you get out in the open and I'll hit you."

In a block of time which we set aside for full-team passing, we always try to have two offensive units alternating and throwing against our best pass defenders. Our defensive line will sometimes be used on defense, but more often they are working on pass rush, screen, and draw in a separate area of the field. This means that a prep line will rush our offensive passing unit and our own linebackers and deep backs will cover. This arrangement allows us to pit our best against our best. But it limits your players to going against your own type of coverage. Therefore, later in the year we will not use this situation; instead, our offense will run and throw against the prep team which has developed defensive coverages likely to be used by our opponents.

Again I cite the importance of the prep team. Our prep defensive backs must learn the basic pattern of coverage used by the opponent; they must give us the best presentation of that look that they can.

More sophisticated coverages beyond man and zone, which wind up being a combination of the two or some form of free safety, are not always discernible in scouting reports or film exchange. To deal with this, we try to put wrinkles into the prep coverage—the kind we imagine *might* be employed against us.

Again, when we pass in our practice schedule it is with a full contingent of players for a full interval. It, like the running game, presents a controlled resistance—close to a live drill—but not as violent. Any interception, however, makes the play "live," except just prior to a game day. The secondary goes all out to intercept or to break up the play and they slap the receiver with two hands upon a completion. I feel that this has helped our throwing game immensely; it most closely simulates what takes place in a game.

Our offensive linemen must read dogs and blitzes and make adjustments to pick them up on the move. Our backs must block, run, and catch, along with our ends, in full traffic. Our quarterback must recognize the de-

#85 Jim Seymour stretches in front of Purdue defender as he gathers in this Hanratty pass on a hook maneuver.

fense and visualize the patterns against the defensive coverage. He is always forced to throw within the normal time limit. He has to maneuver to see through and beyond all the rushing traffic. I can't think of a better way to teach him the importance of concentration, defensive recognition, passing depth and poise under pressure.

As with the run time-up, we always work two plays on the left hash, two in the middle and two on the right hash. The receivers must now contend with all the jostling and "hold-up" techniques that they are likely to face during a game. During this period, as with the running game, we utilize a three- to four-second whistle to mark the end of the interval. What needs to be done in the play must be done in that time.

Most of the patterns which we use are designed to enable one receiver to beat his man. This tight form or man coverage forces the receiver to smooth out his techniques. We use a wide

receiver tree (this will be explained in greater detail in a later chapter). As the starting point we identify the play as a pass and add words to the receiver's tree.

All our pocket passes are labeled with numbers, 40's, 50's, 60's, 70's, 80's and 90's. All our run-action passes are called in the same form used in calling a run. Example: tailback pass right, strong, flanker out and up. The word "tailback" indicates that this is a run-action pass. Our roll-outs are described by words which carry a specific meaning which is also tied to a formation. Example—"fan," "cruise," and so on.

Naturally, formations are flexible by design and as we scout ourselves and chart our own formation tendencies, we adapt our passing game from week to week to disguise a key.

Here we list our trees for a back from the backfield, for the flanker back and for the split end.

142

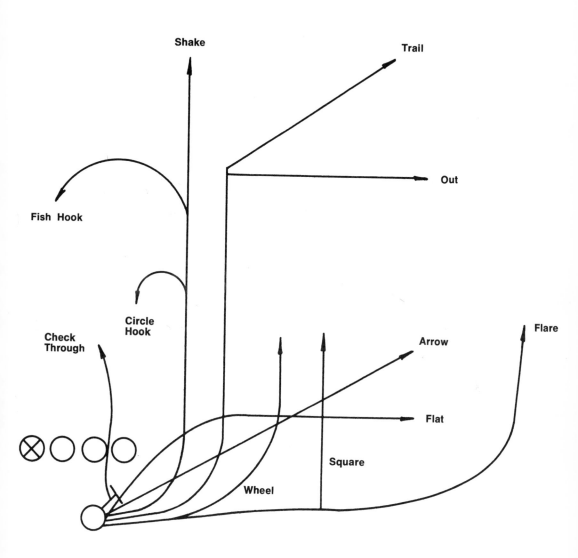

Shake

Trail

Out

Fish Hook

Circle Hook

Check Through

Flare

Arrow

Flat

Square

Wheel

HB—FB Pass Cuts

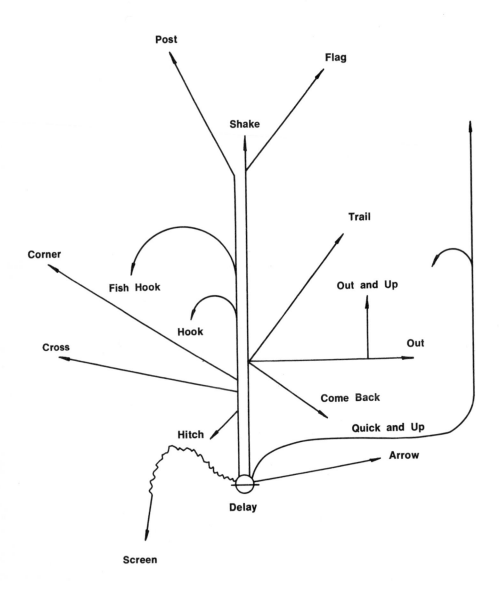

Split End—Flanker Pass Cuts

Next, I'll illustrate three types of passes with the complete call from the huddle:

Run-Action Pass

Quarterback calls "Belly Pass Rt. Weaker Halfback Flat."

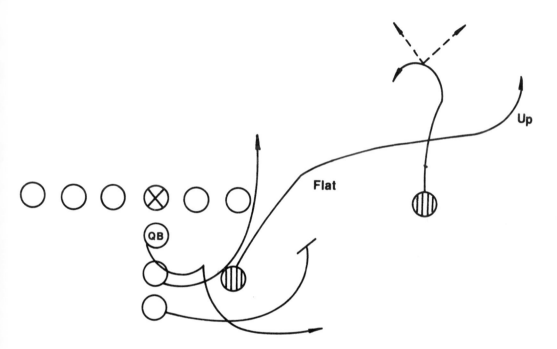

In the above run-action pass you will note that the word "belly" used in the huddle immediately indicates that it is a run-action pass off the belly series. The direction is indicated by *right*. The "weaker" halfback flat indicates where the halfback is to line up and the route that he is to take—into the flat. The end would either run a post, a flag, a hook, depending on how we designed the "flat" cut that week.

Action Pass

Quarterback calls "Fan Right." (The formation is fixed to the play.) (The blocking is fixed to the play.)

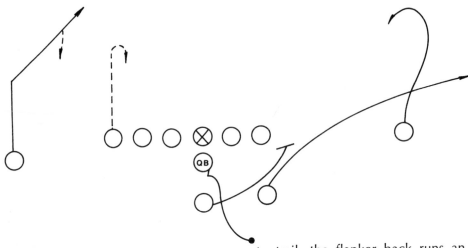

Pocket Pass

Quarterback calls "90 TE Trail." (90 designates pocket and strong right formation.) When the tight end is told to trail, the flanker back runs an associated pattern that we have taught him just as the split end did in the run-action pass.

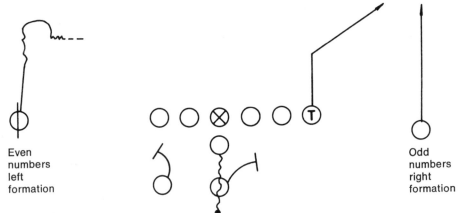

Even
numbers
left
formation

Odd
numbers
right
formation

Our 90 patterns are strong *right* to the *tight end and flanker side*. Our 80 patterns are strong *left* to the *tight end and flanker side*. The *60's* and *70's* put two receivers wide split (combo) to the same side. The *40's* and *50's* work to the *split end side* (weaker).

We reduce the number of words in the call by building into the number a formation, a direction, a pocket protection, a cadence. More refinements can be added by words in the passing tree.

Basic Pass Route Theory Countering Man Coverage

The most difficult pass coverage involves a single defender against a single receiver. This is *man* coverage. Here we think in terms of three elements:

1. Make the defensive man fear you when you go deep and always come off the line prepared to beat him if he will not *run* with you. If he does, cut away.
2. Make him play you head-up for a two-way go. His toughest coverage is to the wide side of the field. If he favors the wide side, entice him that way so you can make a sharp cut back to the sideline.
3. Run a course that gives you an out pattern; if you are open, the quarterback will take it. If you are covered, he will pump the ball to you; you immediately run an up. If your man is faster in recovery than you, and if you cannot beat him to the deep, then you hook up and come back toward the passer.

Against A Zone: (Three Basics)

1. The purpose here is to empty a zone by driving through it deep. A second receiver trails into the voided zone.
2. Flooding a zone: This attack is geared to separate the overlap of a zoning underneath-cover man and a deep-zone man. The first receiver drives as deep as he can, trying to win the race to the deep. The second man engages the shallow coverage underneath. The third man exploits the seam which opens.
3. The third tactic is similar to the second. However, instead of stretching the zoned area vertically, you strain it horizontally. This means you attack the underneath coverage zones and exploit the seams in between.

Run-action passes with interior line fakes help to freeze linebackers momentarily. A wide receiver drives off and finds an inside seam between his zone and the delayed linebacker.

Combined Cuts

Those cuts that attack both zone and man coverage are always useful when you cannot forecast the defensive coverage because of its use of disguise. In this event, we try to determine how many men are involved in the coverage. Probably the most difficult cut to cover—for both man and zone—is one in which a variety of things can happen. If you perfect one or two cuts against an equal coverage, you will cause teams to compensate against it.

In this way, they have to give up something of their total defense. For example, almost every team in college football runs this basic pattern (below). Even though it is predictable, it is still difficult to stop it with only two men on two receivers.

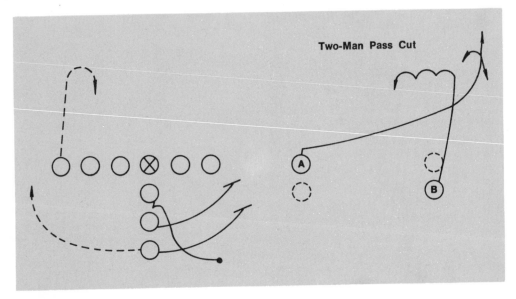

Two-Man Pass Cut

In this pattern, you assume that a defensive man must align somewhere head up or inside of A; otherwise, A can go right up the field on a "quickie."

If the man is at least head up and runs with A to the flat, this opens a seam for the wide man hooking. If the man on A does not run with him,

a roll-out quarterback can hit him quickly for that six or seven quick yards. The man covering A must also be fast enough to turn and go with him to the sidelines and up. The receiver, having no success on the "quickie," the "angle out" or the "up," can always hook up again on the sideline. This is hard coverage for one man. Meanwhile, the wide hooker has much area to explore: He comes off the line going "deep" if he can; if he cannot, then he hooks to the open seam.

Against *zone* coverage by two men, you split the seams by the best method available. If your quarterback can deliver the ball to the open man consistently, he will soon force different coverage. That means that defensively another half-a-man or another whole man will have to align so he can compensate.

If the compensation comes from the inside of the line, it opens up greater running possibilities. If it is from the secondary, then you move your attack to the slighted area.

When you employ word terminology for your communication, you can adapt with greater flexibility. You can use that "universal" two-man cut as an action pass, run-action pass, and pocket pass. It becomes easy now to throw a third receiver into that same side or to the back side . . . thus causing some major problems to most defenses.

In principle, we try for a balanced attack and devote as much time to our passing game as we do to our running game. In fact, a particular game will call for more of one than the other. When an opponent compensates defensively by increasing his coverage at the expense of his rush, we try to run. Obviously, the reverse is just as important.

Areas of Coaching Offense To Be Stressed

Other points we stress are matters of general strategy. But we want coaches and players to be fully aware of the game significance as we:

1. Minimize and coach against penalties.
2. Work and coach against fumbles and interceptions.
3. Run and pass more plays per game by conserving words in the huddle and by reducing the number of words in the cadence.
4. Conserve all time-outs.
5. Exploit the kicking game.

All of our offensive thinking is influenced by number three. This affects all the others.

The prime agent of the offense, however, is the quarterback. His training and the time spent with him can only work for the betterment of the team.

7 Refining the System

Refining the System

There are many systems in football and in time they usually evolve into more refined systems. Having a working knowledge of many different systems allows one a backlog of understanding to use as building blocks for newer concepts. We have attempted a consolidation of the best of all former systems. In the chapter entitled "Offensive Overview," I cited a quarterback call system of blocking. This is practical and workable, but it involves teaching the quarterback a tremendous amount of football and its success rests on one of two strategies: (1) Precall the play to an area with a fixed pattern of blocking because the defense is in the alignment you anticipated all week. (2) Precall the play, but let the quarterback pick the type of blocking and audibilize on sight.

If the defensive look is unfamiliar or if your call blocking is not effective against the look, you must resort to still another method mentioned earlier.

It is simple to audibilize away again from that area to another one. This is risky because all 11 men must achieve effective communication and understand a new assignment in a confined period of time and finally because they do not have the positive knowledge of where they are going until quite late. Splits become hazy and skills less sharp through lack of certitude. There are times, however, when these risks are worth taking.

Let me give an example of allowing the quarterback to call the blocking on a precalled off-tackle play (see diagram 7-1). The first sound he calls is the pattern, and the team leaves on the second and third sounds.

An example of precalling a play, with fixed-rule blocking also called in the huddle is as shown in diagram 7-2.

154

Diagram 7-1. Audible blocking call.

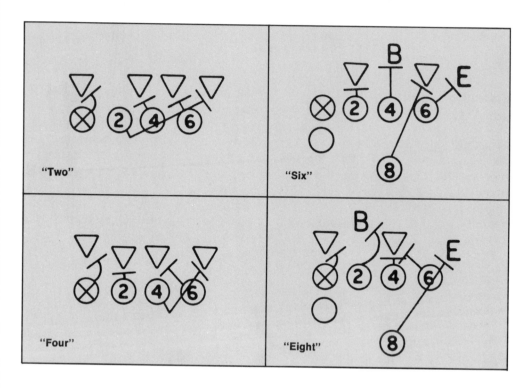

"Two"

"Six"

"Four"

"Eight"

Diagram 7-2. Belly off tackle, right stronger, block "8" on the first sound.

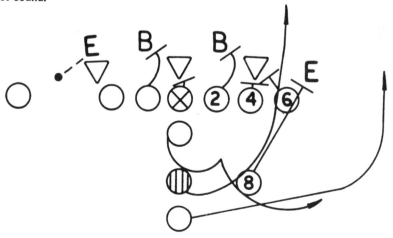

Cadence Employed to Call the Area

The third idea mentioned uses cadence again in the call and is a series allowing the quarterback to direct the attack against a different area. This is hole-to-hole audibilizing.

While I was at Northwestern, with a particularly small team and having a tough year, I found the truth in the adage that "Necessity is the mother of invention." We designed a series allowing two 160-pound backs to combine their 320 pounds with a four-yard headstart in order to hit an area the quarterback had designated. This was our first use of a form of isolation. Here we merely directed the two backs to an area (diagram 7-3).

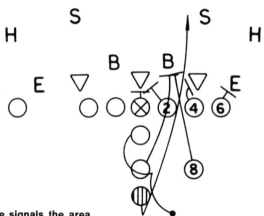

Diagram 7-3. Cadence signals the area.

In this case the area "2" was to be the isolated area. We ran at linebackers and it could have been as easily Hike, four or six, depending on the front. So these three adaptations—1. precalled area and blocking, 2. quarterback selection of the blocking for a precalled hole, 3. a series or hole-to-hole audible with fixed blocking, are really two ways to audibilize and one way to precall. A third way to audibilize is to switch the play from one side to the other. A fourth way is to switch from run to pass or pass to run.

Again, there is a place and a time for each of these; all, plus rule blocking, have gone into our current trend.

Strict rule blocking was an offshoot from tackle calls and eventually to quarterback calls. From this it was a short jump to numbering defensivemen and condensing rules to numbers (diagram 7-4).

This meant highly involved and detailed blocking sheets with a numbering system geared to count single linemen, single backers, stacks of two over a man, stacks of two in a gap. When one man was doubled, it caused improvised ways to pick up extra blockers at the point of attack.

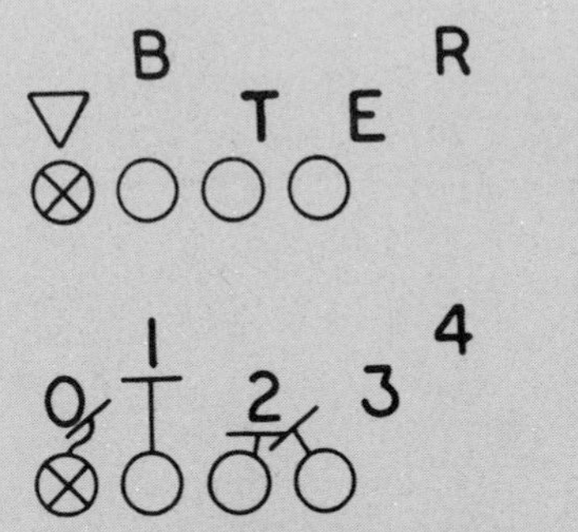

Single-wing Style Modernized to T

Another related method was adopted by teams that carried over single-wing principles of a post, drive, and lead principle. Their blocking calls ignited

Diagram 7-4. Defensive numbering.

The rules would read:

    C—Cut-off zero
    RG—Take #1
    RT—Post #2
    RE—Drive #2

a scheme throughout the line, desig-. nated a post and drive (diagram 7-5), and facilitated a pulling lineman or lead back to block out from that point, hence "trap."

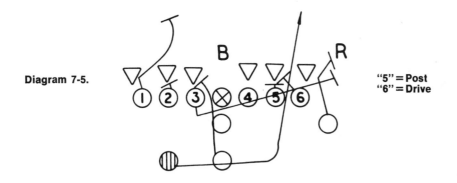

Diagram 7-5.

"5" = Post
"6" = Drive

Master Calls

It is with this backlog of styles and information that we hit upon the concept of master calls. The master call is a *prime* total rule designed to move the line as a unit to a prescribed pattern. Roughly, there are five basic master calls:

1. Reach—to the playside (frontside gap, on, over).
2. Seal—away from playside (full man inside line or LB).
3. Regular—straight up (on over).
4. Divide—isolation, backs fill.
5. Fixed—recognition *or* pattern fits the original master call.

The whole purpose of the offensive line is to create a bubble or distortion when running is into the line and to seal off pursuit when the running is to the outside. You can *reach* every defensive man in the run direction, but you will still need some point of division at the end of the reach — otherwise pursuit will be too great and will run you to the sideline. You can seal every defender down the line and have beautiful blocking angles but you will still need a dividing point at which another lead blocker must kick out away from the seal.

Reach

Seal with kick out from pulling lineman or back to cause a divide.

Reach with double to cause a divide

Divide isolate

Seal

Regular (Straight up)

When a master call is used we are directing everyone to an area. Certain plays have a built-in master call. When meeting blackboard defenses, the master call fits perfectly.

Change-ups in the defensive alignment call for offensive alternatives from the master call (diagram 7-6).

In-line communication between the interior linemen allows alternating moves and diversified blocking schemes.

This flexibility, we felt, would allow us to have a master blocking scheme whenever needed. If it fits the front we encounter, our players' recognition allows the call to "freeze." If it does not, they use intraline communication on the frontside or at the point of play attack.

The divide-point and pivotal man in the scheme is the center, when he reaches frontside right the entire backside must also reach to keep from creating a void.

The exception to this would be the play in which ball-handling or faking action enables a back to fill a void on the backside.

If the scheme was a reach master call to the tight-end side, our players realize that we can now block as many as four men—with a back leading, five. Obviously this effect is reduced if the center must block over or seal,

Diagram 7-6.

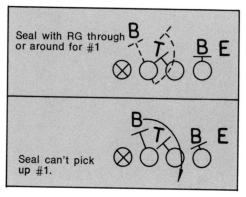

or if you want to double anyone, or if you go to the SE side.

The center then gives the guards a control word. The guards communicate with the center and the tackle their side. The tackles communicate with the guard their side and the tight end when he is there. They simply direct themselves and their teammate knows the alternative and coordinating path. The directions are:

1. *Freeze,* meaning the play will be blocked the fixed way in the pattern of design.

2. *"Regular"* tells his teammate the look calls for straight-up numbered blocking and he is going straight up.

3. *"Down"* tells his teammate that he must block a full man down and to react accordingly on the next vulnerable defensive man. (Seal)

4. *"Up"* tells his teammate he will block a *reach.*

159

Extra words are used to signify things such as *"block down"* and "I'll step around for a backer." This is a *"hold"* call and is used as an alternative in the master call.

The word *"gap"* is a zone call saying to the outside blocker, "There are too many people to my inside for us to block. I'm going to block inside and I need help." This, too, is an alternative type of master call.

An example of each will clarify the use of these calls along with an understanding of two principles.

1. Our linemen always call out words regardless of play side or away.
2. The center, as the swingman, is the control point and must be aware of the backside blocking scheme so that he can be sure it is coordinated with his move.

The development of this scheme has prompted us to call the point of attack into the formation and to add it on at the end of the huddle call rather than setting the formation first as we used to do.

Example: "Sprint Off Tackle Right Strong."

The master call, the design here, specifies blocking *reach* with a double team by the TE and RT. Notice the diagrams of the play (presented on pages 161 through 164) with applied rules of master call, etc.

When we break the huddle, the players know that Sprint is reach blocking. They know we are going off tackle to the right side, and that the tight end and flanker are there because it is into strong right formation. Further, this play has a built-in 1st sound cadence. They know everything they need to know up to the point of adjusting to looks.

Diagram 7-7 — Upon coming to the line, all players or any player first recognizing the defensive front as a 5-4-point-of-attack "look" which fits our master call will mutter and pass along a "freeze" call. Bang! We fire out into our blocks.

Diagram 7-8 — The right tackle and tight end read a wide-six look at the point of attack and adjust the call to "regular."

Diagram 7-9 — The center, right guard, and right tackle see two men arranged in a gap stack; thus we need to call the guard and tackle down to pick up the stack. They communicate "down." Immediately, the tight end knows that if they go inside he, too, must adjust. "Down" is man blocking man. On the backside, the center, knowing the guard and tackle frontside will handle the stack, can now concern himself with backside pattern. Likewise, the backside guard and tackle have communicated an "up" and execute a rake-through technique.

Diagram 7-10 — This 6-1 defense is much the same as the 5-4 look and "reach" applies all the way to the point of the double team—the line being aware that there is one blocker kicking out from the backfield.

Diagram 7-11 — The Split-6 look or 4-4 as it is sometimes aligned, presents a "through or around" situation. Any one of the point-of-attack players who

recognizes this puts the guard in a "hold." The tight end knows that the tackle must block down so he will be on the first man outside the tackle.

The right guard will take the No. 1 man if he blitzes; he will step around for him if the No. 1 man scrapes off. The center knows the frontside backer is accounted for and adjusts to the next man.

Diagram 7-7. Pattern Fixed.

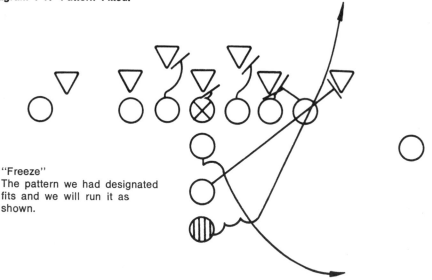

"Freeze"
The pattern we had designated fits and we will run it as shown.

Diagram 7-8. Regular.

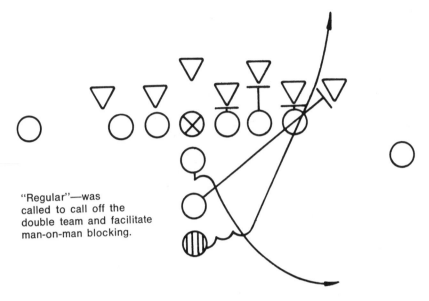

"Regular"—was
called to call off the
double team and facilitate
man-on-man blocking.

Diagram 7-9. Seal.

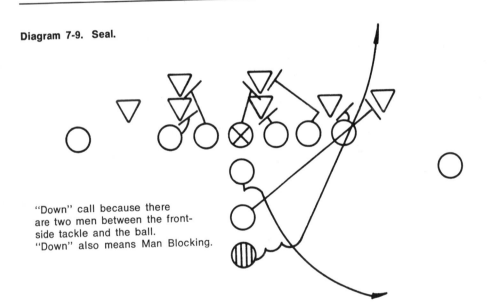

"Down" call because there
are two men between the frontside tackle and the ball.
"Down" also means Man Blocking.

Diagram 7-10. Reach.

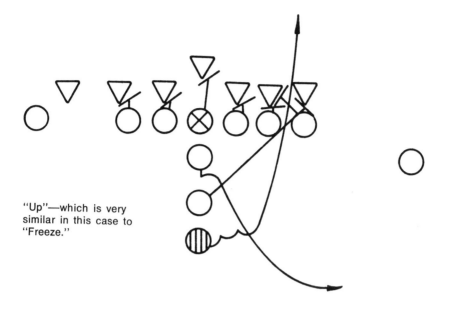

"Up"—which is very similar in this case to "Freeze."

Diagram 7-11. Hold.

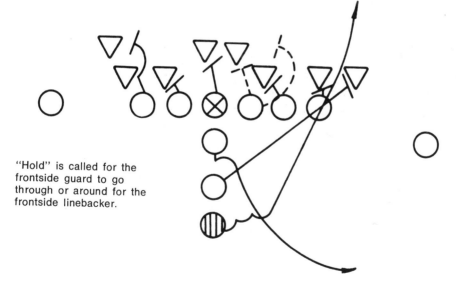

"Hold" is called for the frontside guard to go through or around for the frontside linebacker.

Diagram 7-12. Gap.

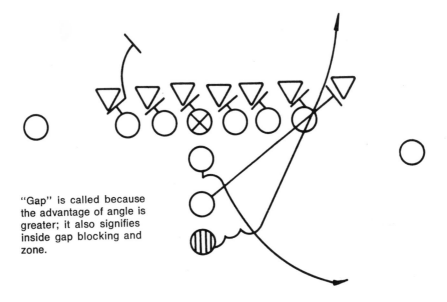

"Gap" is called because the advantage of angle is greater; it also signifies inside gap blocking and zone.

The recognition of all gaps filled prompts a gap call (diagram 7-12), bringing everybody on the frontside to single block his inside gap zone even including the center and backside which differentiates it from "down" blocking a full "man" removed.

Points of Importance:
1. Linemen must be well schooled to recognize defensive fronts.
2. They must spot man stacks and gap stacks when they appear.
3. They must be alert to the number of people involved within their areas.
4. They must master all types of blocks to be employed.
5. They must master the communication to other linemen and know when to block man-to-man and when to block zones.
6. Any player can use any call.

Summary

Master Calls	Communication	Pattern
1 a. Reach	"Up"	Zone outside.
1 b. Reach	"Gap"	Zone inside.
2 a. Seal	"Down"	Man.
2 b. Seal	"Hold"	Alternative to seal.
3. Regular	"Regular"	Numbered blocking.
4. Divide	Pattern fixed	Numbered isolation blocking.
5. Freeze	Freeze	Master call fits.

In the player's notebook, we draw up the offensive formation and block it as we would against a pure blackboard alignment. We then show blocking adjustments for the next four or five possibilities. The master call or rule is built into the specific play and the players soon recognize it. They learn the cadence of the play the same way; it is correlated to area of attack.

When preparing for a specific opponent, we hand out additional sheets showing fronts used by this team and their favorite stunts. We insert the most effective blocking combination against the stunts.

Recognition is the key; we keep in mind that we are not coaching for rote memory, but to develop *player-coaches*. The players take great pride in their ability to adapt the best pattern to attack a defense. Their person-al pride and team coordination make this fairly sophisticated system the best one we have encountered.

Audibles and the Use of Systems

I said before that there are times when each one of these systems has a special strategic advantage. If you try to use a jumble of blocking schemes indiscriminately, you can confuse and overwhelm your players. For this reason we tried to make an intelligent choice of the circumstances under which we will use each scheme—and then we stick to it. In this way, there isn't constant changing, new learning, merely rehearsals of the old.

Middle—Quarterback Calls Blocking to a Hole

In the middle area where traps and double teams are necessary, where there is a need to single block, to finesse block, isolate, and wedge, we use quarterback recognition and audibilized blocking calls. See Buck Trap and Rules in Chapter V.

Inside—Quarterback Calls Hole-to-Hole Audible From Left Inside Through Middle Right Inside

The inside area can present such a great variety of looks that sometimes the wide assortment can cause confusion, so we choose to attack the inside area only if it is there to be run. If it is not, we want to go to another hole. All of our inside attack or two and four holes are, therefore, set up in a series allowing hole-to-hole audibles.

Off-tackle Areas

Because this is the bread-and-butter-attack area of any running game and because it relates so well to run-action passing, we use the Master Call Recognition System when going against it.

Sweeps

All of our sweeps are precalled and use fixed blocking.

Other Audibles (Runs)

We run an audible to either side on any play that attacks the Inside, Off-tackle, and Sweep area — again with fixed blocking. This is an example of the side-to-side audible and is best employed against unbalanced defenses and those which run a lot of stunts or blitzes with a rover back.

Run-action Passes

Passes are tied to runs and are audibilized when field position and down-and-distance allow us the luxury of an "either/or" play. These are good calls for third down with four or more yards to go.

Action Passes

All action passes are precalled with assigned fixed blockings.

Pocket Passes

We use rule blocking for our pocket protection.

Conclusion

This assignment of a system to an area gives great security in blocking. It keeps our players alert to all types of adjustments and offsets the worry that we will face something we cannot attack intelligently.

Some coaches may feel this is too much to teach, too much to learn . . . that any one of the systems would be enough to use against any area. We have found just the opposite—that our players love to feel they have an edge, and they realize that by confining a separate blocking system to a definite area we actually get better focus on that specific area.

Once the idea is grasped by players, they readily accept it. It is then easy to lay out area attacks weekly. What required a long description in print boils down to just a few points for each area. The expanded concept actually reduces what one must know when it is applied to a particular area.

There is no key to the attack in our cadence because our system always uses the same words already in the cadence. The system minimizes our splitting problems and allows us to handle the split more intelligently. The total system, then, is an evolution of many past ideas and we hope that we are incorporating the best of each. Only results can test our judgment.

The Passing Game

The Pocket Pass
Cup Protection
Check-throughs
Numbering Systems
Multiple Cuts
The Roll-out Pass
Universal Cut
Strong Side Roll-out
Weak Side Roll-out
Additional Pass Routes
The Play-Action or Run-Action Pass
Receiving
Sideline Patterns
A Receiver's Individuality
A Receiver's Coaching Point
Beat the Clock
Coaching Aids
Finding the Receiving Lane

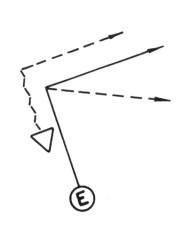

The Passing Game

The Pocket Pass

As noted earlier, the pass threat has become much more refined and polished than at any previous time in the history of football. Perhaps the patterns of professional football dictated the refinements of the throwing game with all of its excitement and spectator appeal. But beyond thrills for the fans, the coach realizes that great chunks of yardage can be gained quickly through the air. A premium, then, is put on receivers who have speed and deceptive moves . . . a line which can protect the throwers . . . and on an accurate passer who can hit more often than not. It is a far more difficult combination to put together than to describe.

Roughly speaking, I have always tried to give about one half of our practice time to the passing game. The practice has helped us both defensively and offensively. I think Vince Lombardi showed in professional football that passing alone is not enough.

This is the last and perhaps most important factor of the passing game; it *paves the way for the running game* and pressures the defense to prepare for and play a total game.

To simplify terminology and blend in our scheme of offensive thinking, we categorize styles of passing attacks.

Some teams use one basic type or small doses of several. We believe that an effective passing game involves three distinct types: *Pocket, Roll Out,* and *Run-Action.*

The pocket pass, again most popularized by the pros, sets a wall of protection from which the quarterback can throw. In the last decade, short escape tosses to backs who sift through the line or flare wide . . . or check through after block protection have added a new dimension to the always growing list of offensive threats. The pro game delights in isolating a swift halfback against a not-so-swift linebacker. This becomes a matter of personnel skills and execution.

1968 Notre Dame Captain #78—George Kunz uncovered in cup protection drops deeper to protect Terry Hanratty's right flank as the Irish quarterback prepares to unload the bomb!

For the collegiate game there are two basic times when we choose to pocket: (1) when you simply must pass, screen, or draw because of the long yardage needed; (2) when your quarterback is not a running threat.

Pocket protection usually offers a greater scope of the field and greater opportunity to pick up stunts and protect the kind of passer who is not primarily a runner or scrambler.

Teams using pocket protection find set-step protection or "cup" (which it sometimes resembles) easy in adjustment. Uncovered linemen drop back and aid backs blocking defensive ends . . . or they can double on a particularly strong interior rushing lineman. Rules for cup protection evolve from strict "area" protection in which your linemen fill their area of the cup (diagram 8-1), to a man-to-man principle in which the left guard is assigned a man wherever he goes, etc. The area of the cup progresses also from the inside out, to the outside in. Here the linemen block on or outside, and backs fill the voids (diagram 8-2). Sometimes backs are used on backers, and lineman on lineman with a combination of "outside in cup" and basic "man" protection.

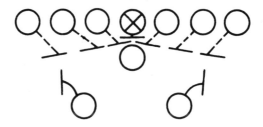

Diagram 8-1.

Cup Zone
Line = inside on.
Backs = outside.

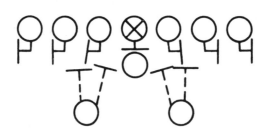

Diagram 8-2.

Line = on outside.
Backs = void.

Whatever the protection scheme, the number of receivers determines the number of pass protectors.

Obviously, the high-risk protection comes with multiple receivers out. In such plays dual responsibility is often employed. As a receiver comes off the line, he will read an unblocked blitzer and look for a check-off throw. This is useful against zone defenses.

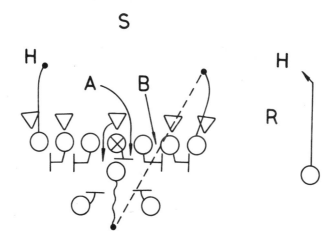

Diagram 8-3. Check-off pass vs linebacker blitz.

As shown above (diagram 8-3), if either A or B linebacker blitzes, the check-off throw is a fine maneuver. If they do not, the pattern continues. Naturally, a man-to-man defense would destroy this tactic as far as the ends are concerned, but this could open areas of flare or halfback check passes since these men are usually covered by linebackers. A numbering system to simplify calls and to provide immediate information about formation, protection, and pattern will contribute greatly to simplicity of style.

Earlier I mentioned that we reserve numbers for the pocket game. The 80's and 90's are meaningful as pocket protection and also tell us the formation. The 90's signify the tight end and flanker to the right and 80's merely indicate the opposite formation to the left.

Diagram 8-4. Pro set formation.

If we deal with the 90's, the formation is a normal pro set, but the backs may vary their formation in the backfield. Example: we number the receivers from the playside across as 1, 2, 3 and backs are 4 and 5 (diagram 8-4).

The nearest back naturally has a lower number since he is in a better position to be called into a playside pattern.

By calling a 91, 92, 93, 94 or 95, you immediately tell the team how many receivers are involved. From week to week we change up the pattern. If 92 is the flanker and TE working together, it may require that the two-man pattern against a man-to-man will not be the same as the two-man pattern against the zone.

If the defensive teams disguise well, it becomes necessary for receivers to read the defense on the move and act accordingly. Following such reactions is part of the quarterback's job.

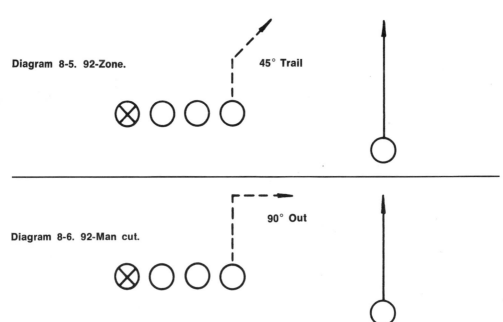

Diagram 8-5. 92-Zone.

45° Trail

Diagram 8-6. 92-Man cut.

90° Out

93-94-95 plus words

Diagram 8-7. Adding to the two-man pattern with words.

Each cut is designed to do a particular thing.

92-zone (diagram 8-5) voids the deepest zone by racing the #1 man deep and allowing the #2 to trail into the voided area.

In the man-cut (diagram 8-6), it is simply a sharper cut forcing the man covering #2 to stay with him hard off the line and then react to his sharp out.

If we decide to drive off #2 and trail #1 in or have #1 do a sharp square in, we use the word "switch" in the call.

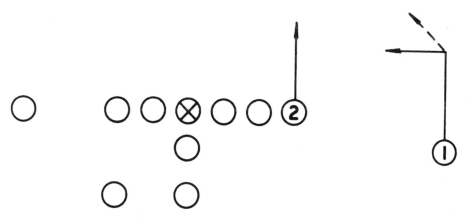

Diagram 8-8. 92-Switch.

By the use of simple add-on words (diagram 8-7), the two-man pattern can be anything you want it to be: 92 Reg, 92 Switch (diagram 8-8), 92 Drag, 92 Double hook, 92 Double post, 92 Double flag, etc.

If your two-man pattern, with its maximum protection moves successfully, fine. If it does not, you may need to throw a receiver into the pattern, the 94 series (diagram 8-9).

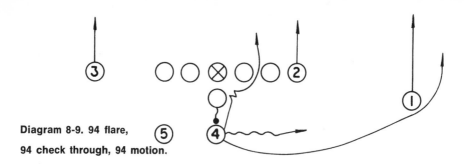

Diagram 8-9. 94 flare, 94 check through, 94 motion.

If the frontside pattern is overdefensed or if the split end on the backside is singled, you can devise a 93 pattern easily. If you want only the #3 man out (the flanker or #1 is out anyway) you merely add the word "single" and get maximum protection (diagram 8-10).

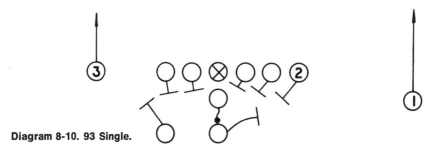

Diagram 8-10. 93 Single.

We also employ the frontside of the play to the weakside of the formation. These calls are the 40's and 50's; odd numbers refer to the right and even refer to the left. The opposite side of the 90's formation are the 40's.

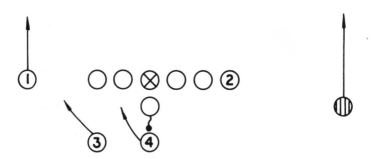

Diagram 8-11. Formation referred to as the 40's.

178

If the quarterback calls 40, he is designating the left side of the pro formation . . . and again the receivers are numbered. There is no need to number the flanker here since he knows he's to run the backside of his pattern (diagram 8-11).

Thus, the 90's tie to the 40's and the formation is strongside right.

The 80's tie to the 50's and the strongside is left.

This simple numbering system tells us: formation, pocket protection, pass pattern, direction. You can even build into the 40's and 50's, 80's and 90's a fixed cadence if you so desire.

The next step in the numbering system is the alignment of two wide receivers to the same side. To the right we label it odd or 70's (diagram 8-12); to the left, even or 60's.

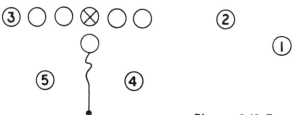

Diagram 8-12. Formation labeled "72."

Here again you have available all the combinations of numbers and words: 73 Hook, 73 Cross, 72 Cross, 75 (five receivers out).

Certainly we do not try to time up every combination; we may throw only five or six pocket passes in a game. The flexibility, however, provides again broad exposure and it is there to be used if the need arises. We rarely throw more than three receivers out at a time, but we are prepared to throw all five.

Again, the determination of how

many receivers to send out depends on how many defenders you anticipate in coverage. If few cover, the probability is that one man will play one man. This, then, does not call for multiple receivers as in a zone, but maximum protection with skilled execution. This is when you see if your preparation of skills is better than those of the people who are attempting to defend.

Versatility of formation is a must, however, and it is also a must that these pocket formations be tied to

179

your normal offense. In my mind, we can't think of the passing game—and specifically the pocket style—without thinking also of the *draw* style of play and the screens. Whenever we time our pocket game, one out of every four plays will be a screen or draw. They go hand-in-hand with the hard rush and help convert the sting of overaggressive rushers into an offensive advantage.

Diagram 8-13. Roll-out Pass.

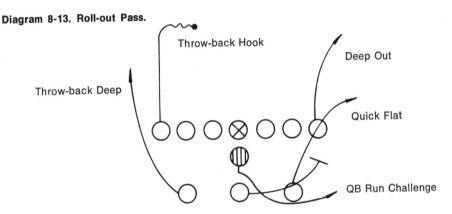

The Roll-out Pass

The next style of pass, most popularized by the collegiate teams, employs the "sprint-out" or "roll-out." The intent here is usually to exploit the talent of another runner in the backfield and tax the defense into a number of concentrated areas.

The basic roll-out style from the balanced-T era was the threat of the pass deep, pass flat, the quarterback sweep, the throw-back hook, and the throw-back long. The symmetry of formation made this play equally dangerous to both sides and forced a balancing of defensive power (see diagram 8-13).

From the basic sprint-out came the need to employ the quarterback as a sweep ball carrier—playing "cat and mouse" with possible rushers or forcers. The flat had to be covered along with the deep outside; one man was needed to box in the sprint-out quarterback.

To the playside, the right tackle, right guard, half of the center, and the fullback represented three-and-one-half blockers. If an opponent covers the flat and deep outside defensively and rushes three men, he has already committed five. The middle deep area must be covered and, therefore, he has committed at least six. Any overbalancing may see the play going to the opposite side.

Diagram 8-14.

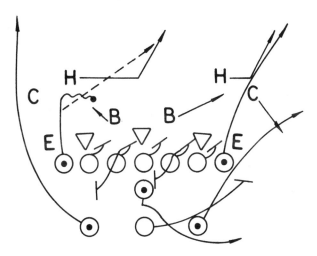

If the fullback blocks a containing end down, the quarterback can then turn the corner as a ball carrier or flip a short lob to a halfback slipping into the flat (diagram 8-14). The defensive tackle cannot work too hard on the outside without facing the possibility of drawing the fullback inside of him. If defenses revolved or rotated to such a sprint-out, the throw-back hook or cross-to-the-backside-hook-area plus the throw-back deep area become fairly vulnerable. It was from this basic situation that the roll-out started to grow in its dimensions.

Defenses soon figured ways to compensate allowing the offense one strength, but taking away the prime threat. Offense then responded by divorcing the receivers from the group and presenting another formation that had to be reckoned with. This was our thought when we went to the combination of two wide receivers to one side (diagram 8-15).

181

#5 Quarterback Terry Hanratty demonstrates the perfect form for rolling out. He is nearly eight yards deep, his vision is directed front-side, his grasp of the ball is in a quickly adjustable position to throw, run, or pull up and throw back.

We tried to force defenses into overcommitting personnel to our two-man wide side. If they did not, we could hope our skills, perfected in these patterns all year, would outperform those of the defense who worked on them just during that week. If they should overcompensate, we would try throw backs or screens.

If the compensation of the defense comes from the basic front, we feel that our best chances are with the run. If the compensation comes from the perimeter of pass defense and leaves the run defense intact, we try to counterthrow or throw back.

8-15. Two receivers to one side.

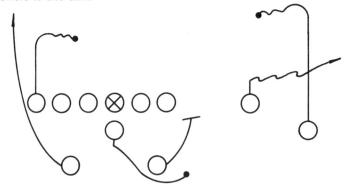

Whatever can be done from one formation, can be done with reasonable similarity from others. We took the same basic idea of the combo formation and used it in the pro set (see diagrams 8-16 below.)

Diagram 8-16.

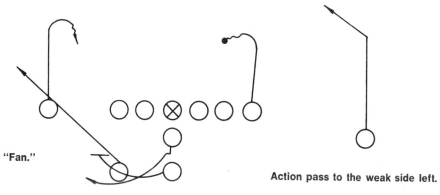

"Fan."

Action pass to the weak side left.

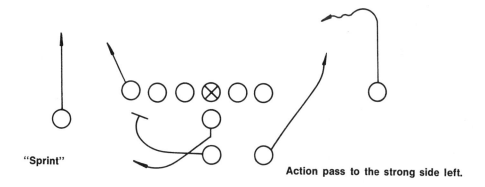

"Sprint"

Action pass to the strong side left.

It is a small chore now to employ a basic cut that taxes defenses, utilize a fourth runner and diversify the formation with similar cuts. The two remaining backs in the backfield add on a new prospect with motion, leading blocking, screens, check through and running straight thrusts.

All of what we do in roll-out is identified with words. If the quarterback calls "cruise right" the response is simply a combo of receivers right; the blocking and pattern are fixed to mean a two-man pattern (diagram 8-17).

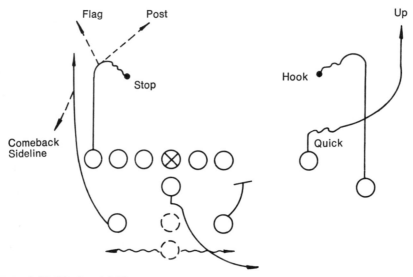

Diagram 8-17. "Cruise right."

We add words and get "cruise, right, stop"; otherwise the tight end stays in. Call "cruise, right, throw-back" and the left half runs a deep sideline; otherwise he stays in. Call "cruise, right, three" and the backs align in the I and the left half will flare playside.

Again, it is not my intention to outline specific plays. Rather, I want to show a system in which one coach or one staff can innovate, developing their thoughts. Our staff evolved the concepts I have stated and we constantly revise and edit, experiment and adapt. Words that are meaningful are employed and never used to mean anything else. "Cruise" is always to the combo side, it is *"cruise"* blocking pattern. "Fan" is always to the split end side, it is always *"fan"* blocking, etc.

In this way, we build an arsenal of cuts geared to go against man or zone, against under-coverage or deep coverage, against over-defense or single-defense.

Naturally, we don't innovate during a game the way we do in practice, but if a play is begging to be run, we have probably touched it somewhere in our preparation and can easily adjust to it.

Another important point for the roll-out style is this—the passer in rolling out never looks anywhere but frontside as he rolls. As he maneuvers with an open drop step, he can see the playside all the way during the time it takes him to come to the judgment point. The judgment point, about eight yards behind the offensive tackle, reveals one of three things: (1) The front side pattern is coming open, release the ball; (2) it isn't open, but the fullback chopped the end and there is leverage—run! (3) the pattern is covered frontside. The end is containing, pull up and throw back. If all of this fails, then as the old-timers used to say, "Peel it and eat it or throw it into the nickel seats."

Much of what we do with the passing game is limited to a few receivers, either two to the same side or one to each side. From the basic structure just described we try to train our most frequent receivers to learn visually and sensibly the patterns of defensive secondary. We further attempt to narrow the options they have to one basically good way to attack the coverage. This holds the margin of error down.

This is not easily done; nor can you really be sure that it will be done accurately by all receivers and the quarterback at the same time. A slight miscalculation may result in a lost play, or worse, in an interception. Still the rewards are greater with greater risks and so we attempt to "school" receivers into running the course forced on us by the defense.

The Play or Run-Action Pass

During most of my playing days in the 1940's, the passing game pretty much resembled the standard pocket pass with basic, stringently run patterns. There were times in my coaching career when just that style was good enough to get the job done.

It has been my good fortune to be able to employ a sprint-out quarterback whenever I've been blessed with a great athlete at quarterback who can tax the opposition both running and passing. This fits into the style of the quarterback, but the run-action pass seems to emerge as the best of two worlds. It helps the running game

Coley O'Brien demonstrates a running pass—correctly turning his torso downfield to afford a more accurate and easier release.

through deception and it generates greater distortion of secondary defenses which overcommit to run fakes.

Trying again to avoid duplication, all the cuts run in our "pattern tree" are virtually the same. There is perhaps a slightly longer time taken in running courses to allow for slow blocks (fake-block-and-then-run pattern). This time element is naturally used to make a good enough fake to defensive men at the supposed point of attack.

In the 1968 season, circumstances forced us to move our second-string quarterback, Coley O'Brien, to halfback. Because of his ability, the running pass became still another facet of the multiple threat provided by a run-action sequence against a defense.

One of the very first and most suc-cessful sequences we used in the run-action category is the basic "speed sequence" illustrated in Chapter 10.

The runner faking the off tackle and sweep area held the defensive men who were involved with fronts.

A wide flanker drove the deeper or secondary defenders into a position far removed from the completion area. The toughest job for the defense was to key the "slow blocking" tight end and discern whether the play was a run or a pass.

Football is indeed a matter of inches and any delay by the defenders gave us the "inches" advantage—and sometimes feet or yards.

Though it is repetitious, the following play diagram (8-18) will recall the total look—both to the tight end side and to the split end side.

Diagram 8-18.

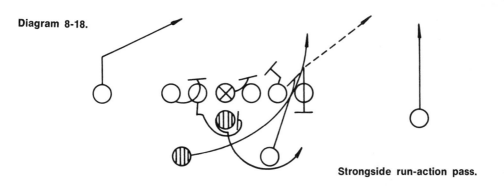

Strongside run-action pass.

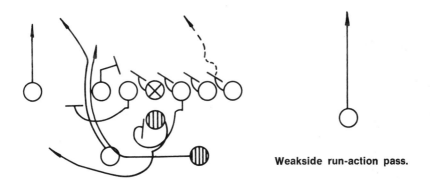

Weakside run-action pass.

From the basic two-back-divided and the speed-sweep, which was the main threat, football evolved to more of the I formations: the true four-man I, or power-I, or just two-back-I.

This development captured the imagination of our own staff along with many other people around the nation. In truth, the I-fake to the tailback seemed a much better fake and easier to tie into some of the more popular running schemes.

With this as a start, we began to use all of our basic formations, strong and weak, combo right and left, power-I with one split end in the run-action game. *If numbers governed the pocket calls and words ignited the roll-out directions,* we had to find a third means of identifying a style of pass.

We chose to label our run-action game exactly as we call a run. The only difference is that we call out the word "pass" at the end of the call (diagram 8-19). This immediately tells the line we are directing them into a fire-out form of protection and that the play is to be a pass and they should not be guilty of being downfield.

Diagram 8-19.

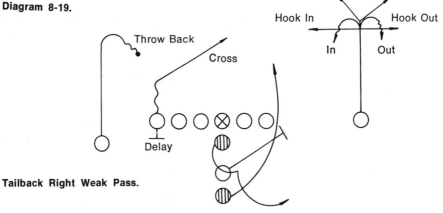

Tailback Right Weak Pass.

If we wanted a specific cut, it became an add-on word (see diagram 8-20). This simple addition would alert the split end to drive off deep.

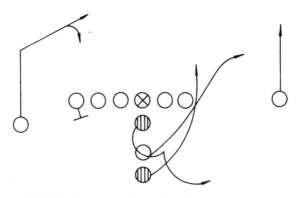

Diagram 8-20. Tailback Right Weak Pass — Fullback flat.

Other run actions were simply labeled "Belly pass" from our belly series, "Iso pass" from our isolation ball handling, "Tackle trap pass" or "Bootleg."

Our players responded readily to this type of communication and we know certain words ignite the particular players whose jobs or duties are to be changed.

An integral part of this form of pass is a screen tied to every action that your offense will use. In 1964, we most often utilized a three-back offense with one split receiver. Our pass offense was at that time 70 per cent run-action. The following diagram (8-21) will tie together some of what we did then and are likely to do again.

Diagram 8-21.

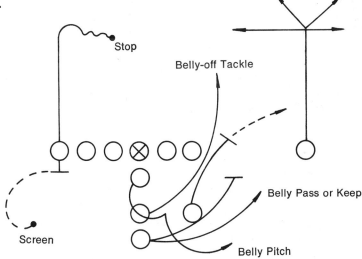

1. BOT—was the base belly off tackle.
2. BP—was the belly pitch or option to the I back.
3. B Pass or B Keep—was the quarterback option of sweeping or passing.
4. B Pass Stop—was a throw back to the tight end.

5. Belly Screen—was a throw back screen to the tight end.

Again, it becomes quite easy to evolve this into a greater variety of formations by permitting either the right half or left half realignment or motion.

Jim Seymour — Notre Dame's All American End, had great concentration while fielding the ball. Here he is shown with the inside of his hands together — in full stride.

Receiving

Bart Starr's comment about concentration being the absolute necessity was a most perceptive point in his description of passing. The ability to concentrate on the ball at the time of the catch, in traffic, under great pressure, is indeed a special talent. We often refer to a player as having "good hands," "fair hands" or "stone hands." Certainly hand size, dexterity, and reasonable touch play a part in receiving, but improving the receiver's ability to catch a ball is most frequently achieved by increasing his concentra-tion—while he preserves a degree of relaxation.

In prepractice warm-ups, our receivers will play catch with the quarterbacks and first try to field softer throws one-handed. They take lobs over the shoulder, to one side, and high throws over the head. We stress "looking the ball into the hands" trying always to prevent the receiver from catching with the body unless the ball is coming into the gut zone.

We feel that extended arms with thumbs together give maximum web-

190

bing to receive the ball. A general rule would be: palms up for a catch as low as the waistline—for a catch above the waistline, palms front and thumbs together. Receivers and defensive backs must be aware that they often catch a ball while moving toward it; this doubles the normal ball force.

Once the ball is caught, it must be tucked away and the receiver becomes a runner. Probably the easiest passes are those most often dropped because the receiver takes the catch for granted, glancing away at the last second and starting to run without the ball. This often happens with short throws or screen passes. Here again we drill into our players: "If you never gain a yard, first catch the ball."

On long throws, we want the receiver to run with natural form and pump his arms until the last moment. The receiver who runs with outstretched arms impairs his speed and coordination. If the ball is underthrown, the receiver must make every effort to come back and field it at the highest point possible — trying for the catch, but preventing the interception at all costs.

Getting a player to run a proper pattern is not easy. He must understand the timing involved within the play—and gauge his speed and moves

so he can approach a point of reception when the quarterback is ready to throw.

Boyd Dowler, the ex-Packer, ran two forms of an out-pattern which illustrate this point. We try to do something similar.

If the action of the pass is a pocket or a roll-out, we have the receiver come hard off the line and threaten the defender deep. The receiver fights for a body lean forward even when he plants his inside foot for the sideline cut. Rearing back and settling the weight lessens speed and clues defenders. The coaching point we make is to have him threaten up to the point of causing the defender to run with him or move backward. He then, at a predetermined point of timing and distance, makes a turn greater than 90°, "comeback" sideline in hope of creating an even larger gap between himself and the defender.

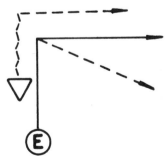

This is a rather routine cut and

191

most teams employ it, but its true effectiveness is governed by: (1) the accuracy of the throw; (2) the timing and trueness of the pattern; (3) the knowledge of the defensive coverage.

If this out-pattern is thrown to a receiver in the area of a corner man who does not have deep coverage, he will merely hang in the area. You cannot threaten him deep.

Diagram 8-22. Out pattern.

If the pass is of a play-action variety, more time is available to get to the same area. The pattern, however, is now different.

As the receiver comes off the line, he tries to run a true "up" pattern and does what is almost a question-mark move that places him in the same sideline area and depth as the comeback sideline (see diagram 8-22).

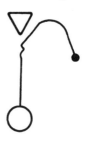

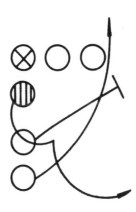

The entire maneuver is one of timing. Naturally, there must be room for flexibility in case you have guessed wrong about the coverage.

This is difficult to grasp and only the most experienced receivers fully master this quick adjustment.

Let us say that we are running the

"question mark" out and the defender will not run with us. The receiver will go all the way on the up until it is obvious it is taken away. In this case, he must make a curl *in* action to a seam for a chance at the reception (diagram 8-23).

Diagram 8-23. Curl-in pattern.

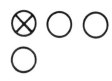

Here again the knowledge of defensive secondary and their reactions must be part of both the quarterback's and the receiver's mastery. This, to us, is the coach's responsibility in teaching. These players, from whom we expect judgment and adjustments, must be informed of all the facets, all the change-ups. They must have adequate preparation to meet all changes if they are to perform with confidence.

Often they will tell us what is happening to them on their routes so we can formulate an adjustment.

An on-the-move-adjustment is technically "reading the defense" on the move. It does involve great risk. To minimize the risks, we limit the options a player may use.

A Receiver's Individuality

Certain players have a "sense" of being open, or better yet, a sense of how to get open if they are not. It is probably past experience—perhaps basketball or much football—that enables this sense to develop. At any rate, there is the fact of a player's individuality. Based on his speed (a rare and important commodity), his height, and his moves, he must constantly refine these moves to develop smooth effortless reactions. As in the sequencing of a football system, it helps to start always the same way, ending in a variety of ways.

Our wide receivers get down in a three-point stance with their inside leg back, with a slight head nod to

193

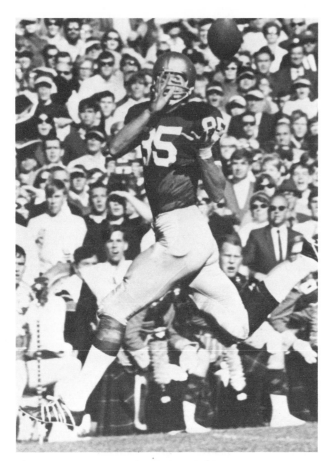

Seymour, again in full stride, focuses his vision on the ball and attempts to catch it in his hands — this route was an out and up.

the inside toward the ball. They cannot leave on cadence because their distance and the noise make it difficult to ignite accurately. They leave on the movement of the ball. They are instructed to come off the line at either full speed or close to it—under disguise. Good defensive backs study the moves and countermoves made by the great receivers. Like it or not, most of us fall into a routine of doing those things most often that we do best or easiest.

Sometimes this routine can work to a receiver's benefit. An example of this would be in running a post or corner pattern deep. A variety of things can happen. Usually the defender will play inside to the short side of the field, outside to the wide side, and head up at any time. His alignment may be a disguise, however, and his true responsibility will not unfold until forced to show.

Trying to force his hand, the receiver on the right offensive side is supposed to run a post to the largest portion of the field.

In doing this, we try to work on the idea that a long pattern needs longer continuity. He will start in the direction he ultimately wants to go, the inside. When the defender eases that direction, the true, hard, sharp cut to the flag is made with all the speed one can muster; just as soon as he gets defensive reaction he will make his final move back to the post.

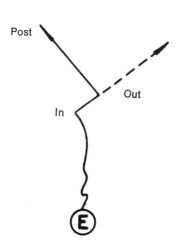

3 Move Post Route

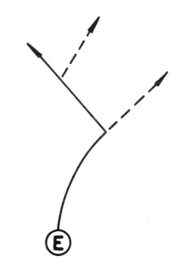

2 Move Post Route

In, out, and finally, in, seems a long route, but the footwork and rapid cutting develop quickly.

Trying to make this post technique look exactly like the flag route is simply a matter of dropping the third move. Another way is to use the three-step move to the flag: (1) move to the outside; (2) sharp to the post; (3) three to the flag.

Combining the variations involved, there are two basic ways to run the post and two ways to run the flag. One uses three moves; the other two. The timing involved is geared to the depth of the pass and the action, roll or pocket of the quarterback.

195

A Receiver's Coaching Point

Never argue with success! I've had great receivers who jumped every time they caught the ball whether they needed to or not. Did they catch the ball was my only question.

I've consistently had receivers reach for an "out" pattern and throw their inside arm across their vision to enable them to have their thumbs on the inside of the catch. Perhaps that violates theory in that your reach is restricted and that vision is impaired. I do know, however, that catching with the thumbs inside can sustain a more forceful throw than if the thumbs are on the outside. The coaching point is simply to know what the ultimate objective is and if it is being achieved. I won't quibble about technique unless it's technique which frustrates the ultimate objective.

The passing game then starts to piece itself together in a knowledge of defensive coverages and in pitting receivers against these coverages with effective patterns. The ball delivery, of course, depends on the quarterback's skill. The style of his pass is built into your system in a way that best utilizes your talents and ties with your style of run offense.

All of this must be perfected in the separate parts (individual patterns, throwing drills, recognition of perimeters, etc.). It must also come together. This goes back to our theory of drilling the most efficient and realistic way that we can.

We pit our full offensive unit against a full defense, trying to get the complete impact of rush and traffic. We constantly throw, screen, and draw against a variety of coverages. Our receivers are harassed, jostled, held up, knocked down, and generally treated as they would be in a game. In the time given to passing within our practice plan, we want it to be very, very gamelike.

Toward the end of our fall preparation and prior to the first game, we try to put on the finishing touches and train to "beat the clock."

Beat the Clock

This phrase, naturally, refers to those times when the clock is running and we are trying to crowd more play into the remaining moments. It could be just before the half or at the close of the game. It could be to conserve time-outs or to play catch-up football. In any event, it is one of those strategies that does not just happen; it must be worked on.

We set a formation with a split receiver to both sides and hustle our huddle . . . do away with huddle completely. We go strictly audible at this point and our first objective is to stop the clock. The second objective is naturally to attempt to score or advance the ball.

We do this at full tilt against the running clock several times a week. The offensive audibles which make up our beat-the-clock series are just enough to keep everybody honest. We insert a draw and a screen, a basic run off-tackle, and a more elaborate passing game.

We try to hit the wide receivers quick or quick and up. There are always two people (the tight end and one of the backs) involved with a check through for an outlet. An audible call can release all four of these men in the event we read a prevent defense.

This beat-the-clock idea is certainly not new, but it is a valuable piece of strategy which belongs in any offensive system. We use the most basic two-wide-receiver formation available. Any time the quarterback screams out "Clock . . . Clock," the formation is automatic.

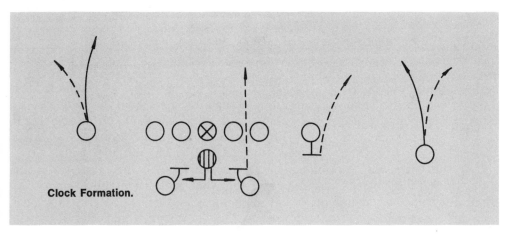

Clock Formation.

With no huddle, the players respond to former drill and past experience. We tune this up at the close of our week. When the clock is stopped, we rehuddle for a more closely planned call.

The quarterback and all receivers are instructed to either get out of bounds or score. If the quarterback can't find an open receiver, he must either scramble to the sideline or ground the ball as an incompletion.

Terry Hanratty follows through in the face of a rush. Proper trajectory allows him this release.

The opposite of this "clock" strategy is the "bleed" tactic. Here we want the clock to keep running or else we want to force the opponent to utilize his time-outs.

Over the years, the importance of both "clock" and "bleed" has shown often. The time we spend on it has been well rewarded.

Coaching Aids

During warm weather, all of our backs and receivers wear wrist sweatbands and use a touch of clear shoe polish or hand spray for tackiness.

We see to it that all receivers have a ball of their own to fondle, toss, and mold in their off moments. It is a small thing, but it develops a feel or touch for the ball.

Another point with reference to the throwing game is: praise the effort of going after the ball, praise the catch in traffic. We insist that after the catch, the receiver run and attempt to advance the ball. Here it is important that ends know how to properly carry a ball and roll with the fall or the tumble without jeopardizing the ball's safety. This isn't mastered unless they are put through a drill or through live

198

pass scrimmage, but ignored, the lack will cause a good completion to wind up as a fumble and turnover.

Whenever a scaled pass scrimmage is involved, it is very important to clock the throw and the reception. If you do not have a working standard, you may fool yourself into thinking you have a good passing game which, in truth, will not hold up under shorter time periods.

We want the release of a throw to be within three seconds. For a wide roll-out, a long pocket, or a play-action —not much longer than that. I feel 3.5 is maximum for a release.

A very quick quarterback who gains depth rapidly may make it seem longer and perhaps there will be times when pass protection will give such a luxury, but a minimum release time is a good point to shoot for.

Finding the Receiving Lane

Depending on the quarterback's arm and his strength of throw, it is likely that he will throw a ten- to 15-yard gain (in effect this is a 20- to 25-yard throw) on a direct line. This being true, he cannot throw through people but only in seams.

The trajectory of a throw is governed by its depth. Thus, he must look to seams and sometimes throw to a spot that forces the receiver to move to a spot away from a nearest defender. The receiver must also sense the nearest defender and slide to a vision point where he and the quarterback are in "lane."

On longer throws, the ball must loft according to the quarterback's calculation. He will turn the nose up and loft a ball for a receiver to run under when he is clearly in the free. If hotly pursued, the ball must be on the money. We preach simple slogans:

1. Never throw behind the receiver if he is running a crossing pattern.
2. Never lead him into trouble.
3. Never force the ball.
4. Don't stare down your prime target.
5. If he is covered at the time you are ready to throw, pump and regather.
6. Think completion by imagining the flight you want the ball to take.
7. Always know where you are attempting to place the ball.
8. Never hang the ball on a short horizontal throw or on a screen pass—drill it!
9. For the right-handed, turn your torso toward downfield on a run pass right, your left hip forward on run pass left.
10. Never eat the ball for negative yardage, unless absolutely necessary.

199

9 Training the Quarterback

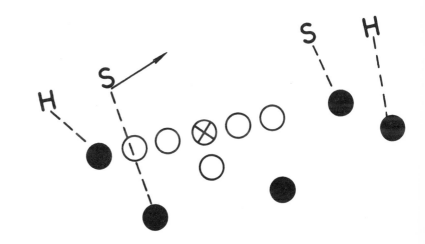

Training the Quarterback

The skills in football have progressed rapidly in the past 20 years and in particular this has been evident in the many fine quarterbacks across the country. A great football team rarely emerges without a top signal caller.

I think that over the years I've been blessed with some really fine talent and perhaps that is the best point I can make regarding the position of quarterback. To begin with, the boy must be an athlete. He must obviously have leadership qualities, dexterity of feet and hands, the ability to shoulder responsibility under pressure and, certainly, the ability to throw.

I have never attempted to mold an image of the ideal quarterback because after handling them—with our offensive backfield coach — I realize that they come in a variety of packages.

While at Miami, my first quarterback was a fine passer and leader. Since then, in nearly 20 seasons, I've witnessed many quarterback styles and skills. At Northwestern, there were two especially good athletes who played well, with dramatically different styles. One, a versatile, triple-threat athlete, was perfectly suited to a roll-out and run-action style of play. The other, because of his incredibly accurate passing ability, caused us to change to a pocket style of attack similar to the pro offense.

Moving from Northwestern to Notre Dame, we were challenged to select a quarterback from personnel we did not know much about. After our first spring practice, I was completely convinced that a certain young man was our best prospect. He threw the ball in a peculiar side-arm fashion and even a bit off balance. He did have great perception and a speedy delivery, however, plus a knack for spotting secondary receivers. The greatest abilities he had were his quickness and maneuverability. He was an excellent ball handler, but lacked real game experience except for a few spotted plays.

Again, we tried to evaluate what it was that he could do best and then, of course, put together an offensive scheme which would be able to take advantage of it. In 1964, with one great receiver, we became virtually a run-and-run action team employing a formation with but one split end. It proved a fine combination.

Shortly after, Notre Dame was blessed with several good passers. Our offense then opened to a point at which all of their versatility could be employed.

The point I want to make is that our offensive thinking and the evolution of our attacks changed radically with the style dictated by the skill of our quarterbacks. Other players and positions naturally were taken into consideration, but the skill of the quarterback was the prime consideration.

There were years when we did not have a great passer, but even then the selection of the quarterback was based on his other abilities. In those instances, the best athlete we had was not a great passer. We worked accordingly and continued trying to refine our limited passing game.

Much has been written on the mechanics of throwing the ball or the strategy of a quarterback. We work on a few principles and stress them.

Throwing the Ball

Innate ability is aided by several physical assets concerned with throwing. Hand size is important, perception, strength in the wrist and forearms, body balance, previous training, and, lastly, the boy's dedication and concentration.

Bart Starr, in his book on quarterbacking, touched on a "prime" point that probably was passed over too lightly by many. He called it "concentration." This ability, to blot out all else and focus on what needs to be done, is the essential quality for a passer.

I believe that the delivery can take many forms with respect to the height of the ball when released, but a good quarterback must always finish his release with a fully extended arm. There will be times when he will have to throw almost standing on his head, but I'm speaking of the times when a normal pass can be executed. By fully extending the arm, the wrist snap

205

Quarterback Terry Hanratty throwing.
Observe: 1. Arm fully extended
2. Wrist revolve inside out, palm down
3. Lead foot and off arm close to body — air under back heel
4. Elbow of throwing arm shoulder high
5. "Vision" and concentration to target

at the end is more inclined to revolve in a palm downward motion. This is almost diametrically opposed to a baseball release and involves the most common fault of young quarterbacks.

To stress this point, have a young quarterback grip the ball and lie flat on the ground. Tell him to attempt to throw the ball from this position straight up about eight to ten feet and have it return straight down. If his wrist revolves from the outside in, he will not be able to do it. The straight throw necessitates a straight, almost "handshake" release that causes the wrist to revolve inside out.

The grip of the ball varies and I believe Terry Hanratty violated an old and questionable norm in that his entire hand grasped the ball. Terry gets a very tight spiral and much downward action upon the release. His ball rifles through the air and wind does not affect it very much. His index finger is usually braced on the hump of the lace and it is the last thing to touch the ball upon release.

We drill our quarterbacks several ways and each drill is designed with a special purpose in mind.

In prepractice when they warm up their arms, we have them play catch at different distances over the crossbar. Here we stress *trajectory* and ac-curacy. The boys attempt to see how close they can come to the bar without hitting it and still drop it at a designated point.

They also play a "flash" game of catch in which the receiver flashes his hands at the intended spot of reception. In this instance, it is good to have a player stand very close to the passer on the side of his throwing arm. This will cause him to elevate his arm or throw the ball with a release higher than his shoulder. If he does not, he will brush the person and disrupt the throw.

Body balance is one of the most difficult of all things to master in throwing. To stress balance, we try to make the passer aware of pointing his *lead foot* and holding his off arm in close to his body making sure the back foot has air under the heel at the completion of his delivery. The weight of the body in this position is upright or even a little forward. If a man is covered, we want the quarterback to pump the ball at him and regather balance.

It is the repetition of *grip, extended arm, wrist revolve, lead foot, holding in the off arm, back heel up, trajectory* and *release above the shoulder* that we stress. All of these are to govern the mechanical, but we also stress that he concentrate on where he wants the ball to go and, frankly, *"think"* completion. The best practice a passer can have is to simply pass as often, as correctly, and under conditions as similar to a game as possible.

Footwork and Pivots

One of the many skills a quarterback must master is taking the snap from center and pivoting to fake or make a handoff. There are many ways of doing it and the best way for a particular coach is the one he understands best or the way which has served him most successfully. Following that formula, we choose to have the quarterback form his hands with thumbs together so that the right thumb fits in the groove of the left thumb. The right hand keeps pressure up and forward on the center with a wrist-high insertion. The left hand is moved slightly left and the right hand slightly right. The reason, simply, is to utilize the left hand as a clamp and not a backstop. A backstop hand will suffer "stoved" fingers with an off-center snap.

The center grips the ball with laces up and is instructed to bend his elbow and forcefully bring the ball up and back to the quarterback's right-hand pressure. In doing this, there is a slight and natural rotation inward of the center's wrist, almost a quarter turn. It is not done on purpose; the normal action of bending the elbow and using force causes this turn. This, then, causes the meat of the ball to pop into the palm of the right hand and the left, joined at the thumbs, clamps the underside of the ball.

A quarterback with large hands can easily handle a snap with only one hand if the entire procedure is accurately carried out.

An important point here is that the quarterback should align himself as far from the center as his body build will allow and still be able to be wrist deep with about a 120-degree bend in his arms. It is this bend that allows the quarterback the cushion to extend his arms for a completely solid impact of the snap. In doing this, he can exert a slight ride forward with his hands and still be moving his feet.

His foot position is parallel and separated by about the width of his shoulders. The weight distribution is based on the pivot to be employed. Our quarterbacks are taught all the basic pivots by name and we direct them to shade their weight on the push-off foot. We liken their pivot area to the face of a clock, the cen-

#3 Coley O'Brien gathers his body with ball cocked. He will shortly jab with his front foot and use the left arm for ballast. We employed Coley's versatility by playing him at flanker, halfback and quarterback.

ter being 12 o'clock and the fullback being six. If we call for a pivot, it is by name.

Option pivot — first step to one or 11.

Boot pivot—first step to five or seven reverse.

Pocket pivot right or left—first step to six.

They learn the terminology of the pivot in association with the backfield action employed. From this point we merely stress the coaching points each pivot requires.

One of the basic pivots on roll-out, pocket, screen, draw and off-tackle plays, is a drop step to six o'clock.

There is no possible key to run or pass or even to which side the play will hit. The execution of the drop step is simultaneous with the snap of the ball.

Many coaches have gone to this particular style because it does afford a quick, smooth departure from the line. We call it a depth step, because most often they are inclined to work too close to the line.

Immediately upon receiving the snap, the quarterback is instructed to bring the ball close to his body with both hands on the ball unless he is faking with the off hand.

209

Handoffs

Much of offensive football is based on misdirection or deception in order to cause defenses to react incorrectly. Offense is action and defense is reaction. This being the case, deception becomes important. Because of this and a number of safety reasons, our backs accept the ball with the inside arm up. The quarterback lays the ball in flat in an area within his own vision and rides both hands along the runner's hip until he is past him. In the event it is a fake, he will put the ball into the pocket formed, allow the faker to run the length of the quarterback's arms, and let the ball slip out naturally.

Pocket Action

For a pocket-action play, the quarterback will drop-step either right- or left-footed (whatever seems to be the smoothest and fastest for a particular boy). This drop step is straight back with the lead foot to six o'clock, at which point the toe is still facing the line. It is then pivoted up on, and a near crossover step employed with the other foot. This, opposed to straight back out, may impair vision to the opposite side, but it has proven a much faster method. Johnny Unitas was quoted in an article concerning this technique and put it very well when he said, "The first step is a position step . . . then a sprint to your depth . . . the last step is a position step for balance and cocking the ball." This is pretty much our thinking also. If we do use a straight back-out style, then we work very hard on having the quarterback pump his arms and bend his legs as he backpedals. We stress speed and depth, coaching with phrases, the most common: "Rush everything but the throw."

Beyond taking the snap, pivoting, handing off or faking, pitching out, pocketing, rolling out, or keeping on a quarterback run, most of the quarterback's duties are mental. These physical things are mechanics or refinements of the mechanics. We try very hard to make his movements an economy of motion geared for quickness and smoothness.

Most gifted high school athletes will have to be altered to the style you use. This is not easy because you are trying to rework the grooves of many past habits. For this reason, pivots, getaway . . . pitches . . . first steps, etc., are stressed daily. Soon your quarterbacks become habituated so that the "forced" concentration becomes their own natural execution.

I think this is the reason coaches constantly seek newer and better techniques—to guard against teaching an improper or an inferior method of execution.

The Big Picture

Almost every coach has looked back with nostalgia at his own playing days and said or thought, "Boy, if I could have played then and know what I do today." Obviously, that feeling is generated by the great awareness one realizes in coaching the total or "Big Picture." It is precisely this total concept, total awareness, that coaches strive to give all their players and especially their player coach, the quarterback.

The easiest task for a novice or non-coach to perform is to spot the obvious error. "He should have cut in there" or "Why didn't he throw a screen pass?" etc.

In football, these people have become known as Monday quarterbacks (having Saturday and Sunday to arrive at a decision the quarterback had to make in a pressure-filled moment). Whether you know them as alumni, relatives, friends, well-wishers, or those who don't wish so well, they usually mean little harm and are totally unaware of all the circumstances. This is a big—a very big—point! There are a lot of things to know other than the physical mechanics of the quarterback.

The game has become subtle, sometimes delicate, very intricate with strategy and deception. To be sure, in essence it is still blocking and tackling, but "where," "when" and "why" render blocking and tackling powerful or useless.

The great task is to teach your young quarterback everything he can possibly know about his team and the opponent. This must be approached with the idea of giving the opponent more credit than may be his due. Opponents may not employ all that you anticipate, but there will be a day when one does. Exposure then, is the first order of the day. The quarterback must understand "fronts." This term, front, means the line and linebacker alignment in all the multiple "looks" possible. Not only must he know the looks, but the probable stunts, team tendencies, and defensive concepts of coverage employed with a particular front. Learning fronts is something like learning a multiplication table; they must be recognized and memorized, but they are not worth anything if they are not understood.

We try to depict all the base defenses with 4, 5, 6, 7, and 8-man fronts. We attempt also to term them and the stunts employed from them.

211

By use of small flash cards and film—among other means—the quarterback will also mentally assign a weakness or strength to a particular look. We will allow him the benefit of all we know about the opponents' veer tendency, stunt tendency, dog or blitz tendency, and who on the defense is a cover man or a rush man.

If he understands and recognizes fronts and their manifold possibilities, the next step is to teach him associated coverage. This is all based on possibility because exactly what a team does from a base look is conjecture until the ball is snapped. The more I see of football, the more I credit the ingenuity of coaches. They will often give you a look or disguise it so that you think you have an opening; then, a devised game or coverage will snare you once you've taken the bait.

Some teams will reflect heavily the pattern of their past history and say by their style: "To hell with everything, we're coming after you and if we're to lose, you'll have to beat us passing and that's that!" Others employ another strategy, saying: "We'll give you the short pass and bend, but won't break, or play solid pass zone and force you to play a ground attack that must be errorless and flawless." Still other teams will cover every man and play a man against a man with a "destroy the blocker and read to the ball" style. Whatever the style or the deployment of defense, attacks are forced into great variety to get through an entire season.

When we attempt to teach the quarterback pass defense, it would realistically be better to allow him to play pass defense. Time does not allow such a practice usually, and so it must be accomplished by drill and much concentrated work.

We start out by showing him the seven basic zone areas and all the basic ways of covering them with a three-deep secondary. We then progress to four-deep secondaries and all the ways a zone can be used. After basic zone, we expose the quarterback to true man. From this point on it becomes the "extra" coverage of a free safety, a double-free safety, a half-zone, half-man combination.

He is taught to recognize double coverage on a single receiver and the various tactics to avoid or adjust to this. Over and above all the possible coverages being exposed and explained to him, we ask him to study film of the opponent in his free time. Most teams are not given to making wholesale changes as their personnel will limit this, as well as the ever-constant restriction of time spent in perfecting a new concept.

When a young quarterback understands defensive fronts, secondary perimeters, and multiple coverages, he must drill on them over and over again. We give him this kind of drilling at least 50 percent of the practice time.

If defenses were perfect, no one could ever score. The same is true of offense; no one would ever stop you. The last word then, is starting off with an equal chance and then, finally, executing.

Personality Factors of the Quarterback

In any training situation, there are thousands of ways "to skin a cat." I have heard coaches exclaim loud and long on their "philosophy" of how to treat the quarterback. Some insist they never bawl him out in front of the team; others inisist they do, merely to rally the team behind him against the "tyrant."

I confess that I never tried to be, nor will I ever be, quite so subtle. I merely praise him or criticize him, correct him, or learn from him as befits the occasion. I do the same with my own children, as I'm sure most parents do. Even when I'm angry with them, I can't say I love them any less and, frankly, in the name of love, don't want to waste time being anything other than straightforward with them.

Again, this pressures the quarterback, but he will, of necessity, learn to live with it. If he is too much the shrinking violet, too inhibited, not wise enough to know that I and my staff are only working for a better team, we have selected the wrong player to lead us.

People speak of confidence and the many great benefits exuding confidence can bring. I agree, but I'd rather be less than confident and have my quarterback that way, than to have false confidence that is not built on prior work, study, concentration, repetition, and, lastly, game execution.

Quarterback Drills

I have already stated that we firmly feel committed to drill on only those things that we actually do in a game. Therefore, our quarterbacks practice pivots, cadence, handoffs, pitchouts, and passing during the entire practice. They do little else except that in off-drill moments; they work on their option throws or rotating the trunk so they won't throw across their bodies when on the run.

During the season, if their schedules can be so arranged, my backfield coach will have a daily 30-minute informal meeting with them and cover our next opponent's film or game-plan

A coach's pat on the behind, an assistant's applause, all spontaneously given as praise to a quarterback's job well done under the pressure of battle.

theory. Sometimes, if it can be arranged, they'll have lunch together and just talk about the opponent and the plans we have worked out to use against them.

I hold staff meetings with the offensive and the defensive staffs separately during the season, but whatever we've discussed concerning the offensive game plan, the backfield coach is charged with relaying and teaching the quarterback. In this way we are always on the same page. When time permits, I like to brief them myself. It keeps me sharp on our game plan and the practice lends itself toward having the quarterback see the game plan as I view it. No egotism is intended but, as a head coach, I feel

you must make decisions and have the courage to shoulder them, right or wrong. If things go right, it is easy to be gracious and share credit; if they go wrong, I think it a necessity to accept all the blame. If you operate this way, then you must always be aware of what is going on.

After nearly ten years with the same backfield coach, a young man who played on my first team at Miami, Ohio—Tom Pagna—I don't feel any great need to worry about communicating with the quarterbacks. I mention this point because it does bring out the importance of staff coordination. Obviously, the longer people work together, the more likely it is that you will have an efficient opera-

214

tion. By now Tom knows my thoughts almost as soon as we leave the offensive staff meeting and gets an early start in the week at attempting to convey and teach new items to the quarterback.

In the prepractice time on the field, the quarterbacks will begin warming up their arms and even try out a new footwork pattern with any early arriving backs. All of this is taxing, both physically and mentally, but we stress over and over that the season is ten games and each game is 60 minutes. If you give your maximum effort, both in practice and concentration, the rewards are the winning of games.

For this reason, I heartily endorse the practice of the young men who get interested in another sport outside of football in the off season. You can be hungry for ten weeks, but not much longer. I want them to stay in good physical shape through basketball or handball.

They can watch film if they desire in the off season. There is always reading material about f o o t b a l l around; this, too, is at their fingertips. The 12-month job is the coach's. The player needs to get away from it to retain his playing enthusiasm. Spring football comes soon enough for most of them.

Understanding Coverage

As mentioned earlier, the quarterback would do well to play in the defensive secondary for a greater understanding of coverage. To aid his understanding, we attempt to build defensive looks (fronts and perimeters) and label them. This serves as a base for the quarterback and he studies them in his off moments trying to fit offensive patterns against them which are the most suitable. Our offensive staff does the same, naturally, but the quarterback must have the experience of his own understanding; therefore, it is best done through his own study but under our guidance.

Listed are some of the more common coverages we expect to face during the course of the year. We position these opposite the formations we expect to use and identify all the eligible receivers. Our strong and weak formations, along with two receivers to a side (combo), are the base formations we employed in 1966.

The alignments do not always present keys as to which coverage a team is in, but when a young quarterback is facing the alignment and knows through film and study what the various possibilities of coverage are from a particular alignment, he is more apt

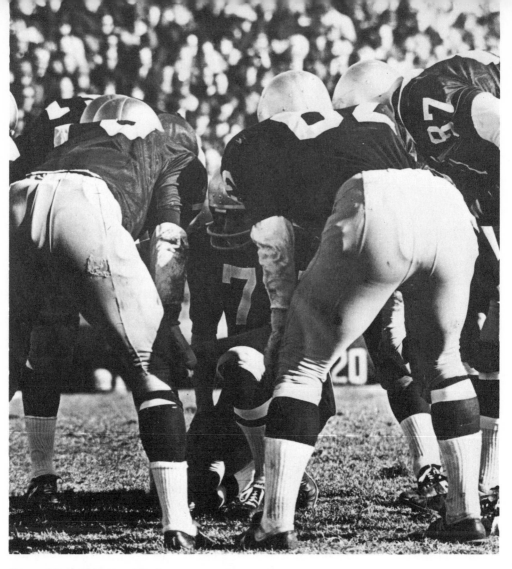

Recognizing coverage, knowing what plays work best given this field position, down and distance . . . these are the things a quarterback must keep in mind in making the proper play selection.

to recognize patterns. Teams will do the slightest of things that tip off the coverage. Still others don't care whether or not you know they are going to play that coverage on that down! They evidently feel their decision to use the defense was based on our tendency, field position, down and distance, and is more likely to be their best bet. This, I am quite sure, leads to the cliche in coaching: "It's a guessing game."

This is true up to the point of anticipating what the opponent plans for a particular down, but the evolution of offensive automatics which take advantage of a new look on defense causes the defense to disguise the look more often than not.

Coverage vs. Strong and Weak

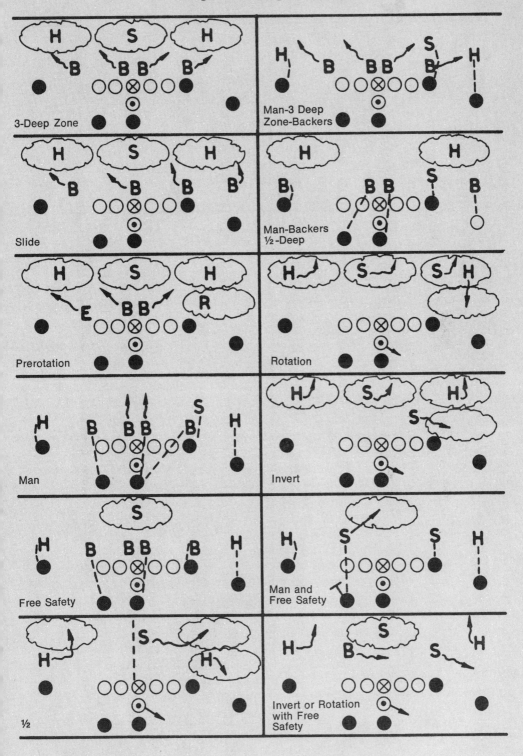

3-Deep Zone

Man-3 Deep
Zone-Backers

Slide

Man-Backers
½-Deep

Prerotation

Rotation

Man

Invert

Free Safety

Man and
Free Safety

½

Invert or Rotation
with Free
Safety

Coverages vs. Combo

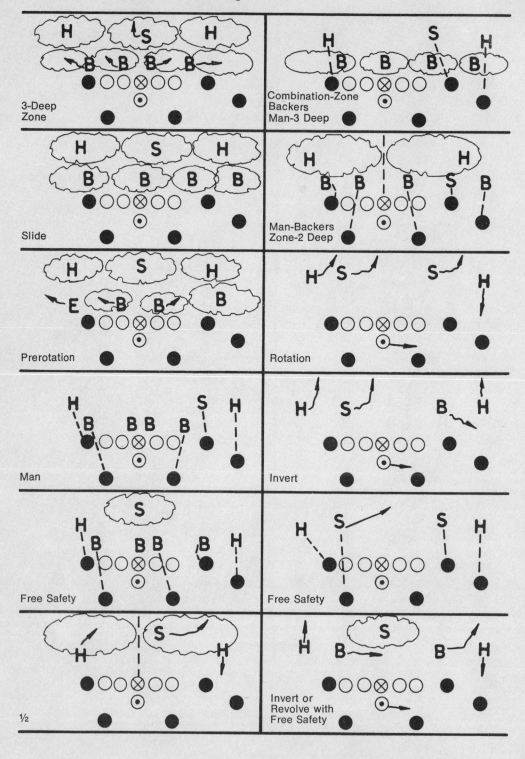

3-Deep Zone

Combination-Zone Backers Man-3 Deep

Slide

Man-Backers Zone-2 Deep

Prerotation

Rotation

Man

Invert

Free Safety

Free Safety

½

Invert or Revolve with Free Safety

Several years ago Tom Pagna was asked to write an article for *Coaching Clinic* dealing with the preparation of the quarterback and the laying out of a game plan. I take the liberty at this point of including the article in its entirety, even at the risk of being repetitious. The article says, in brief, what we undertake to do when preparing a game plan.

Preparing the Game Plan and the Quarterback

"When you prepare a game plan, it is of paramount importance that you impart your theories and expectations to the quarterback directing the attack. In a very confined period of time he must understand the complete overlay of many defensive looks, along with possible offshoot variables. Within this recognition must be an equal awareness of what in the 'game plan' best attacks this look. NOTE: To merely strive for simplification is not enough because, as in all things, the simplest method is not always the best. Our method of presentation is relatively simple, but entire digestion of the plan itself is quite involved.

"Our teaching theory revolves around basic knowledge taught long before the playing season is under way. We attempt to teach the quarter-back all of the fronts employed numerically and give word terminology to stunts and alignments. In this way, a quick reference point is established and the quarterback can begin to perceive for himself possible defensive adjustments to formations."

Current Fronts

"As a beginning, we align the 14 most prevalent and current fronts which we expect (see Chapter V). These are formulated on cards and the quarterback has a summer to flash them about so that at a glance he can recognize them.

"An extension of learning fronts is recognizing the basic perimeters or secondary combinations. The quarterback learns, for example, that eight-man fronts are three deep, seven are four, six are five, etc. By no more than classroom instruction, we attempt to teach him coverage. We want him to understand a true zone utilizing seven people with four rushers. We want him to comprehend true man with four or five covering and the remainder rushing. We also expose him to the multitude of combinations that are an employment of combining man and zone. NOTE: We also categorize and name these secondary coverages, which then serve as basic knowledge utilizable for quick reference.

219

Diagram 9-1. Game plan chart.

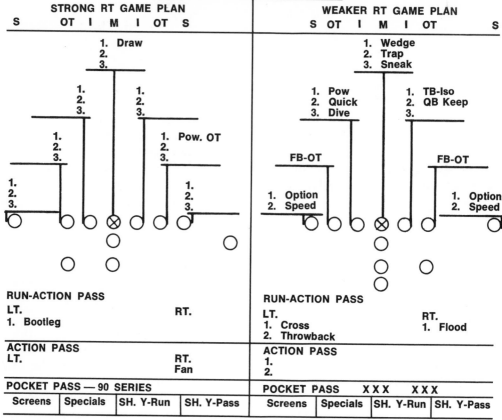

STRONG RT GAME PLAN							WEAKER RT GAME PLAN						
S	OT	I	M	I	OT	S	S	OT	I	M	I	OT	S

STRONG RT GAME PLAN

1. Draw
2.
3.

1.   1.
2.   2.
3.   3.

1.   1. Pow. OT
2.   2.
3.   3.

1.   1.
2.   2.
3.   3.

WEAKER RT GAME PLAN

1. Wedge
2. Trap
3. Sneak

1. Pow   1. TB-Iso
2. Quick   2. QB Keep
3. Dive   3.

FB-OT   FB-OT

1. Option   1. Option
2. Speed   2. Speed

RUN-ACTION PASS		RUN-ACTION PASS	
LT.	RT.	LT.	RT.
1. Bootleg		1. Cross	1. Flood
		2. Throwback	

ACTION PASS		ACTION PASS	
LT.	RT.	1.	
	Fan	2.	

POCKET PASS — 90 SERIES				POCKET PASS X X X X X X			
Screens	Specials	SH. Y-Run	SH. Y-Pass	Screens	Specials	SH. Y-Run	SH. Y-Pass

"Before we even attempt to design our own offense, we hope to have the quarterback master the following: defensive alignment and stunts, zone coveragé (rotation, inversion, revolve), man coverage (safety blitz, corner blitz), semi-zone and man, free safety and rover. These will serve as a base to which new knowledge can be added. TIP: Ideally, it would help to have the quarterback actually play defensive halfback or safety in skeleton drills during the preseason work. When the complete cycle of the teaching method is fulfilled, the quarterback should have been exposed to 'blackboard theory,' 'film recognition,' 'actual physical experiment,' and many, many hours of practice."

Attack Zones

"With this basic knowledge, we begin to simplify· our attack zones by breaking them down as follows:

Areas to Run	Ways to Pass
Sweep	Run Action
Off Tackle	Action
Inside	Pocket
Middle	

"All other types of attack fall under these basic categories, as illustrated on the game-plan chart (diagram 9-1)."

Offensive Thinking

"The same theory that we employ on recognition of defenses applies to our offensive thinking. We start with a very broad base and run the gamut of about everything. We throw a multitude of formations with and without motion at our team. This is done for a threefold purpose:

1. It exposes our defense to many possible looks.
2. It helps the staff to better formulate the talents of our offensive players, learning their weak and strong points.
3. It creates an overwhelming backlog of exposure when we begin to add new plays during the actual season.

"When we finalize our weekly game plan, it will appear on a 4"x 6" easy-to-carry card enclosed in a transparent plastic folder. On that card appears everything that has been prepared for that week. Space permitting, we will draw each formation set and all that we will attack with it. To conserve space the formations are only drawn one way and are mentally transposed. NOTE: From this card the initials of a play indicate what goes where. The quarterback is schooled to know our selections by formations against their fronts and our pass choices against

the opponents' perimeters. In reviewing the plan we also teach him a field breakdown of red, amber, and green areas. These areas dictate his calls with a respective 'safe,' 'caution,' and 'go' offense.

"Each game and each quarterback has taught us something about our preparation. From this comes reevaluation, refinement, and constant evolution toward a better way. There is a quip that goes, 'Hindsight, anyone's, is better than all of Napoleon's foresight.' Through the reconstruction and analyzing of game film and our planned attack, we learn how well or how poorly we have set our game plan.

Establish a Flexibility

"The basic thought that smolders behind every coaching scheme is to do enough—but not too much. We try to maintain a flexibility in our formations, and we tie in the run areas with this same idea. For example, we may plan three ways to attack an off-tackle hole, each with a different backfield action or at least a blocking change. Included in this is one way to hit (a) quickly, (b) with power, (c) and finesse. If this planning is merely to a tight-end side, a completely new attack to a split-end weak side must be employed—otherwise defenses will

221

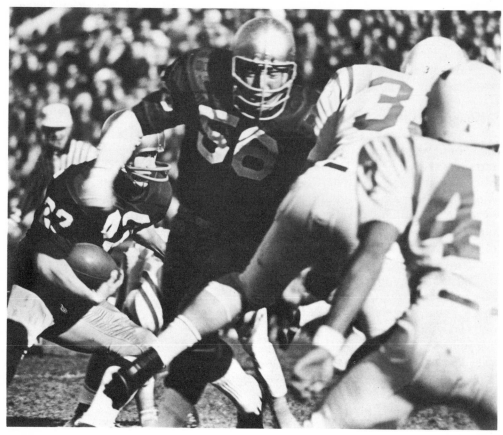

#56 Larry DiNardo seals off two defenders while the ball carrier, halfback Denny Allan, makes his cut to daylight.

veer or overadjust to the strength of your formation.

"For this reason many teams do not mirror plays. They simply employ an offense to and from a given formation. When great variances from full-house T and balanced lines evolved, this became almost a universal practice. An extension and by-product of this un-mirrored running attack was the great concept of sequence football. We, too, try to sequence a run-action pass to every run, a counter to every action, and a screen to every sequence. NOTE: When screens and draws are laid out on the game plan, they are described as 'Specials' and placed in a category adjacent to the offensive formations from which we run our basic offense. We also attempt to coach the quarterback on our best short-yardage plays, our surest possession passes, and when these are best used."

222

Finalized Game Plan

"A full game plan should be finalized by Wednesday, using Monday and Tuesday for experimentation and crystallization. A review on Thursday and Friday, allowing the quarterback to explain our strategy back to us, insures his complete understanding of it. TIP: Along with the red, amber, and green areas of the field, there is much to discuss with the quarterback along theoretical lines.

"He must be abreast of your intent of play selection with the most frequent down, first and ten. Where he is in the color area of the field—and what the opponent's defensive first and ten down tendencies have been in the past—must govern his call. The same is true for second and long (plays over five yards), second and short (plays under five yards), third and long (over three yards), third and short (one yard or less).

"All fourth-down choices are governed from the area the quarterback occupies on the field. If he is in fourth-down area, he will select our best short-yardage plays against what will probably be a short yardage or tight defense.

"We do not force the quarterback to hold a consistent pattern of play selection. He can pass any time; there is no such thing as sure passing downs or running downs. Each opponent and each year stretch our thinking; therefore, we try to maintain a great flexibility. We scout ourselves with a formation, down, and hash chart, from game to game. It is easily done and, when graphed, strong tendencies become quickly observable. NOTE: When the game is over, the quarterback has taken the final exam. We grade the film and with him observe all that we had previously planned. Some things will go astray; some will work well with poor execution; still others will miss being perfect by inches."

Sequence football

Over the years I have always held in high regard the explosiveness of the basic concept of sequence football. I have seen properly sequenced plays storm the castle, but this was not so much the result of strategy as the natural impulse of the defense. When plays look or start out like previously run successful plays, a team reacts to past knowledge. Some of these plays may not even employ the most advantageous style of blocking, but the large factors of deception and sequence make them successful. Darrell Royal's "Wishbone T" at the University of Texas is a great example of the value of sequence plays.

It is apparent that quick reacting and pursuing teams, which are well drilled and well coached, are more susceptible to sequence or deception than are poorer teams. Giving the opponent full credit, sequencing has long been a sound style of attack.

In theory, it is categorizing of "like" plays and attacking different areas from formations which look alike. Although we use several isolated plays, even these have companion plays to be run if they are successful. With this thought in mind, it is imperative to have your quarterback understand fully the arsenal he has at his disposal.

Certain defenses will pretty well take away the sweep game, but leave interior plays. We then attempt to pick away at the interior. Even though the defense may not change, your sweep game in sequence with the interior game is likely to be more successful. The same is true of run-action passes tied to successful running plays.

There are two basic sequences that have been very successful for us over the years. They are built on the premise of a sound running play at one point and then a complementary sequence of attacks. The two sequences that I refer to are the "Belly" and the "Speed." The quarterbacks who operate these attacks are drilled on the "down and distance" idea of the opponent we face. Knowing our opponent's tendencies in these areas, we confine our quarterback to a group of plays in a "series" and allow him to select the best one. His guideposts, again, are the opponent's tendencies, their alignment, their front and perimeter. Usually it is necessary to incorporate such a series into an audible system. If the defense is more predictable, we will precall the play in the huddle.

The Belly Sequence

The belly sequence as employed by Notre Dame in 1964's power-I offense was a primary weapon for us throughout that year. I choose to call it the *sequence* rather than *series* as a matter of description. The plays start out the same, but attack the different areas of middle, inside, off tackle, sweep, and pass. Here are the assignments and theory behind the belly sequence plays.

1. *Off Tackle*—The belly off tackle is a basic fullback-off-tackle play and is not especially subtle or complex. The most natural of the four plays, it has to earn the respect of the defense by the sheer power and positiveness of its threat.

   Whenever the defensive alignment will allow us to send our fullback off tackle, that is the play we'll run. It is the bread-and-butter play that either causes delay or re-

action by the defensive linebacker, defensive end, and defensive tackle.

2. *Belly-Off-Tackle—Coaching Point—* The fullback's footwork is rather uncommon and until it is run over and over and over, the correct timing may be difficult to attain. The important thing for the fullback is to get to the offensive tackle hole as quickly as possible with shoulders parallel to the scrimmage line. This last item is vital for the defense will not usually read this play outside the offensive tackle. Almost always, it will hit the hole and then be read inside to which area overly quick linebackers will move.

   We ask the fullback to take a parallel stance, an open first step and around into the hole, eyeing daylight from the offensive tackle in. He is to accept the ball or fake with his inside arm up. We insist that he bleed yardage, never gaining less than the length of his body falling forward.

   The quarterback's pivot on a belly-off-tackle right is a push-off with his right foot and a dropping and turning of his left foot (reverse pivot) to the point of 5 o'clock. His next movement is a correction or shuffle step forcing him to reach as far and as deep as he can to catch the fullback as quickly as

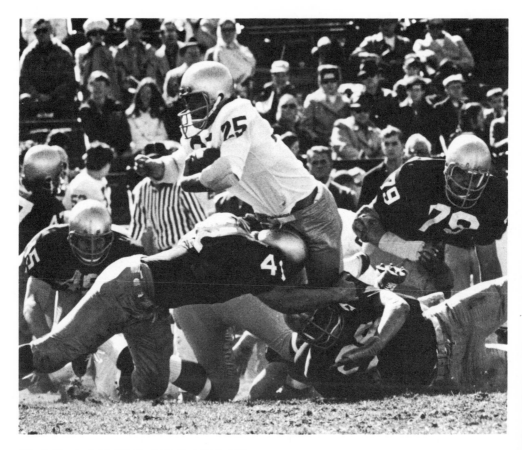

The fullback must bleed yardage, never gaining less than the length of his body falling forward.

possible. He then places the ball in the pocket and rides it the full length of the fullback's run to the line. As the fullback, racing past the quarterback, causes the quarterback's arms to ride back toward the center, the quarterback pulls out and continues his sequence faking.

This play is simple, but basic in the attraction it causes in the defense which sets off the rest of the sequence.

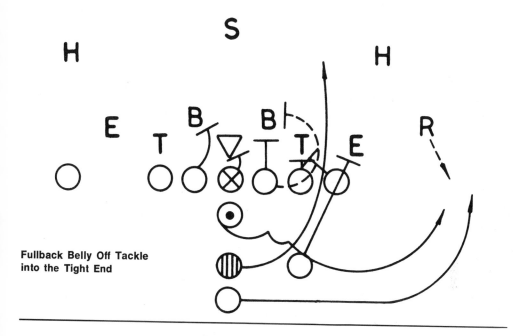

**Fullback Belly Off Tackle
into the Tight End**

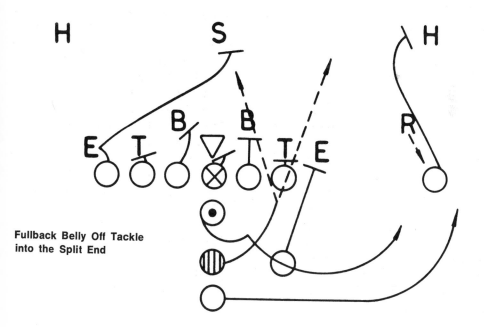

**Fullback Belly Off Tackle
into the Split End**

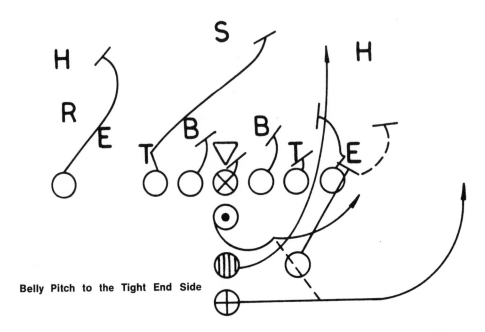

Belly Pitch to the Tight End Side

3. *The Sweep*—Once the off tackle is established, the next step is to capitalize on its strong draw of the defensive tackle, linebacker and end, by going outside. Devising and describing blocking schemes is not my intention, as most coaches will suit their style to what their personnel can handle. However you attempt to block it, you gain a slight edge by the tailback's alignment and there is no need for motion. He can get very wide very quickly and allow the fullback's fake to hold interior linebackers and linemen.

3a. *The Sweep—Coaching Point*—We ask the fullback to run the play and read the hole exactly as he does the off tackle. His fake makes the play. We ask the quarterback to reach deep and cause as long a ride and fake as possible. When he reverses and places the ball in the fullback's pocket, he allows the fullback's momentum to "cock" his two-hand grip of the ball toward the line of scrimmage. This natural "cocking" will also necessitate locking or fixing the drop-back leg of the quarterback. It then acts as a fulcrum over which the already cocked arms allow the pitch to be released.

The tailback is to fly as wide as he can, not gaining any ground or giving any until he receives the pitch.

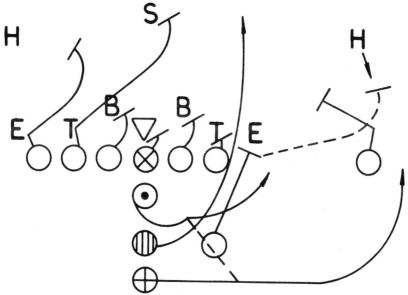

Belly Pitch to the Split End Side

Naturally, the defensive end's penetration can destroy the play. Three things help the offense obviate this eventuality.

1. The fullback's success on the off tackle and good faking when he doesn't have the ball.
2. The quarterback's ride and eyeing the area to which he'll pitch.
3. The nearback and end combination block or devised blocking on the defensive end.

233

4. *The Pass*—The off tackle and the pitch can attain success but may be shut off by a monster or a quick supporting corner; hence, the need to involve the sequence attack with the threat of the pass.

Belly Pass to the Split End Side

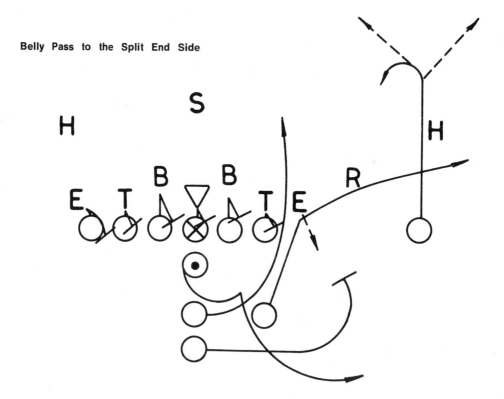

1. The fullback's route is identical to his off-tackle route.
2. The tailback's route is the same but now he wheels and "logs in" the widest lineman who rushes.
3. The nearback must be an actor and not immediately reveal his intent to run a pass route. He maintains position that will both enable him to gain blocking leverage and still be

elusive and free enough to get into his route.

4. The quarterback's role here is to avoid showing pass through skrimping his ride and fake to the fullback. This portion of his assignment is exactly the same, but slightly less drawn out. He reaches back and catches the fullback as deep as he can and as quickly as he can after his ride ends, he fights to gain a depth of six to eight yards with a slight roll to the play side. His perception and delivery are vital. There is usually a fraction of a second when "defensive uncertainty" can cause a nearback in the flat to be free. On more rare occasions, the deep receiver of the two, might be free. In any event the play, if perfectly covered, can become a quarterback sweep since the tailback has position on the widest lineman.

Quarterback Keep Off Belly

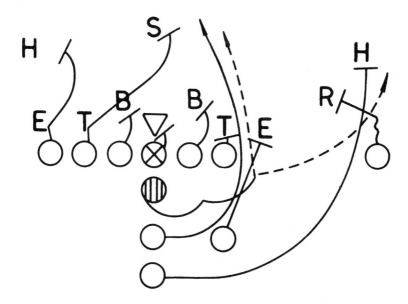

Quarterback Keep "Change Up"

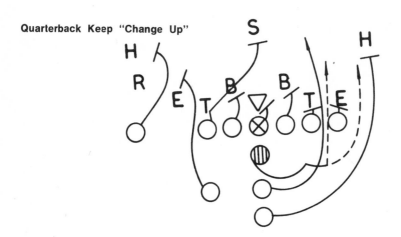

5. *The Inside Play*—Each of the three plays mentioned is full flow, and the inside play, naturally enough, is a counter. We incorporate it into our belly sequence because it starts like a belly play.

Most teams refer to it as "tackle trap" and the action again sets up a suitable run-action pass or "bootleg."

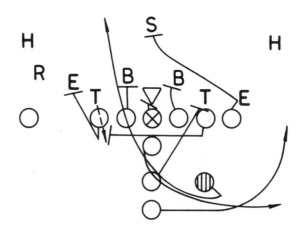

Tackle Trap

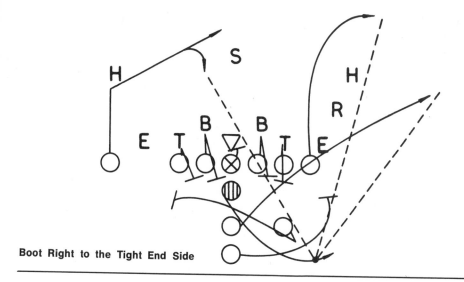

Boot Right to the Tight End Side

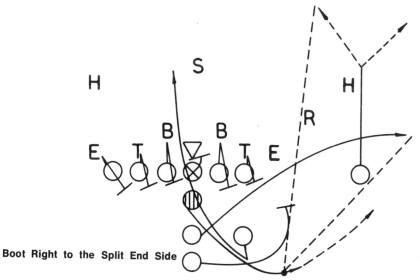

Boot Right to the Split End Side

6. *Coaching the Belly Counter—*
   1. The fullback takes a much straighter path to the tackle area, sealing it for the pulling and trapping tackle.
   2. The tailback runs the same flare and log-in course.
   3. The nearback starts as Belly, hitches back and receives an inside handoff.
   4. The quarterback reverses more tightly, dropping the shoulder or dipping it to the side he moves back first. In this way he can get a tighter pivot, facilitating a front handoff or a close fake.

237

The Speed Sequence

The next sequence we are discussing combines the sweep with the pass and we feel it best attacks a monster or "unbalanced team" or a team which invests to a full flow. It can also attack defensive sets when those defenses adjust. Those adjustments are the very factor that aids the sequencing theory.

To be effective, the most basic play must bear the brunt of your attack. The speed-sweep fills this need for us. This is the play we feel we must make go well enough to justify an opponent's spending much time looking at it in preparation. The more they look at it and the better we run it, the more it allows the possibility of success with the sequence plays.

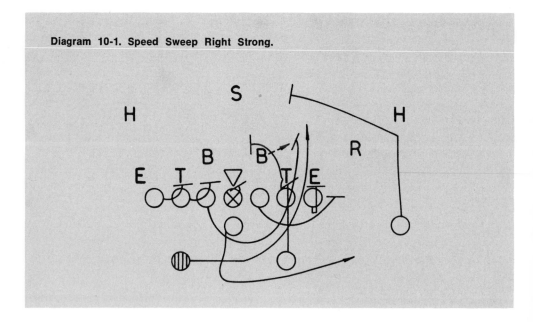

Diagram 10-1. Speed Sweep Right Strong.

This play (diagram 10-1) is designed as an off tackle as well as a sweep, depending on the backside guard's choice of a point of attack. The ball carrier keys the backside guard to daylight. The extended flanker back, split up to 12 yards, is always a receiver threat. This reduces the support naturally and when combined with a pass will cause an uncertainty or momentary defensive "waiting."

The rules of the sweep are as follows:

F.S. end—split two yards, draw block the second man from head up on the offensive tackle.

T.—slam, on, outside, release for backside linebacker.

G.—pull half-moon course for widest man.

C.—frontside.

B.S.G.—pull half-moon and read end's block, read in or out.

T.—seal guard's area.

E.—seal tackle's area or release.

L. H. B.—line up behind tackle, staying parallel, follow backside guard.

Nearback—line up behind tackle, technique block the man slammed on line (over to outside) of our offensive tackle.

QB—open to side of ball carrier, straight back, fake to flanker backside.

Flanker—drive off and read coverage, on run; block safety outside in, after forcing halfback to deepen.

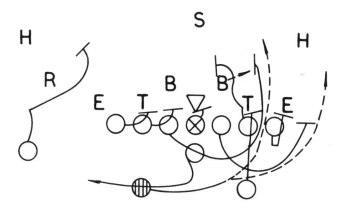

Diagram 10-2. Speed Sweep Right Weak.

The above play has been run as a counter with the guards running opposite the flow. This we do on occasion to keep defensive linebackers from flowing or blitzing too recklessly. In the sequence (diagram 10-2), the guards "opposite" will also simulate the "waggle" play.

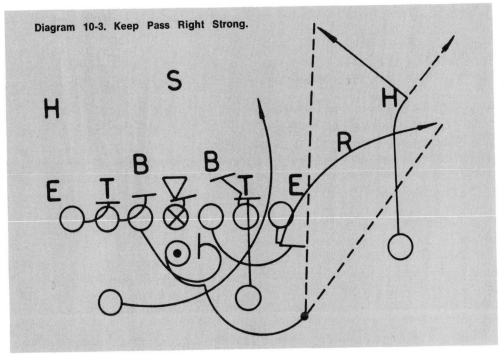

Diagram 10-3. Keep Pass Right Strong.

The play here (diagram 10-3) resembles the sweep, but now the quarterback puts the ball into the left halfback's pocket and the left halfback is told: "Run the sweep and gain five yards." He also turns in tighter, as in an off tackle, to keep pursuit from stretching out. The flanker back tries to drive off any deep covering halfback and breaks in or out depending on the safetyman's reaction. The frontside end after he simulates his "wait" block, sneaks on his angle course beyond a man zoning the flat.

If a team cannot read, run or pass quickly and accurately, or gambles with a rushing corner, this play is a deceiving one. Naturally, the coverage of the defensive backs aids or hinders the play. Some types are more easily attacked than others.

If there is an overload to the flanker backside or "unbalance," we might call the sweep away (diagram 10-4).

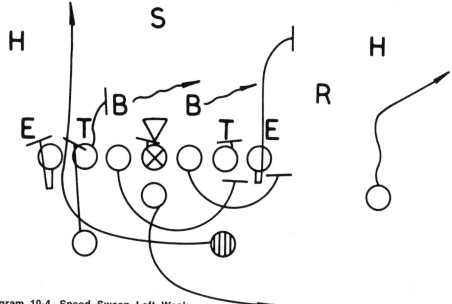

Diagram 10-4. Speed Sweep Left Weak.

If the defense likes to veer away from the monster, we can employ another sequence play as shown in diagram 10-5 below.

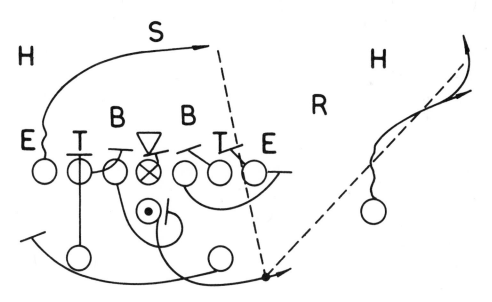

Diagram 10-5. Waggle Pass Right Strong.

Diagram 10-6. Keep Pass Left Weak.

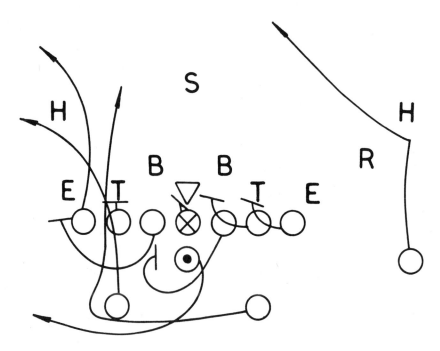

The other possibility is the pass to the weak side off the sweep, called "Keep Pass Weak." It employs a slightly different cut as we are now shy a flanker back. The line necessarily has to block a frontside gap, on; backside, rule (see diagram 10-6).

The quarterback must know why each play is designed and he further must base his sequencing on the defensive reactions to stop our basic play. If the defensive team is balanced, try wide side plays. If they are unbalanced, does the unbalancing member play pass or run best? Does the unbalance go to formation or to field? All of these points are strategic questions and factors governing the proper choice of the sequence of Pass and Run Strong, or Pass and Run Weak. It also may be time to take away true flow by employing the sweep with guards "opposite" or the waggle play pass.

It is now the play choice that causes the confusion to the defense: "Where is it coming?" as opposed to, "Here it comes regardless of how they blocked it." This is the difference I wish to point out. In sequencing, you need not devise many blocking schemes as you employ the theory of "where" as your factor to keep the defense "uncertain."

NOTE: Though the formation is referred to as strong and weak, the split end who aligns opposite the flanker side has an option of aligning tight or split. The key word for determining this is "Speed."

11 The Kicking Game

The Kicking Game

Perhaps the most underrated phase of football is the kicking game. I call it underrated because it is both an attack weapon and a tremendous defensive measure. It gains or loses for a team that important element, field position. In each of our practice sessions there is some portion of time allotted to the kicking game.

Normally speaking, this is every phase of kicking: the kickoff, the extra point, the field goal, and the punt. It also involves the complete defense against and return of kicks.

The Punt

The most frequently employed part of the kicking game is the punt. It is the surest gain in football if it is carried out successfully. One of football's cardinal sins is to have a punt blocked.

In punting the ball it is imperative to have a center capable of accurately snapping the ball to the punter. Our long snappers practice this phase every prepractice moment they have. Their stances require a little more stagger of the feet, especially to the side of the primary hand-snapping. A right-hander, then, will stagger his right leg to keep it from hindering his follow-through arm. We expect the snap to be a tight spiral, waist high, directed at the middle of the punter aligned 13 or 14 yards deep. The complete snap from the center to the punter should be executed in no more than 8/10 of a second.

The punter with his punting leg slightly forward or parallel must first field the ball. Ideally, he will be a two-step kicker; a slight jab with his punting foot, a firm step with the off foot, and the punt.

The punter should never reach for a snap to his side, but, rather, should slide laterally to place his body behind it. He must truly concentrate on hitting the ball with a fully extended leg. His toe at the completion of the punt should be pointed downward and slightly inward, allowing the full impact of his instep to meet the major portion or "meat" of the ball.

Everything should be in line. The hold of the ball, the leg kick, and the drop of the ball.

The drop of the ball should be as level as possible so as to avoid the erratic contact of a vertically inclined surface.

A major fault of many punters is dropping the ball. The drop should consist of as short a period of "free ball" as possible. On windy days it may even be necessary to restrict this to nearly kicking the ball out of the hands. The arms holding the ball should reach out to allow full leg extension. Technically, the body weight from above the waist should be forward and actually carry the punter that way after impact. The arms are used for ballast.

When the ball is on the offensive right hash it should be kicked to the greater part of the field. This is true when on the left hash also.

Naturally the ideal kick is high and long. The higher the kick the more time available for deploying players into positions for punt coverage.

The entire punt should not take longer than two seconds to get off and when possible, 1.9 or 1.8.

Some players punt without pads and when they have pads on it changes things just enough to disrupt the punt. For example, shoulder pads do not allow the arms to be as close to the body as without pads. Kicking with pads on, then, must be compensated for by holding the ball slightly inside to prevent the "off-the-side-of-the-foot" kick.

Whatever the kick, it is enhanced if the punter will keep his toe pointed in or downward. The front of the toe does not come in contact with the ball on a good punt.

Our alignment for the punt is a simple one and it is executed according to line splits. Since the defense has the last move, the spacing must be adequate to handle an 11-man rush if necessary.

Each man splits to protect his teammate to his inside. We block numbered rules or slide. If we block numbered rules, it is simply a numbered process and counting who is yours at the snap of the ball.

If we slide, it is everyone blocking a gap area left or right. If one area is voided that man can release downfield.

Spread Punt

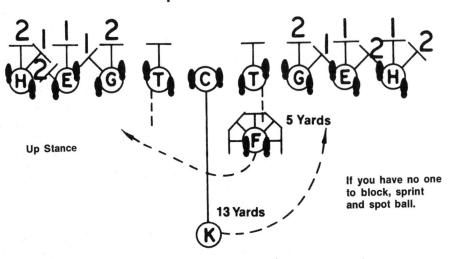

Up Stance

5 Yards

13 Yards

If you have no one to block, sprint and spot ball.

QB calls—shift if you have less than 5 and field position. Spread punt first . . . then silent count, punter's name, direction and type of kick. Snap should be .07 seconds; kick away in 1.3 seconds. QB replaces the kickers - blocking assignment.

Up Stance—Left Half has inside leg back. All others have outside leg back. Heel, toe relationship in a two-point stance.

Split Rules—All linemen split according to inside gap.

    Tackles: protect center
    Guards: protect tackles
    Ends: protect guards
    HB's: protect ends and themselves

Assignments

Tackles—Block gap and beware of possible shooters from over center to over guard.

G—Outside gap, over, release. Keep inside foot planted.

E—Over, outside.

RHB—Over, outside gap, release. Be aware of frontside split.

LHB—Take second man from head-up end.

FB-1. Never back up.
   2. Never block low, as a rusher may go over you.
   3. Keep your head on a swivel to the man most endangering the kicking cone.

250

4. Don't give ground.

5. Cover side opposite the one you align on. Align to the same side as the kicker's kicking leg.

We use an up-stance for better vision and to avoid lunging out thus creating gaps.

Immediately on impact of the ball the punter will yell out "Left" or "Middle" or "Right." We then react in our lanes to the ball.

On the pursuit downfield for coverage it is important that the two widest men protecting the punt coordinate on who spots the ball and who contains from the outside. This is dictated by who is the most free of blocking responsibility.

The five interior people must maintain lanes and intervals. The center will *spot* the center of the ball and the remaining linemen must maintain comparative leverage. They must not follow a teammate; that will cause a voided area.

They must cup the opponent, hem him in, never allow a wall to become set. They must not be fenced off. They must guardedly judge the flight of the ball and not spend time looking up for it for this is a critical and vulnerable period in which they can be chopped

down easily.

Pursuit does not guarantee not getting blocked, but we preach scramble and don't "stay" blocked. "Make yourself responsible for the tackle." Punt coverage is hustle, desire, and heart. In platoon football this is the only time other than on an interception that they can tackle! "Take advantage of this," we tell them.

Spread Punt Coverage

It is imperative that we have good coverage of our punts to prevent our opponent from returning them for any significant yardage. Our center and our halfbacks are the ones most frequently assigned to get to the ball first. They should attempt to reach the ball just as it hits the ground or is caught to destroy any punt return pattern.

Our ends should cover to their outside, to get wider than any possible wall of blockers. Our guards go straight downfield, favoring the wide side of the field. The deep back will cover outside left, and the kicker, outside right.

We are now legally allowed to down the ball anywhere on the field *even inside an opponent's ten-yard line.*

251

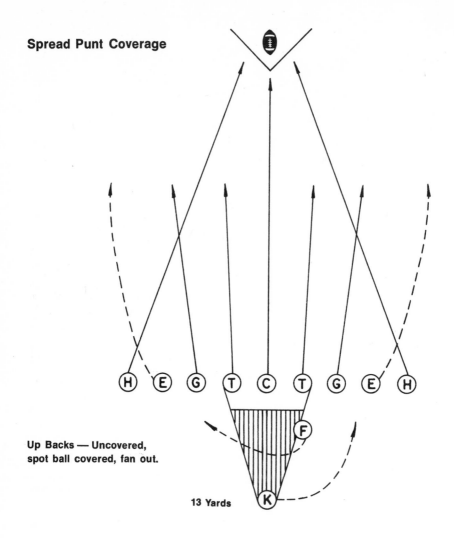

Spread Punt Coverage

**Up Backs — Uncovered,
spot ball covered, fan out.**

13 Yards

When we practice punting, it is with the wind and against the wind, right hash, left hash, and middle. We will kick with our backs to the goal line and also from the 50-yard line on in. From the 50 in, we fight to bleed every inch out of the punt and down it as close to the goal as we can.

We do this daily under full rush, everything full go except tackling.

We utilize every rush we can think of and tax our protection to the maximum in practice.

In this same section of time we employ our quick-kick game and *punt run* or *punt pass*.

We always stress to the players the importance of this phase of the game, lest they not recognize that *breaks* are made within the *kicking game*.

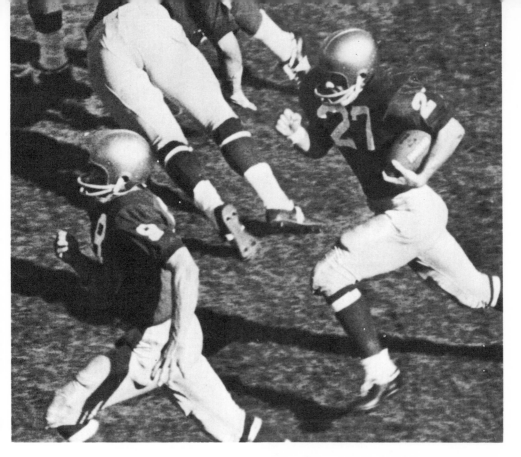

Punt return specialist Nick Rassas found the opening on this play as he races for six points with #8 Tom Longo providing the escort.

The Punt Return

There are many styles of punt return, but to begin with, you must have a sure-handed receiver handling the ball. He must have judgment when to return and when to fair catch. It must be a decision he has made in practice under pressure, often. His hand dexterity and his breakaway speed are factors that will undoubtedly predict the fate of your return game. Whatever the devised scheme of return, it is rarely combined with an all-out rush. This decision, whether to rush for a truly attempted block, or rush to set up the punt return is the decision of the defensive team captain. He will base this on prior knowledge of the opponent's snapper, his protection, his punter, field position, and the game circumstance as it unfolds.

With all plays designed to advance the ball, the scheme of return must force a distortion of the pursuing wave. It must seal off one area and steamroll another. Several years back, Tom Schoen and Nick Rassas gave us tremendous scoring threats as punt-return men. The following diagram shows the punt return we employed.

253

Punt Return Right

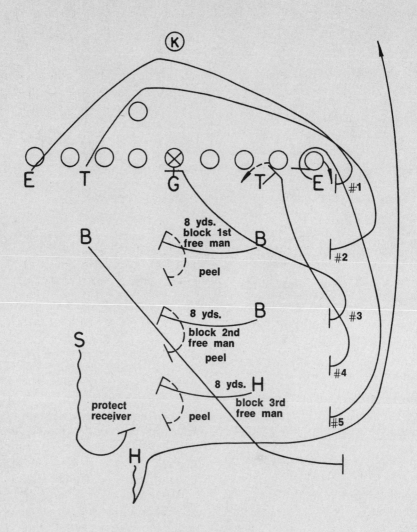

Four don'ts in our punt return.
1. Don't be offside.
2. Don't rough the kicker.
3. Don't let the ball hit ground.
4. Don't clip.

Both ends rush and force the kick, both tackles and the middle guard follow suit. They will then sprint to their wall position of #1, #2, #3, #4, #5, at five yards distance apart, respectively. The fullback away from the return side sprints deep to take out any wide contain man. The center and guard seal and then peel back for protecting backside pursuit.

The nearest outside linebacker fakes a rush and glides to cut off interior pursuit. The away-halfback protects the catch and picks off the first man down his side.

Again, we return to the short and wide sides, right and left, trying always to avoid showing a pattern. The easiest punt to return is the quick low drive that is easily fielded and yields little time for the offense to cover it.

Coaching Points

In fielding punts it is desirable to get your body in the path of the ball flight and not off to the side. We teach the player to field the ball in the air, wherever possible. You've probably seen a ball drop through the receiver as through a bottomless bucket. To avoid this we stress tight elbows and staggering the hands, as shoulder pads will prevent elbows from being in tight. The catch, whenever possible, should be with the hands and then nestled into the body. A punt return is one of the many ways for the defense to score. It is a source of pride, a great morale factor, and a surging of team play when this happens. We preach this and constantly ask our players to be prideful in their effort and execution. The play itself is most vulnerable to clipping and we really try to discourage any questionable block. Again, the kicking game and its phases represent those moments where game-breaking "breaks" are made.

Extra Point and Field Goal

The field goal and extra point tries are treated as one and the same with the notable exception that a field goal after the kick must be treated as a scrimmage punt. It must be covered! We lay stress on this so that the team never relaxes and allows a missed field goal to bounce around or be picked up and returned free of pursuit.

The stress point in executing this kick is the formation of a protective triangle or cone much the same as with a punt. We take maximum leg spreads to widen the base of the offensive line.

We also do this from an up position. The center blocks high, the area and width of his body. Each of three linemen on both sides of the center attempt to step up to the inside, staying in as wide and as parallel a stance as possible. It is uncomfortable at best and you cannot deliver a blow from this position, but it does block the area of the cone which we are attempting to block for a period of 1.3 seconds.

Point After Touchdown And Field Goal

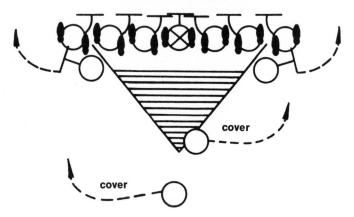

1. Holder at seven yds.
2. Up backs behind second man in. Block out on first man to show from outside end.
3. LINE—Up position with inside foot back. No splits. On snap of ball, step up and in with inside foot, keeping outside foot planted. Put head across inside gap. Move with snap.
4. Center—Check team before snap. Center ball when ready and fill over.
5. Line and Backs—Always cover on field-goal attempts. Holder and kicker flare out after kick.

We set the holder at seven yards and never wider than either leg of the center. This is to insure that, regardless of the angle of the kick, the kicker will strive to kick over the center; thus, there will not be a short side but an equal balance for protection.

Place-kicking is timing. It is proper footwork, with sound leverage and exact impact. Again, we ask the kicker

Mike Eckman shows good form on this kick having his shoulders erect and his vision focused on the ball.

to edge up his kicking foot, take a tiny position lead step, another step and kick.

We ask that he meet the ball squarely, in line with the target at which he is aiming, and keep his shoulders erect. Too much weight over the ball detracts from leverage and causes a low hit. His head is downward, with vision on the ball but his weight is behind the ball. After impact it is important for the kicker to stride straight through the kick and place the foot squarely in line with his intended plan of flight.

Again everything is in a line, no sidewinding kick, no jumping or lung-ing. We strive to make him especially conscious of *approach, impact,* and *follow-through.* If he concentrates on this and does it under pressure often, he will improve.

Most kickers either lock their ankle for an intended angling up of the toes, or tie the toe of the shoe up with a lace. Some specialists even conjure up their own special shoe with a built-in angle from the instep forward.

The idea of this is to attain immediate height and prevent a blocked kick.

Wind is a factor, angle is a factor, and a really key factor is the holder.

257

The Holder

The holder should be a man who holds all the time for the same kicker. He should possess excellent hands and poise. He kneels with his chest facing almost squarely to the center and his outside leg up. His inside knee is close to the kicking tee, but far enough removed to give great freedom to the kicker's follow-through. The holder reaches his hands out and leans as far forward as he can comfortably maintain. Once the ball hits his hands, he secures it quickly and places it on the tee in one continuous motion. He strives to avoid placing the laces so that they face the kicker. Concentration and relaxed poise must allow nothing to interfere with his maneuver. When he places the ball down, the arm nearest the kicker is usually the one that is dropped, thus removing any barrier to the kicker's advance.

The kicker will strive to place his off foot roughly within a six- to eight-inch area of the kicking tee. The holder must watch the ball actually kicked off the tee before changing his vision or following the ball in flight.

The Kickoff Return

One of the most exciting plays in football and the least used form of defense and attack is the kickoff. I feel it is an unusual defensive play in that it is usually the only time when a single wave of defenders combs the field horizontally at nearly the same time. It is true that you always face one or two selected safety men, but for the most part there is little in the way of a secondary defense.

For this reason, the kickoff appears as an exciting play. Any time the initial plane or leading edge of onrushing defenders is pierced, there is the possibility of a long gainer.

It is for this reason that we attempt a concept of return very much akin to that of a scrimmage running play. Our main objective is to cause distortion in the wave of defenders. It is through both horizontal and vertical distortion that runners advance. A safety man dare not pursue the initial wave too closely, nor can he allow too large a gap to develop. If he does, he may be forced into the hardest tackle to make, a solo tackle in a completely open field.

Shown in the kickoff-return diagram is a simply drawn-up return. It stresses the basic idea of distortion by recoil and cross-blocking to create greater and easier blocking angles.

1. If the ball is kicked to the middle, return middle.
2. If the ball is kicked to either side, return is to that side with same blocking responsibilities.
3. Timing is the key: When ball is kicked, give ground and block man for whom you are responsible.

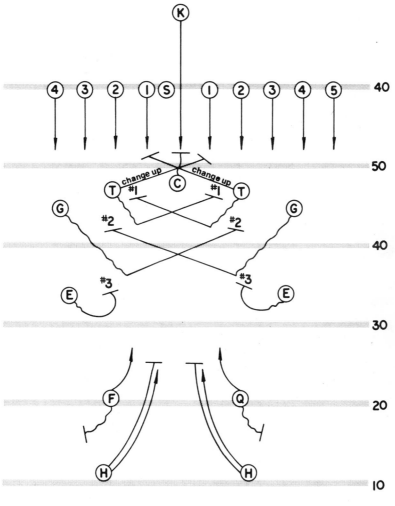

GL.

(See next page for return assignments)

Center—Give ground and block kicker or man who comes down for him. Sustain.

Tackles—You are responsible for first man to opposite side of kicker. Give ground, cross, block. On change-up, go, throw, sustain hustle.

Guards—You are responsible for second man to opposite side of kicker. Give ground, cross, block inside out.

Ends—Give ground toward ball and block out on third man from kicker to your side.

Fullback & quarterback—Time up your blocks and turn out on the next widest man from the end's block, or lead up middle.

Halfbacks—Call out which one is the receiver, the other leads and blocks. Take the quickest route upfield and always field the ball in the air.

If we can reach our 30 or 40, we are close to four-down area. This is the prime factor in any drive for a touchdown.

The center man is aggressive, at once trying to pierce or delay the center of the wave.

As a change-up, both of the tackles may also be aggressive. Normally, however, the tackles cross, and the guards cross deeper. The ends recoil and turn out. The four remaining backs hustle to an apex, attempting to run at the largest area of distortion.

We employ tackles in the kickoff as we do in the punt—they are the players nearest the center. We do this simply because we feel the tackles have greater heft; the smaller guards, who have a longer way to run, will be more able to perform their job.

We practice the kickoff return frequently during the last two days before a game. We also work against onside kicks and various alignments that create a better deployment for coverage.

Nothing that may take place in a game should come as a surprise if we can make our players truly exposed to all the possibilities.

Kickoff Coverage

Kickoff coverage is predicated on speed, pride, hustle, and dedication.

You must employ your fastest men, who will take pride in making the tackle. They must hold their lanes and refuse to be blocked as they converge on the receiver. A large part of their effectiveness will be in direct proportion to the kicker. Our kickers work on their specialty daily. We want height for time, and distance for field position. Often you can predict the emotional readiness of your defensive team by watching how they cover a kickoff return. We also practice onside kicks and coverage as a weapon in time of need.

Kickoff Coverage

1. Both Ends and Center must keep the ball in a triangle.
2. All others spot the ball.
   * Fullback always replaces the kicker.
   * When using an ON-SIDE kick, always kick the ball from one side.
   * Safety—Never allow too large a gap between the wave of your teammates and yourself.

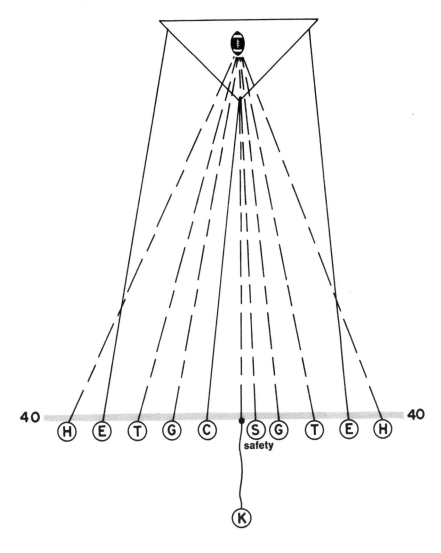

The Quick Kick

The quick kick can be a very definite advantage in a particular game situation. We have set forth below two diagrams illustrating two versions of the quick kick, one from the power-I and the other from the normal split backfield (that is to say, from the three-back and the two-back type of offense).

Quick Kick Ideas:

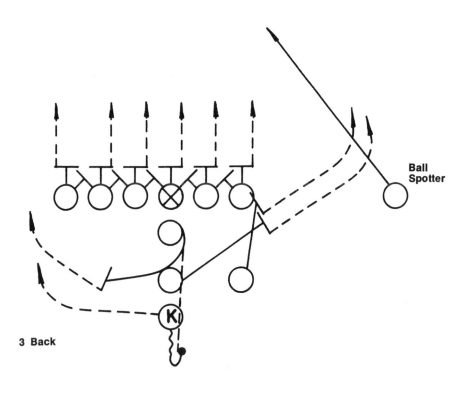

Ball
Spotter

3 Back

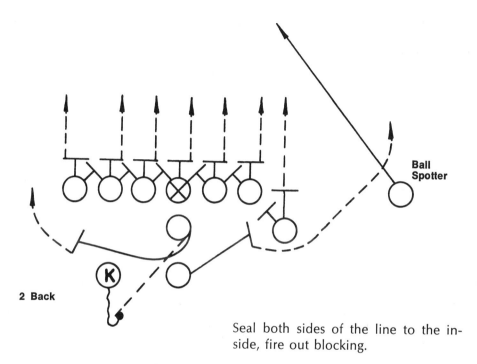

Ball Spotter

2 Back

Seal both sides of the line to the inside, fire out blocking.

In concluding my remarks concerning the kicking game, let me say that each phase is an important part of the game. It must be a phase that you and your team have worked on with legitimate effort and time. It seems that it will pay off in just that same proportion.

To be blessed with the native talent of a punter or place-kicker, snappers and holders, return men and kickoff men is one thing. If you face a year without that blessing, you will encounter your most unforgettable teaching aid regarding the importance of the kicking game.

In the years in which our normal talent is not as good as we would like, we spend much time in trying to develop it. It is time never wasted.

12 Scouting

Basics
Breakdowns
The Punch Card System
The Scouting Final Report
  a) Cover Sheet
  b) Formation Summary
  c) Breakdown Sheet (Formation)
  d) Statistical Breakdown
  e) Opponent Patterns
  f) Defensive Alignments

Scouting

In most major college football conferences and leagues, scouting is a twofold process. Most teams and coaches have a reciprocal film-exchange agreement. Since we are a major independent we deal with each opponent separately. Most often we work out a film exchange for the films of our opponent's last three games. I think that the last three are really quite current enough, though some people feel the need for more. Our own experience shows us that the normal progression of change in offensive and defensive planning in the course of a season lessens the value of looking at all the opponent's games or films.

Too often, more than this provides such a vast amount of information that it will cause a staff to offense and defense ghosts. Normally speaking, it is enough to exchange three films and have a scout present for the three prior games that the opponent plays. The scout will not see as much in one glance as a staff will in reviewing and breaking down the opponent's film, but he will sense the opponent's tempo or pulse which film cannot provide. It is precisely for this reason that we bother to scout at all.

A keen observer of football can almost sense and discern the actual "personality" of a team after observing them three consecutive times.

He will concentrate on the basics of offensive and defensive alignment, personnel performance, overall team speed, strengths and weaknesses.

Our scouting system is relatively simple in that we work with a basic offensive card and a worksheet. Examples of all of this will be shown later in the chapter.

The first premise of scouting is that one has an organized system, a system which will enable you to ascertain tendencies quickly in a minimum amount of time.

Normally, the scout will return late Saturday evening or Sunday morning from his trip. From the time the game has ended until our staff meets Sunday at 1:00 p.m., he must consolidate his most recent game report with the previous two.

Our scouting system is, again, similar to our own offense and defense in that it deals with "word terminology." We even employ numbering, much the same as in our own system.

Before the team breaks the huddle, the scout will have marked the three basics—1) down, 2) distance, 3) yard line and hash mark—across the top of his card. Each play calls for a new card and the cards are numbered in the sequenced order that the plays were run.

When the opponent moves into a particular formation, the scout will quickly pencil a word or combination of meaningful words that depict the formation. At the snap of the ball, we find it most advantageous to have the scout keep his vision about one yard behind the quarterback. This will en-

able him to see the quarterback's pivot, pulling linemen, and backfield action. Knowing the numbers of the people playing will also aid his observations.

We ask the scout to write down only what he sees and no more. If he cannot see it all, and obviously he cannot, we will pick it up in the film exchange.

From the formation he will label a backfield action, direction, and the gain or loss. He may make a quick note that is a personnel or personality tip. He will immediately flip to the next numbered card in progression and restate the new down, distance, yard line and hash.

What I have said here is concerned simply with the fundamentals of scouting. An example of one card's information then, would contain the following:

---

1. *Down:* 1st   *Dist:* 10   *Yd:* Opponents 40.
   Hash: L-M-R

   The down is first, the distance to travel is 10, the ball is on the 40 of the opponent of the team we are scouting.

2. Scribbled quickly: Pro-eastern
   Belly off tackle right +6

This information signifies the formation and the backfield action. Perhaps later, after the game and on the flight home, the scout will fill all this in with pencil, though this would not really be necessary. Pro-eastern, belly off tackle rt. +6 would look like this when pencilled in:

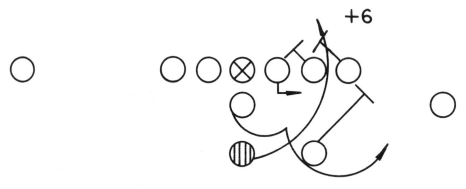

In this way, if the scout saw the blocking at the point of attack, he would pencil it in or designate a pulling lineman, or crackback flanker, etc.

Just as in our offense, the dual system of words and numbers tells him that off tackle is the six hole. The direction was right, therefore, this information is transcribed later on as "six hole right."

After an entire game is scouted and each play is represented by the individual card in sequence, the card's perimeter is stencil-cut with a simply operated cutter. This permits the insertion of an "ice pick" through the six hole and all the cut "six holes right" fall out of the stack. In fact, it is man-ual data processing. I suppose a computer could handle this quite easily, but when working with only 80 to 100 cards it does not seem practical.

With this method it becomes merely a matter of organization to find what you want to know. We can take note of all the two, four, six, eight hole plays run right from the left, middle, and right hash marks, or all the two, four, six, eight hole plays to the left.

We divide all pass patterns into: pocket, run-action and sprint-out. All of the kicking game and fourth-down plays, are separated. In this system, you can arrive at how much information you want or need. You can separate data indefinitely and arrive at the breakdown of plays in many ways. Example of breakdowns:

1. All first and ten plays.
2. All second and long (seven and over).
3. All second and short (three and under).
4. All third and long (five and over).
5. All third and short (three and under).
6. All two, four, six, eight, holes, Rt. Runs.
7. All two, four, six, eight, holes, Lt. Runs.
8. All formations and runs.
9. All Left, Middle, Right hash plays.
10. All pocket passes.

The point here is that any combination you wish is now readily available.

The breakdowns must be presented in some final order which can be easily and meaningfully inspected. If we are to put this in a scouting report form, then it, too, must be consolidated with prior games. We will often use three different-colored stencils to discern easily one game from the next when the report has been totally consolidated.

What most staffs are looking for when they attempt to defense a team are tendencies, the tendencies of what play, from what formation, using what player and from where on the field. Sooner or later a hash tendency or a down tendency, or a particular formation and play tendency appear as a result of frequent use. This, then, is what scouting is all about. Find the team's strengths in the order they employ them. Find their formation ideas, one of which may be multiple use and frequent change. This will then affect your preparation.

We strive to stop those six or seven best "bread-and-butter" run plays they employ. You expose your defense to their most frequent and most successful patterns of pass. You hope to do this by alignment, by execution, and by calculated anticipation based on tendency.

Scouting the defense is a little more difficult since the play-run against the defense may happen in such a remote area or so quickly that it would be impossible to read coverage. Here you must have the scout record the down and distance, position on the field, the basic alignment against which formation, and any stunt or dog he can catch through his fleeting glimpse. More than this is too much. The exchange film can complement the cards of defense just by sequencing them with the film. By charting them and breaking them down, one might be able to grasp part of the defensive game plan thinking that was employed.

271

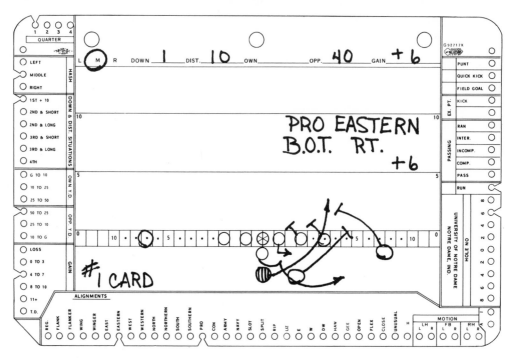

When this is compared to other game charts, a tendency may arise.

The individual abilities of skilled players, such as defensive backs, linebackers, quarterbacks, halfbacks and receivers, must be dealt with as separate data. Any remark the scout feels may adequately describe the opponent is a bonus. We would also prefer to have his feeling on interior linemen's size, speed, reaction. We definitely want to know which are their best and their weaker players who will be on the field against us on game day.

In order to give an overall idea how the complete scouting report is put together, I have attempted to take a sample brochure and make a few remarks which explain the function of each particular page (see pages 273 through 280). They are naturally bound together and along with a weekly offensive and defensive game plan, they will become part of the player's permanent notebook.

Only the top of the card and the words Pro-Eastern, BOT Rt, +6 need be written down before the card is flipped to the next one (see above). Going back after the game, the scout will punch the following from the perimeter: first quarter, middle hash, first & ten, 50 to 25, four to seven gain, Pro-Eastern, six Hole Right, Run. This completes the first play and he immediately sets up the second play card by listing right hash, second & four, ball on the opponent's 46.

272

The Scouting Pamphlet

The following pages are the composite report broken down and a small explanation with each portion.

#1 Cover Sheet

Offensive Unit #1

Pos.	No.	Name	Ht.	Wt.	Cl.
Split	89	Al Miller	6-3	196	Sr.
LT	72	Paul Smith	6-3	225	Jr.
LG	63	Larry Charles	6-1	225	Jr.
C	50	Greg Brown	6-3	228	Sr.
RG	68	Jon White	5-11	226	Jr.
RT	75	Melvin Fisher	6-2	235	Jr.
TE	82	Ray Johnson	6-4	193	So.
QB	14	Ed Martin	6-1	193	Sr.
TB	44	Dennis Doe	5-11	188	So.
Flank	42	Barry Ray	5-11	170	Sr.
FB	32	Tim Jones	6-2	221	Jr.

Offensive Unit #2

Pos.	No.	Name	Ht.	Wt.	Cl.
Split	23	Alan	6-2	178	Jr.
LT	77	Jim	6-2	220	So.
LG	60	Louis	6-3	210	So.
C	51	Allen	6-2	230	So.
RG	00	Charles	6-2	220	So.
RT	70	Gary	6-3	230	So.
TE	86	Herschell	6-4	196	So.
QB	13	Larry	6-2	200	So.
TB	26	Bill	6-1	185	Jr.
Flank	22	Kerry	6-0	172	So.
FB	40	Tom	6-0	225	So.

Defensive Unit #1

Pos.	No.	Name	Ht.	Wt.	Cl.
LE	83	Dan Dole	6-3	220	So.
LT	67	Mike Small	6-4	228	Jr.
MG	61	Greg Aiken	6-1	225	Jr.
RT	78	Layne Ford	6-4	237	So.
RE	85	Ken Michaels	6-2	197	So.
LLB	31	Rod Barns	6-2	203	Jr.
RLB	80	Mike Fields	6-1	232	Jr.
Rover	27	Charles Gray	6-3	190	So.
LH	41	Tom Golden	6-0	175	So.
RH	35	Ray Church	5-10	180	So.
S	45	Steve Wiley	6-1	178	Sr.

Defensive Unit #2

Pos.	No.	Name	Ht.	Wt.	Cl.
LE	88	Bill	6-3	218	Sr.
LT	65	Bob	6-2	208	Jr.
MG	52	Charles	6-2	205	Jr.
RT	73	Duane	6-4	228	Sr.
RE	87	Scott	6-2	205	Sr.
LLB	55	Marcos	6-2	205	So.
RLB	10	Dave	6-3	200	So.
Rover	30	Lane	6-0	183	So.
LH	17	Roy	6-2	185	So.
RH	27	Charles	6-3	190	So.
S	21	Pat	6-2	183	Jr.

The Cover Sheet (a two-game scouting report)

The cover sheet or page one is merely the two-deep alignment of the opponent by position. His number, height and weight are listed accordingly for total familiarization.

#2 Formation Summary

Pro		**Con**
52 times 26 runs 26 passes		38 times 21 runs 17 passes
	Total	90 times 47 runs 43 passes
Close Pro		**Close Con**
16 times 9 runs 7 passes		12 times 6 runs 6 passes
	Total	28 times 15 runs 13 passes
Close East Slot		**Close West Split**
9 times 6 runs 3 passes		13 times 9 runs 4 passes
	Total	22 times 15 runs 7 passes
Flank		**Wing**
2 runs		1 pass
	Total	3 times 2 runs 1 pass

Formation Summary

The second sheet gives a summary of the formations most frequently used by our opponent. It also shows how often each particular formation has spawned run or pass plays and the total number of these plays from this formation, either left or right.

274

Figures three, four, five, are statistical frequencies as one is viewing specific formations from the defensive viewpoint. It tells how many times each hole was attacked and how many yards gained plus the action used to get there.

#3 PRO

	GAME 1	GAME 2	TOTAL
PASSES	10	16	26
COMP.	2	4	6
INCOMP.	2	9	11
INTERC.		1	1
RAN	6	2	8

	GAME 1	GAME 2	TOTAL
RUNS	16	10	26
PASSES	10	16	26
TOTALS	26	26	52

									TOTAL
		Belly K (TD) +4 / 12		HB Draw O / Qb. Sn. +3	Qt +2	HB Draw +3	BOT +34 +20 +4 +1 +5 +9 +3 +3	Sprint Keep —1 / FB Toss —2	
2nd Game	Sp. Sw. 9	Belly K —2 1 3 / BOT 5			Qt 5 1 1 4	HB Draw 13			
TIMES	1	6		2	5	2	8	2	26
GAIN	9	13		3	13	16	79	—3	130
AVERAGE	9	2.3		1.5	2.6	8	9.9	—1.5	5
TOUCHDOWNS	0	1		0	0	0	0	0	1

CON

	GAME 1	GAME 2	TOTAL
PASSES	5	12	17
COMP.	2	6	8
INCOMP.	2	2	4
INTERC.			
RAN	1	4	5

	GAME 1	GAME 2	TOTAL
RUNS	6	15	21
PASSES	5	12	17
TOTALS	11	27	38

									TOTAL
		BOT +14 +2 +2		Qt +2				Sprint Keep +2 / Belly Opt +1	
2nd Game	FB Toss —1	BOT 3	HB Draw 9 / FB ISO 0			BOT 3		Sp. Sw. +4 —5 +7 (TD) +63 +3 +9 (TD) +25 +1 +1 Belly Opt 14	
TIMES	1	4	2	1		1		10	19
GAIN	—1	21	9	2		3		122	156
AVERAGE	—1	5.25	4.5	2		3		12.2	8.2
TOUCHDOWNS	0	0	0	0		0		2	2

	GAME 1	GAME 2	TOTAL
PASSES	5	2	7
COMP.	2		2
INCOMP.	1	1	2
INTERC.			
RAN	2	1	3

	GAME 1	GAME 2	TOTAL
RUNS	3	6	9
PASSES	5	2	7
TOTALS	8	8	16

	Speed Sw. +19				Rev. +10	Belly Pitch +7
2nd Game	Sp. Sw. 5 / Sp. Sw. 8			QB. S. 3	Rev. —1 / BOT 1 BOT 3	
TIMES	3			1	2 / 2	1 / 9
GAIN	32			3	9 / 4	7 / 55
AVERAGE	10.6			3	4.5 / 2	7 / 6.1
TOUCHDOWNS	0			0	0 / 0	0 / 0

CLOSE — CON

	GAME 1	GAME 2	TOTAL
PASSES	4	2	6
COMP.	1		1
INCOMP.	2	1	3
INTERC.			
RAN	1	1	2

	GAME 1	GAME 2	TOTAL
RUNS	2	4	6
PASSES	4	2	6
TOTALS	6	6	12

	Belly Pitch +4				Sp. Sw. +10
2nd Game	Sprint Keep 5	Rev. 3	Qb. Sn. 4		Sp. Sw. 2
TIMES	2	1	1	2	6
GAIN	19	3	4	12	38
AVERAGE	9.5	3	4	6	6.3
TOUCHDOWNS	0	0	0	0	0

#5 CLOSE EAST SLOT

	GAME 1	GAME 2	TOTAL
PASSES	2	1	3
COMP.		1	1
INCOMP.	1		1
INTERC.			
RAN	1	(TD)	

	GAME 1	GAME 2	TOTAL
RUNS	5	1	6
PASSES	2	1	3
TOTALS	7		9

2nd Game				Delay Snk +2	Tear T —1	Long T +2	BOT +5 +4		
	Sprint Keep 2								
TIMES	1			1	1	1	2		6
GAIN	2			2	—1	2	9		14
AVERAGE	2			2	—1	2	4.5		2.3
TOUCHDOWNS	0			0	0	0	0		0

CLOSE WEST SPLIT

	GAME 1	GAME 2	TOTAL
PASSES	2	2	4
COMP.	1	1	2
INCOMP.	1		1
INTERC.			
RAN		1	1

	GAME 1	GAME 2	TOTAL
RUNS	9		9
PASSES	2	2	4
TOTALS	11		13

2nd Game	Belly Opt. —1 (TD) +9 Sprint Keep +4	BOT +2	Long T +6 +4					Sprint Keep —4 —3 FB Toss +6	
TIMES	3	1	2					3	9
GAIN	12	2	10					—1	23
AVERAGE	4	2	5					— .3	3.3
TOUCHDOWNS	0	0	0					0	0

277

#6 Opponent's Offensive Statistics

Rushing

Hole	8	6	4	2	0	2	4	6	8	Totals
Times Ran	13	13	2	2	7	6	5	15	18	81
Yds. Gained	73	36	15	1	9	13	29	108	131	415
Avg. Gain	5.6	2.77	7.5	.5	1.3	2.1	5.8	7.2	7.3	5.1
T.D.'s	1	1							2	4

▼ **Offense Is Going** ▼

Passing

Attempts	Complete	Incomplete	Intercept	Ran	T.D.'s	Yds. Gain	Yds. Ran
70	20	24	1	25	1	262	72

Hash Mark Data

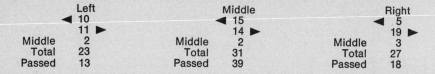

	Left		Middle		Right
◄	10	◄	15	◄	5
	11 ►		14 ►		19 ►
Middle	2	Middle	2	Middle	3
Total	23	Total	31	Total	27
Passed	13	Passed	39	Passed	18

Down & Distance Data

* 1st & 10
  63 plays
  41 runs, 22 passes

* 2nd & less than 5
  9 plays
  7 runs, 2 passes

* 2nd & more than 3
  44 plays
  21 runs, 23 passes

* 3rd & less than 3
  8 plays
  7 runs, 1 pass

* 3rd & long
  25 plays
  4 runs, 22 passes

* 4th & long

* 4th & short

* 4th and 1 on opp. 24
  Speed Sw. Lt. — Con
  4th and 13 on own 41
  Pass Pro

In Figure six are the complete totals of all plays including all formations.

In the hash mark area it shows whether the team runs right, middle, or left, and in what proportion.

The down and distances are self-explanatory.

278

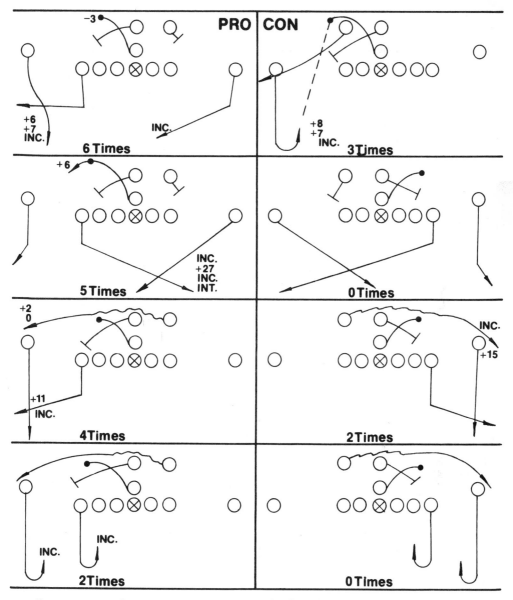

All passes are drawn up in patterns as the formation appears to the defense. The counterpart of that formation appears adjacent to it whether or not it was run. Here we assume that teams can do anything they use to both sides.

If the quarterback ran the ball it is noted next to him. If a particular pattern was incomplete, intercepted, or completed, these, too, are noted next to the receiver.

DEFENSIVE SHEET

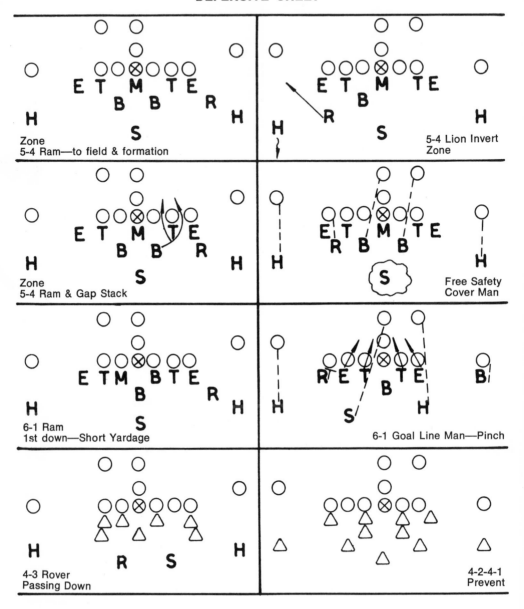

Zone
5-4 Ram—to field & formation

5-4 Lion Invert
Zone

Zone
5-4 Ram & Gap Stack

Free Safety
Cover Man

6-1 Ram
1st down—Short Yardage

6-1 Goal Line Man—Pinch

4-3 Rover
Passing Down

4-2-4-1
Prevent

The defensive sheet merely shows basic alignments, and any blitzes or coverages observed. They are all given names; we will identify them this way to our team.

From this report we will have our offensive prep coaches use the opponent's tendencies. He will tell the prep quarterback to stress their most consistent runs and passes tied to the basic formations. The same is true of our defensive prep team against the offense.

Every boy must become familiar with his opponent, as a player, and must understand the part that player plays in the entire scheme. Recognition of formation and anticipation is important.

13 Loose Ends

Spring Practice Begins Monday

By JOE DOYLE
Tribune Sports Writer

It might seem like only yesterday that Notre Dame defeated Texas in the Cotton Bowl, but it was 86 days ago and Coach Ara Parseghian his staff and squad are ready for another adventure that hopefully will end in a third straight bowl appearance.

Bowl games, or any talk of them, aren't on the agenda for Parseghian and the squad when spring practice starts tomorrow. About 90, give or take a few "fresh air" candidates, will be on hand, perhaps on Cartier Field or the surrounding parking lots or maybe indoors in the ACC.

The weatherman and the condition of the Cartier Field turf will decide the site of the early practices, but with only a brief break on Easter weekend, spring workouts will be compacted into a five week period ending with the Gold-Blue game on May 1.

Co-captains Tom Ga_____ (offense) and Walt Patulski (defense) will head _____ _____ starters from the Cotton Bowl, alth_____ _____ _____ _____ missing is sizeable. At least thr_____ _____ _____ _____ _____ during the year but mis_____

M_____ _____ _____ _____ _____ _____ an and the offe_____ _____ _____ _____ _____ e Theis-
m_____ _____ _____ _____ _____ endous
s_____ _____ _____ _____ _____ Theis-
_____ _____ _____ _____ _____ teen-
_____ _____ _____ _____ _____ and
_____ _____ _____ _____ _____ his

are _____ _____ _____ _____ _____ _____
bega_____ _____ _____ _____ who already h_____
prove_____ _____ _____ records. The co-ca_____
privileg_____ _____ more in the 1970 C_____
most of _____ _____ re before he was i_____
elect _____ _____ wl game this ye_____
Bowl. _____
(pulle_____

That's 132 passes or only six behind Jim Seymour'_____ record 138. And for good measure, the new passer, _____ at the moment, will also throw at Mike Creaney, _____ receiver a year ago with 18 catches.

Offensively, the other vacancies are those at _____ (Larry DiNardo), right guard (Gary Kos), left ta_____ Martin) fullback (Bill Barz) and right halfba_____ Allan) But John Cieszkowski had moved ahead _____ Larry Parker ahead of Allan by Cotton Bow_____ DiNardo, out with knee surgery, had been rep_____ Humbert.

Thus, after a new guard, quarterback, and _____ Irish could go into 1971 with a solid first-team lin_____

Defensively, linebackers Tim Kelly and _____ end Bob _____ _____ are the top graduates. Re_____ mov_____ _____ _____ _____ serves or freshman team _____ the _____ _____ _____ d be stronger than a yea_____ per_____ _____ _____ ws that each squad _____
_____ _____ _____ er who is a regular _____
_____ _____ _____ he next. Linebacker John_____
on_____ _____ _____ a soph, but after surp_____
eno_____ _____ ough corner, so he had _____

_____ _____ vear. Mike Crotty _____
_____ _____ and won the p_____
_____ _____ e defensive back_____
_____ _____ ground gainer. H_____
_____ _____ urns to rejoin hi_____
_____ _____ er in the backfield _____
_____ _____ n asked the likel_____
_____ d. "Why ask me?_____
_____ gna."

_____ t h_____ _____ ater was quick to r_____
_____ d have _____ _____ arterbacks when he _____
_____ d Theismann, but now _____
_____ ly kidding.
_____ both will have quite _____
_____ Steenberge has an e_____

Loose Ends

Everything that is done in organizing a football team and program is directed to one goal: having a winning team. This is not to say that winning at all costs is the ideal, but winning in such a way that the achievements become worthwhile and valuable to all concerned. From the equipment he wears to the training he receives—the reason he plays till graduation—the player is undergoing a learning experience that will forever be a large part of his physical and mental makeup. Knowing this full well, we attempt to understand the young man who is part of our team in the fullest capacity possible.

We know that he will react to discipline, but recoil at tyranny. We want him to feel great loyalty, but not fanaticism. All that he does or all that he is exposed to must be within the confines of good judgment.

I once heard a great man eulogizing his former coach and he paid a verbal tribute to him with these following phrases. I repeat them since they are exactly the goals an excellent coach should seek as his own. To teach your players to be "tough but not toughs," "relentless but not ruthless," "hard but not heartless." This is far easier said than done, but certainly those of us who are entrusted with the minds and bodies of youth must aim at the highest goals of our profession.

The Coach's Personality

Truly the head coach must be something of an enigma to outsiders, for it is necessary that he be the last word when decisions are to be made, yet also be open to suggestion, sensitive though sometimes adamant. His energy must be constant, his enthusiasm catching. There is an entire column on enthusiasm that adorns our office bulletin board and, though the author is unknown, there is one paragraph well worth remembering: "Enthusiasm —if we have it, we should thank God for it. If we don't have it, then we should get down on our knees and pray for it." Certainly you cannot feign it, for it is the spontaneous ease and love of coaching that imbues all those connected with you. Such things cannot be faked—they just are or they aren't.

Player Evaluation

Spring practice for us is the time for strategical experimentation along with player evaluation. For several years now I have made it a practice to have each coach conduct personal interviews with the players in the position he coaches. These are informal get-togethers where the basic idea is to communicate to the prospect how he fits into the overall picture. The coach will try to sound out the player's feelings and intentions about football, and about the position he'd like to play. The coach will also state, matter-of-factly, the boy's strengths and the points on which he needs work. He will further prescribe summer drills and a returning weight for the young man. All these interviews are noted on index cards and brought up for discussion in our staff meetings prior to the fall practice sessions.

It is my great thrill to behold the immense perceptiveness of young men in recognizing that they won't all be stars. Be this as it may, they want very badly to be a part of the team.

It is for this reason that I have never refused anyone an opportunity to come out for spring practice. By the fall most of the nonscholarship boys will know from the previous spring in what capacity they can aid the squad.

Courage

Courage is a nebulous thing and I will not tolerate any blanket statement that implies lack of courage on the part of any player. There may be a moment when his courage is not what it should be, but the courageous state is not always a steady one. True courage is not the absence of fear, it is having fear and overcoming it. For this reason great patience and great understanding are necessary in handling very young players. As time passes and the players become more familiar with what is expected of them, more adept at performing their task, confidence will replace immobilizing fear. I'd venture that the Wright brothers were scared out of their wits the first time they were off the ground at any height. Again, this is not lack of courage, and I attempt to have my staff and my players understand this.

Show me a player who doesn't feel great pressure when he lines up to run back a kickoff in front of 60,000 to 70,000 fans. Show me a speaker who does not get sweaty palms and

287

It sometimes happens that conditions aren't always the best for football. In times like these, that little extra effort is often the difference between a win and a loss.

a quickened pulse rate when his turn comes. Show me a great performer who doesn't worry about the success of his upcoming performance. When you find these people devoid of anxiety, I'll show you someone whose fire has dwindled to dying embers. Competitors on the football field, like competitors in all of life, are not cold or even lukewarm; they are full of the fire of life.

The Practice

Each practice is discussed and every minute of time on the field is a planned period. This time is so important and valuable that lack of planning will subtract from total preparation.

Every practice task sheet (see page 289) presents the intended time periods of the practice and below this the players, by position, who will be engaged. We prepare two offensive units and two defensive units. The rest of our players make up the preparatory teams.

Practice Task Sheet
Date: November 6, 1968

3:45 Jog-Cal
3:50 Sprints
      Iso
3:55 Drills

QB & C	Backs	Line	SE	Def Backs	Backers	Big 4
Ara	Tom	Wally Brian	Mike	Paul	George	Joe

4:00 Kicking Game (Punt Coverage) + Returns Set Wall

Offense	Defense
4:05 Run Time	Pass Drill
4:40 G.L. & Specials	Run & Pass
4:55 Pass Time	5:15 G.L.
5:30 Showers	

	1	2	Off-Prep		1	2	Def-Prep
TE—	Winegardner	Poskon	Lawson	LE—	Kuechenberg	Nash	Hartzel
SE—	Seymour	Eaton	Bergquist	RE—	Lauck	Lambert	Malone
		DeArrieta	Stark			Stenger	
RT—	Kunz	Martin	Maxim				
LT—	Reilly	Brennan	Bars	LT—	McCoy	Mudron	Wisne
			Ruzicka	RT—	Norri	Ziznewski	Cotter
RG—	McKinley	Kos	Fischer				
LG—	Tuck	Kennedy	Hildebrand	RIB—	Olson	Hempel	
			Bossu	LIB—	Freebery	Wright	Kiliany
C—	Oriard	Holtzapfel	Leahy				Swearingen
			Buches	LOB—	Schumacher	Merlitti	Kondrla
			McCon	ROB—	Tim Kelly	Wittliff	Haag
Q—	Hanratty	Theismann	Gardner				McHale
		Belden		RH—	Gasser	Standring	Witchger
							Johnson
FB—	Dushney	Ziegler	Bill Barz	LH—	Zloch	Wack	Sigrist
							Snow
RH—	Gladieux	Criniti		S—	Reid	Lewallen	Heneghan
							Quinn
LH—	O'Brien	Landolfi					
	Allan						

289

An intent Notre Dame bench watches game action—each eager to do his part in bringing home the victory.

Pregame Preparation

I feel it is a very important factor to insure that the team is together the evening before a game. After our evening meal we meet at the quarters designated for our stay (in our case it is the fourth floor of a very quiet seminary). We bring in a movie to be shown at 8:30 p.m. By 10:30 p.m. the boys are in their rooms and lights are out by 11:00 p.m. We have an early rising at 7:30 a.m. I think this, too, is very important so that the boy does not loll in bed too long. Active people who are energetic are most often early risers. I want them up and about. At 8:30 we attend a Mass right at the seminary. The non-Catholic squad members are given an opportunity to attend their own services if they wish. Most of them prefer to sit in the rear of the chapel and observe the proceedings. After the Mass is over, the entire team will take a leisurely stroll about one quarter of a mile around the lake to our dining hall. For a 1:30 p.m. game we plan on a 9:30 a.m. meal.

At roughly 10:30 a.m., when the meal is over and the players have enjoyed the quiet of such an atmosphere, we attempt to cover the remaining items which pertain to the game.

There is no format for this, as it is merely the culmination of all the things we've done through the week. It is my task to convey to the team *why, how* and *when* it must be done. At the conclusion of this talk, we have a short ten-minute breakdown meeting by position and the boys are released till dressing and taping time at 12:00 noon.

The Game

During the process of a game a coach is caught up in all the chaos and noise of a contest. It becomes difficult to communicate. We insure what we must do by simply running a rehearsal before our first game. Players on the offense are assigned a bench area. Players on the defense are assigned another area and their replacements have specific areas. Specialists and kickers are in the middle of the areas.

Bench Assignments

#1 Offense	#1 Defense	Specialists	#2 Offense & Defense	Alternates

← Coach →

Sideline

My staff members are all placed and briefed on their duties during the actual game. It is very important that quick, efficient and smooth communication obtains between coach and coach and player and coach.

It is for this reason that I use two offensive field coaches, two defensive field coaches, and one each in the press box. They are in constant touch with one another and ready to funnel any information to me at an instant's notice.

Postgame

Our players are excused until 4:00 p.m. Sunday when they will jog a mile in sweat suits on their own. This leisurely jog allows them to smooth out the kinks from a trying battle.

All injured personnel are treated immediately after the game or Sunday morning, depending on the extent of the injury. At 6:00 p.m., Sunday evening, the entire squad and staff view the game movies. This enables our staff the period of time between 1:00 and 6:00 p.m. Sunday to grade the film.

The Press

After a game, the media people will often press players for comments or observations. I only ask of our players

291

that they be kind to our opponents and humble both in victory and defeat. I try to assure them that as no one player can win a game, so it is also true of a loss. We feel that we win together and any losses must be assumed the same way.

Many times, an eager young man will not state thoughtfully all that he meant to say or what he has said will be out of context. When this happens, it can sometimes be embarrassing to the young man who has spoken the words or to the opposing team to which he has made reference. It is precisely because of this that we caution them to be truly humble and guard against any anger or emotion which will not appear a fair remark when the emotion has subsided.

Regarding interviews with myself and my staff, we simply try to state the facts of the situation as we see them.

For the last 50 games at Notre Dame we have been the underdog once. This was the last game of our 1968 season. Being the favorite is not always an easy thing, for the press and fans in general take too much for granted. That attitude can easily affect a team. It can lull us into complacency or hurt us too deeply if a loss occurs. The exact superiority of one team over another is essentially a myth. Nothing remains static and players' emotions can overthrow all odds. I tell our players quite frankly before any game, that no game was ever won in the papers. If we are fortunate enough to win, I also insist to them that "nothing is as old as yesterday's news."

I always try to allow the press time for an interview both before and after the game. My one condition is that it must not subtract from my own, my staff's, and my players' time for game preparation. Most knowledgeable writers understand this and will respect your time if you always try to be honest, candid, and fair.

The Player's Academic Life

As a football coach who of necessity bears the pressure of wins and losses, strategy and conditioning, injuries, conflicts, details, family life, *ad infinitum,* it is a task not to become so fragmented that you lose control. My experience here is that you must never lose sight of what is the real purpose of it all.

Most young men employ their physical talent in return for a financial grant-in-aid that will enable them to complete their formal education. This education, their particular degree and, ultimately, graduation, are paramount.

This is the number-one obligation and athletics are simply number two. Realizing this I feel a deep obligation to make certain our players have proper guidance for their curriculum selection, their study time, and their class attendance.

I ask of them three basic things to aid themselves fully in their academic standing.

1. Never cut class without authorization.
2. Always take notes.
3. Budget their time.

If a player has more than one unexcused absence, I am informed immediately. If his average is dropping or his attitude less than what it should be, I, or a member of my staff, will call him in to find the problem.

We do not coddle him or necessarily make these meetings fun. The boy must either rise up to the reality of the task or own up that he cannot. Certainly he can, for he could not have come this far. Some younger people may resent the stringent controls, but when they understand that the discipline is imposed only for their own benefit, they are truly grateful. Our graduation percentage has been one of the achievements of which I and my staff are most proud.

A statistical survey conducted several years ago revealed an unsuspected bit of information to the staff and me. Our players actually received better marks during the season than after. Offhand, it would appear that they perform better when they have more to do; in truth, I think that this is merely human nature. Great accomplishments are born of pain, sacrifice, and elbow grease. The relaxed atmosphere of "off-season" doesn't appear to be the climate for "hustle."

14 Coaching: Of What Value Is It?

We are "people coaches," not just "football coaches."

Coaching:
Of What Value Is It?

It seems to me that a book written about coaching for coaches should end with some remarks about why people coach. My reasons may not be the same as yours, but I want to put some of my thinking on paper as part of that continuing discussion which helps all of us to clarify our thoughts.

Possibly at no other time in the history of America has there been so much confusion, so much dissension, so great a strain on the minds, hearts and integrity of our people. Because we are a part of these times and because we are in athletics, we need to reexamine what we represent.

I mentioned fragmentation of mind experienced by persons who are subjected to excessive demands on their attention and energy — demands pulling them in opposing directions. Doctors have seen this happen to the executive who pursues too many goals without adequate, unifying principles; now, however, we are beginning to suspect that this same kind of shat-

tering pressure can afflict a nation.

Political upheaval, religious change, restless youth, social conflicts, racial fears and hatred — all these pressures of our time argue for a great search for values. Not because our activity is the most important human effort, but because we are part of our times, we coaches must recognize, pursue and communicate the value of athletics . . . and the other values which athletics tends to emphasize.

There are some who deny any value in athletics other than its ability to generate dollars and cents. There are many — as we all know — who claim that an athletic program simply detracts from the real value of university life; that it inevitably becomes too professional, that it is too time-consuming, too commercial. These people obviously do not recognize the values many of us see in our programs. For them, if not for ourselves, we should be prepared to formulate those values.

In any time of change, we expect

traditions and values to be questioned, but today much of this questioning seems to have become cynical, corrosive and, at times, disruptive. We should not be surprised that our work comes under the same challenges. Most men in coaching do not feel any great enthusiasm to justify their contribution. But we cannot simply isolate ourselves, ignoring the questions and challenges raised by people who are often sincere — even when they are under the influence of special interests.

Educators (and citizens concerned with education) began to seriously question the investment of time, effort and money for athletic programs when Sputnik I was launched into space. The immediate reaction was a kind of panic effort to catch up, with a heavy stress on the "core curriculum"—sciences, mathematics, physics, etc. This emphasis was accompanied by a tendency to "weed out" the soft subject, the recreational program, the untalented student. As a nation we started to program our schools as though we believed that only the students with highest IQ's and the highest college board scores were educable . . . were worth the effort.

I suppose it was natural to place a more intense emphasis on the teaching of core subjects, but we seemed to forget parts of our history. We seemed to forget that man is a sum total of all his living experience, *which experience comes in many ways.* We seemed to forget that the actual channels of learning differ with each student . . . and that each student will tend to stress those channels which give expression to his own best talents. The right of the individual to express and achieve according to his own talents and decisions seemed to get lost in our national effort to compete in space research.

In this whole process, we tended to overlook the great distinction between knowledge and wisdom. We achieve wisdom only through living experience. The classroom can be anywhere, any time for anyone.

In our present situation, we seem to give little thought to those values of wisdom which are usually described in abstract terms. Nevertheless, qualities such as loyalty, respect, service, sacrifice, pride, love, dedication, camaraderie, wisdom take on a special importance when society is confronted with the tensions and controversies of our time.

When one endures the physical and mental hardship of being a team member, when he accepts all the unpleasantness of weather, outside pressures, bruises and aches, the disappointment

297

of losing, when he subjects his performance to the judgment of all spectators and critics, . . . through all of this a player can achieve a special discipline of character.

This kind of discipline, we all know, contributes to the strength which helps us to face hardship, responsibility and the demands of duty throughout our lifetimes.

As I watch players grow in their understanding of what it means to be part of a team, as I watch them face the difficulties of a challenging schedule, I've seen many qualities emerge, especially:

The ability to reach out. I have seen a tense, self-doubting individual demand greater effort of himself. In doing so, he has risen above what many others would have settled for as their best. This growth in self-confidence remains with a man convincing him that he can demand much of himself, that he can achieve far more than could be accomplished with a mediocre effort.

Sacrifice. None of this comes about without great effort, great energy. Having faced the demand for that kind of performance, the young man realizes that worthwhile achievements are usually difficult . . . they usually demand sacrifices. If he learns this truth early in life, he has gained an advantage over many of the problems he will face.

The ability to bounce back. Each of us has faced situations which had shattered our faith, tortured our emotions (and, in some instances, our bodies). If we have been fortunate enough to have escaped the heaviest difficulties, we have certainly seen them in the lives of people close to us. We know that it is heartbreaking to come face to face with death, deep suffering, crushing disillusionment. It is agony to have to stand by and watch pain, frustration and waste. Still, each man as he lives through these things or faces them in the lives of friends must respond. Will he despair and fold under the pressure of sorrow? Or will he be able to draw on the past discipline of competition in order to bounce back for another try?

I have watched, played with, and coached men who became far better persons through their participation in athletics.

Again we all have known many needy young men who have been able to financially achieve a college education because of their athletic ability. Their presence enriched the experience of their companions in college. Many brought different experiences and backgrounds into the groups they lived with in college. A good many brought an experience of military combat (though I've heard of very few athletes who were ever involved in the waves of campus destruction). Somehow, the social concerns of the athletes seem to be controlled by the fact that they have lived with high emotion, with a sense of honor, fair play and compassion.

Loyalty . . . compassion . . . personal pride . . . enthusiasm . . . self-discipline . . . faith in one's self . . . surely these are qualities worthy of respect. They are not acquired through merely reading; these are achieved through living!

It becomes increasingly difficult to satisfy everyone's demand and still fulfill a demanding job. New obstacles emerge, along with the traditional ones, to test and try the serious college athlete.

The traditional obstacles that have threatened athletics for years are illegal recruiting, professional gambling, the corruption of a celebrity system, and the like.

More recently our athletic programs have been attacked by the same pressures that pose problems for all our institutions. Across college campuses today there is great unrest. Many young people reject direction, advice, counsel; they are impatient with following, waiting, struggling. Racial prej-

udices and minority group consciousness have surfaced in college athletics as they have elsewhere in our society. In general, though, I believe that athletics has been one of the most open dimensions of our life. There were and are abuses, and there are still individuals who have suffered as coaches or players because of racial bigotry. Still, the world of sports can claim it has done as much for the honest acceptance of the individual as has any other segment of our society.

When the shrillness of social conflict moves into the world of sports through racial boycotts, through players' "strikes," through rejection of honest authority, then this very special world of ours which has meant so much to so many of us is in danger of collapse.

My hope and prayer is that those of us in this world will continue to respect the values we have traditionally honored . . . that we shall refuse to let these values be distorted into tools of social pressure.

Today, more than ever before, the enthusiasm and conscience of our young people have generated a tremendous response in the sensitivity of the adult society. This insistent pressure from the young has compelled an examination of traditional "systems." In this sense, the generation tension is constructive and useful.

If our dynamic, idealistic young people are on one side with hopes and dreams . . . and our thoughtful, older people on the other with experience and judgment, then we have hope for constructive solutions to any of our problems.

As coaches we represent one of the few remaining organized systems for demanding discipline of young men. Their education will not be complete if it does not include the discipline and generosity that can come from being a team member, if it does not include an awareness of responsibility to others. We are "people coaches," not just "football coaches."

These are my personal convictions, but I react strongly against any attack on athletics in general. I have seen too much in it that is good and important for the lives of the athletes themselves and for the welfare of our society. I hope for and work toward the goal that our athletes should be men able to cope with hardship, able to respect law, able to face disappointment, to give loyalty, to know justice, to find that each has his place and his contribution — able to achieve some good, to win if he can, to lose only if he must — but above all, to live up to the limit of his ability.

Ara Parseghian's Coaching Record

Year	School	W	L	T	Pct*
1951	Miami (Ohio)	7	3	0	.700
1952	Miami	8	1	0	.889
1953	Miami	7	1	1	.875
1954	Miami	8	1	0	.889
1955	Miami	9	0	0	1.000
1956	Northwestern	4	4	1	.500
1957	Northwestern	0	9	0	.000
1958	Northwestern	5	4	0	.556
1959	Northwestern	6	3	0	.667
1960	Northwestern	5	4	0	.556
1961	Northwestern	4	5	0	.444
1962	Northwestern	7	2	0	.778
1963	Northwestern	5	4	0	.556
1964	Notre Dame	9	1	0	.900
1965	Notre Dame	7	2	1	.778
1966	Notre Dame	9	0	1	1.000
1967	Notre Dame	8	2	0	.800
1968	Notre Dame	7	2	1	.778
1969	Notre Dame	8	2	1	.800
1970	Notre Dame	10	1	0	.909
	20 years	133	51	6	.723
	At Miami (5 yrs.)	39	6	1	.867
	At Northwestern (8 yrs.)	36	35	1	.507
	At Notre Dame (7 yrs.)	58	10	4	.853

*Winning percentages are exclusive of ties.

A Glossary of Coaching Jargon

Across the grain—The angle of a throw or the cutback angle a runner takes in a completely opposite direction from the pursuit. The advantage is surprise, the disadvantage is negative yardage.

Action—The word action refers to a scheme or pattern—or path—by the offensive backfield.

Action pass—A pass from a quarterback who is sprinting or rolling out. No fake to a back is involved.

Action time—The actual period of time that the play is "live." The time from the snap of the ball until the whistler blows it dead.

Area block—An offensive blocker seals an area by blocking it with his body. As in defensive "zone," he does not block a specific man but the zone.

Alignment—Offensively, the formation. Defensively, the positions, taken in response to the formation.

Area—Some coaches use the term hole with identifying numbers. The *area* is the hole; we identify area as, *Middle, Inside, Off-Tackle* or *Sweep;* points of attack.

Audible — Synonymous with "automatics." The QB verbally changes the play at the line of scrimmage by his cadence. It allows for a last-minute modification against the viewed defensive alignment.

Audibilizing—See automatics or audible.

Automatics—See audible.

Backfield action — The complete meshing pattern of the backs. Full-flow, split-flow, counter-flow are the direction patterns of offensive action.

Backside—The opposite side of the play from the center of line.

Balanced "T"—A full-house backfield in normal T position, with a balanced line on either side of the center-guard, tackle and end equally spaced.

Beat the clock—Plays that are geared to stop the clock without calling a charged time-out. An incomplete pass, an opponent penalty, a sideline run or pass, stepping out of bounds are all methods of beating the clock drills.

Bleed the clock—Allowing the clock to tick off by using every second of huddle time, running all plays inside the sideline and delaying normal hustle to allow the official clock to run out or force an opponent to call time.

Blitz—A defensive action calling for the extra rush or unexpected involvement of a linebacker or a deep secondary member. It is a variation added to standard rushes to confuse offensive blocking patterns or to outnumber the blockers.

Blocking call—A huddle call by the quarterback to specify a blocking pattern in a play. The QB can also make a call at the line in cadence. If the QB does not specify, linemen can make a call to one another.

Boot—To bootleg or boot is to split the flow of the backfield in order to pull guards to the roll-out side of the

QB. Many people refer to waggles as boot, but we think of boot as split-flow.

Boot, waggle or counter—Any pass action that involves a fake of the run one way and allows the QB counter-flow protection to pass.

Bread and butter—Those plays or defenses or players which are of greatest, most consistent value. Those actions that are timeworn but fully tested and are the bulwark of any team function or plan.

Breakdown drills—Drills by the relative positions—offensive line interior, receivers, offensive backs, defensive front four or line, linebackers, deep secondary.

Bubble—Causing a "give" in the defensive wave by force or sheer number of blockers at the point of attack.

Cadence—The ignition or starting sounds that spark the offensive unit to start the players simultaneously. Words, colors, numbers, states and names are used as sounds in cadence. Some give information about where we are running or in what pattern.

Check thru's—A halfback or fullback after checking the rush on his passer

303

sees everyone accounted for and slips through the line for a dunk pass as an outlet for the QB when needed.

Chop—A technique in pass protection when a rusher is overpowering you or running too deep to your outside. The chop is a cross-body block.

Clinch—A defensive linebacker action to hold up and tie up—legally — a receiver coming off the line. A delaying block or "squeeze-clinch."

Comeback—After running his initial pattern a receiver will angle back to the QB to cause a greater angle of separation between a defending man and himself.

Come to a point—A term for defensive line play. It describes the action of the defensive lineman penetrating to a predetermined area.

Contact drills—The live, hitting "full go" action of simulated game conditions. At times only a "one vs one" drill or a "few vs a few."

Contain man—A defensive term. The widest responsibility for a defensive man. Not his alignment, but his assignment. No one is to get outside of "contain" with the ball.

Corner man—A secondary coverage man outside of a defensive end and deeper. He supports against wide plays and protects flat and deep zones. The term is usually connected with a four-spoke, or four-man defensive coverage in the secondary.

Coverage unit—Those defensive men who are committed to the pass coverage.

Curl pattern—A wide semicircle that explores a greater area, but very similar to a hook pattern.

Deep secondary—The alignment and players involved with pass cover and run defense beyond the underneath coverage defense.

Delivering a blow—Uncoiling, on the snap of the ball, from the starting stance with leverage to neutralize an opponent.

Direction—This is merely the determination of the backfield action, right or left, designating the point of attack—or frontside. The opposite side is backside.

Distortion—Offensively, breaking the wave of defense by forcing through power, finesse, or leverage, a broken wave. Also multiformation distortion for disguise. Defensively, false alignment before the ball is snapped, with veering, looping or stunting back to an apparent weakness.

Divide or iso—See "Isolation Block."

Dogs—A defensive term usually calling for man-to-man coverage to enlarge the rushing corps. "Dogs" — red dog — green dog — mad dog — imply types of LB rushes or secondary blitzes.

Double free safety—Similar to single free except there are two center-fielders and each is now concerned with only half of the field.

Double team—Two men teaming to block one defender. Techniques vary but the ratio of 2 to 1 is double teaming. Defensively, two men assigned to one offensive man.

Drag pattern—A receiver route that is a controlled across-pattern or a delayed move to allow expansion by underneath coverage.

Draw—A fake of a pocket action to force expansion of pass defenders and to entice the rush to come harder, "drawing" it inward allowing the ball

carrier to slip into a secondary, running-to-cover pass.

Draw block—To draw block is to set-step, as in pocket protection, and take one side or approach angle of the defender away by positioning your body from the inside out or the outside in.

Drill the ball—This phrase refers to trajectory. A QB should never "hang" or ease up on a horizontal field throw or screen pass. He should drill it — to shorten defensive reaction time.

Drill periods—Those practice periods simulating game situations in a teaching and learning breakdown sequence. The daily staple of renewed work for mastery.

Drive blocker—The offensive blocker driving in or out on a man posted. His duty is to get the defensive man moved laterally to cause a distortion in alignment or "daylight" for the backs to run through.

Drive off—A receiver voids an area against a zone defense to allow a second receiver to run into that area.

Eat the ball—QB action when no one is *open* and the situation is critical —

when he should not risk putting it in the air. Obviously, accepting negative yardage is the best of two choices.

Effort—An ingredient in the great interval that calls for the maximum physical and mental concentration to perform the prescribed duty.

Either/or—Usually refers to a choice of pass to the frontside or a throwback to the opposite side. It can also be a play series, either a pass or a run depending on the front.

Eligible receivers—Those who are allowed to catch passes for the offense. All backs and two ends, six players.

Execution—Another element of the great interval theory — the proper technique to allow the best leverage, hitting surface and economy of effort in performance.

Endurance — The third element, the great interval; the sustained effort through physical conditioning allowing maximum body control and force.

Field balance — The horizontal distribution of defensive players to allow balancing the field, without allowing too much open area to too few defenders.

Field position — Strategic location of the ball. On whose side of the 50? Within four-down area or punting area?

Fire—Much like a stunt with a linebacker or secondary man offsetting or stacking with a defensive lineman to rush the offensive alignment.

Fire out—A term of offensive line action. The linemen simulate a regular running play and give no clue that it is a pass play; then they recoil after the "fire out" to protect the pass action.

Fixed—There is no blocking adjustment; the play is a pattern block; offensive players attack specific areas versus any defensive alignment.

Flank backs—A variation from the balanced T formation placing one of the three deep backfield men just one yard behind the scrimmage line, but beyond the end lineman.

Flanked—General term meaning a man wider than the normal end man on the line. Defense must always be aware of contain and compensate for flank people lest they sacrifice contain.

Flaring backs—A halfback on offense leaving from his normal position in the T and running a shallow pass route parallel to the line.

Flat area — The area of underneath coverage on pass defense when zoning. Its boundaries are as deep as 12 to 15 yards, and the outside one-fourth of the horizontal field.

Flat pattern—A direct line; an arrow-like course of a receiver into the flat area looking over his outside shoulder while gradually gaining ground up to eight yards.

Fold—Offensively: blocking one man inside out and allowing a wider offensive man to "fold" underneath. Defensively: much the same — the widest man coming behind and underneath.

Forcer—A defensive player who has responsibility of containing the outside plays and *forcing* the play in or the passer to pull up. Usually an end or linebacker. On rare occasions a corner or safety.

Forcing the ball—A poorly conceived pass; a throw into a crowd of defenders or at one receiver who is obviously covered.

Forcing unit — The rushing defensive lineman in combination with linebackers; they force the play.

Formation—A single offensive alignment that has one fixed name when it is to the right and another fixed name when it is to the left.

Four-back I—The same as "I" or four people aligned in the backfield behind the center. Kansas City Chiefs use this as a base formation and then move into other formations.

Four-down area — That area where the offense does not have to punt on fourth down to maintain reasonable safety or field position. Also, the area said "within field goal range."

Free safety—A defensive call utilizing everyone in the coverage on a man-to-man basis except the safety. The safety who is free acts as a centerfielder.

Freeze — A communication between linemen telling them to block the fixed pattern on the play because the defensive front fits it perfectly at the point of attack.

Front four — The defensive ends and the defensive tackles who normally are in a down stance to rush the passer or stop the run; usually a 4 - 4 - 3 alignment or a 4 - 3 - 4, etc.

Fronts—The defensive line and linebackers' positions as the QB views them while calling cadence.

Frontside — Interchangeable with "playside" (see playside).

Full house — A balanced T offensive formation, the QB under the center, a left halfback, fullback, and right halfback in the classic T alignment. Usually a balanced line with mirrored or the same alignment to both sides.

Game plan—The organized format of offensive and defensive schemes prepared for a particular game, for a particular opponent and his forecasted tendencies.

Gang tackling — Pursuit to the point where not just one person is trying to stop the play. The swarming of defensive men with great hustle and pride; not derogatory, with no implication of intent to injure.

Gap stacks — When a lineman on offense has defensive men in the gaps to either side, no man on him and another defender stacked behind the gapped man.

Goal line and specials—Those plays that attack the short-yardage defense and goal-line alignments. Also those defenses that are geared to stop goal-line and short-yardage attacks. Specials: screens, draws, misdirection.

Goal-line defense — The defense or defenses selected to protect a shorter area of field; a more hostile and aggressive attitude; a more intense pursuit, usually from a different alignment or front than what a midfield position would call for.

Half a man—In the line, when a defender covers only half of an area. In the secondary, when a LB is walked halfway between a split receiver and the remainder of the offensive alignment; also called a "walkaway."

Half-moon course — A deeper than usual course followed by a pulling lineman allowing time for a wide play to develop.

Hook area — The area of underneath coverage in zone. Its boundaries are as deep as 12 to 15 yards and the two inside one-fourth areas of the horizontal field.

Hook block — Offensive technique block, often called "scramble." It is a shooting out from the down stance at a man aligned wider than yourself and a crabbing on all fours so rapidly as to hook him in, despite his wider alignment.

Hook or curl pass—An offensive pattern or pass "cut"; a receiver runs hard as if on a deep route but seeing people in the deep zone, pulls up quickly, curling into the QB's line of vision.

Head up—An offensive or defensive term; head up or "nose on nose" says simply that offensive and defensive players are squarely opposite each other across the scrimmage line.

Hook pattern—A pass route in which a receiver fakes a *shake* and comes back toward the passer in a tight semicircle. Against a zone, the hook is between defenders. Against man, it is in front of a defender you cannot outrun.

I or I formation—A backfield alignment of two, three, or four backs in one vertical arrangement behind the offensive center.

Ignition—See cadence.

In lane—A receiver finishing his pattern gets "in lane" when he moves to an unobstructed view of the QB. Also, the width of one's own shoulders; in reference to a QB pivoting and staying "in lane."

Inside—The offensive area of attack running from head up the offensive guard to the outside shoulder of the offensive tackle. There is, then, an inside area left and right.

Interception—The reception of a pass by a defensive man covering a receiver.

Invert—A term used to describe getting to defensive zone coverage from a four-deep secondary alignment. The two interior safeties *invert* or race up to action when it is to their side. From here they usually cover flat areas or attack the run play from the inside-out angle of pursuit.

Isolation—Line blocking to the left and right of a point of attack, leaving that area or person occupying that area isolated for a back or backs from the backfield to block.

Jam — A defensive term meaning to deter a receiver, to hold him up; to double cover; or, "bump and run."

Keys—A general term meaning the

person or persons on offense or defense who will give hints or information about the upcoming play by their actions. Coaches give "keys" to players. Players "key" on other players.

Leverage—A blocking or running advantage by reason of the angle of approach one player has on another.

Live—Whenever a coach makes a scrimmage "live," it is full-scale contact just as in a game.

Log in—The technique used by a man to the inside by reason of alignment, blocking a wider man *in*. "Logging in" is not done with force or leverage, but finesse, speed, and influence.

Looks—The countless "fronts" and alignments the defensive line can face.

Loop—A defensive line term similar to a line veer only a bit less direct. One veers on a straight line, but loops or "squirms" in curved semicircle.

Man block—The offensive blocker is assigned by rule or call to block a specific man. He must go anywhere that man does to get him unless there is no rush threat; then, he can double.

Man cover—A man assigned to each

eligible receiver. There are no zones involved here, only one man defending against one receiver. The maximum is six, the minimum, one.

Man cut—A prescribed route to run against man coverage. Either on-the-move adjustment or predetermined adjustment based on alignment.

Man stacks—When a lineman on offense has a man on the line directly opposite him and a linebacker stacked squarely behind the defensive man or slightly offset.

Master call—An offensive term referring to a scheme or pattern of complete line blocking. It is the base call and all adjustments are made within the particular base or "master" call.

Middle—An offensive area of attack delineated from head up the left guard through the center area to head up the right guard.

Mirror—A "mirror" is exactly the same play, formation, or action to the opposite side of a formation.

Monster—Almost synonymous with the name "rover." The usual name for monster is the playing team's nickname: the "Spartan" or "Wolfman" or some suitable term for isolating him from the standard defense.

Motion—A man legally in motion is a player moving parallel to the line or at an angle away from it after the "set" call; short motion (two to three steps) or long motion (across the field) is an attempt to distort the offensive formation and help learn more about the defense's coverage by noting who picks up the motion man.

Nearback—The back nearest to the playside in a normal three-back alignment. It does not mean the FB or any wingback, the LH's or RH's true position in a balanced T.

Numbered blocking—A method of refining and consolidating rule blocking by numbering the defensive people in multiple fronts. E.g., any man over the center is 0. A man stacked behind him is No. 1, the man to the playside is No. 2, etc.

Off tackle—The off-tackle area is the next widest area of attack adjacent to the inside area; it is delineated from the outside shoulder of the offensive tackle to the outside shoulder of the offensive end.

Opponent look — The physical ap-

pearance, alignment, personality and action of the opponent both offensively and defensively; the "look" the prep teams try to give the varsity.

Option running — When an offensive blocker assigned to a defensive man blocks the man in the direction the defender wants to go; this gives the ball carrier the option of running to daylight on either side.

Out pattern—A receiver route straight up the field with a sharp cut to the sideline at a 90° angle (or less) coming back in the direction of the QB at a prescribed time and distance.

Pattern—Generally, a standard way of doing something: (1) A pattern block is one kind of offensive-line blocking. (2) A pass pattern is a basic route or routes a receiver may run. (3) A team's pattern of play is determined by scouting reports.

Pattern blocking—A blocking scheme which looks to blocking areas and not individual people. Such a pattern obtains with reference to predetermined ways of blocking. Example: all linemen sealing the area to their inside or outside.

Pattern tree — The repertoire of pass

routes, usually called "cuts," within the scheme of an overall formation. Examples: in, out, delay, hook, etc.

Perimeter—The secondary coverage "look" as the offensive QB views the field balance of the defense.

Pinch—A defensive maneuver, usually involving coordination by linemen and linebackers, directed toward closing off the inside attack area; can come from one or both sides. Normally used in a goal-line or short-yardage situation; almost the opposite of "squirm."

Playside—The point of attack side from the center to the right or to the left. The opposite is backside or away side.

Pocket—True drop back passing tied to draws, screens, backs checking through; popularized by the professional ranks.

Point of attack—This is the exact spot or hole or area the play is designed to hit. This is always the playside or frontside.

Post blocker — The offensive blocker who fires into a defensive lineman, stopping his penetration across the line. He does not attempt to take him any particular way, just neutralize his penetration, thus "posting" him for a "drive" blocker who, hopefully, will move the defensive man laterally. (Double team.)

Post, drive and lead—An easy method of calling a double team (post and drive) block at a specific point while taking the next widest man out by a trap or back's block.

Power I—Is the vertical alignment of QB, Fullback and Tailback behind the center. The fourth member is at RH or LH. The side on which he assumes position is the power side; hence, Power I right and left.

Pre-Align — To show the offensive or defensive alignment before the ball is snapped.

Pre-Call—A huddle call made by the offensive QB or the defensive captain prior to breaking the huddle. Any voiding of a pre-call is known as an "automatic" on offense and a "revert" on defense.

Pre-Practice—The period of time (usually 15 min.) before the official practice of the team as a unit. (Players work on individual specialties.)

Pre-Rotate — A defensive secondary move before the snap of the ball causing "rover" or "monster" to show unbalance.

Prep team—A team not actually preparing to play in the game but playing the role of the next opponent so that the offense and defense may become familiar with that opponent.

Prevention defense — The coverage and alignment that will bend but not yield the long gainer or long score when you are waiting for the clock to run out or have your opponent in need of a long gainer. The surest and safest defense against the long bomb.

Pro set—A common offensive formation setting a TE and flanker one way and a split end to the opposite side. The backs can divide, align in the I, or remain in normal position of HB and FB.

Pump—A QB maneuver of faking a throw to get defensive reaction and also to tell a receiver he is covered and to go on from there.

Pursuit—A defensive term meaning to overtake a ball carrier or receiver "away" from a defensive man's position. Team pursuit is a practiced

phase not just a "pep" talk about hustle and desire. The angle and speed of approach is pursuit.

Quick pattern—A wide receiver taking a few quick steps forward and then breaking sharply in or out for a quick throw from the QB.

Quickie—A tight end or slot back comes off the line and reads LB blitz; immediately, he turns his head inside and expects a little quick dunk of the ball over the line by the QB.

Reach—A verbal command to establish a whole progression of blocking rules: (#1) block a down lineman to the playside gap. (#2) A LB in that same gap. (#3) A man on your nose. (#4) A man over you but off the line. (#5) Seal away from the play.

Read—Offensively—to read is to discern the coverage, the stunt or defensive move tipped off by alignment before the snap of the ball; also, receiver's and QB's discerning coverage after the snap. Defensively—means hitting and controlling on the line and then sliding to the ball laterally.

Reading the defense — Discerning from the defensive alignment before the snap of the ball the ratio between

313

possible rushers and coverage men. It might further tell what style of coverage it is when read by a QB. "Reading" the defense on the move by a QB or receiver is to discern who covers what area and where he's coming from and whether he's playing a man or a zone, aided or alone.

Recruiting — Follow-up salesmanship extended to future prospects by inviting them to visit your own campus and selling the worth of your academic programs. A highly competitive and tiring search for new prospects.

Regular — Straight ahead numbered blocking as in a 5-2 defense: C on #0, G on #1, T on #2, E on #3, HB on #4.

Revolve — A defensive secondary move; the same as "rotate." It is, ultimately, the same position as prerotate but based on the flow and action of the ball after the snap.

Robber—Similar to free safety or a "roverback"; he adopts a "lance" style, affording a surprise element in pass coverage or secondary blitzing.

Roll out—See sprint out (pass style).

Roll side—The offensive or defensive side which the QB attacks by running an option sweep or pass; also known as "rolling out."

Rover—Defensive term meaning the 11th man, the "odd" man who tips the scales of balanced alignment. Normally used when the team is aligned and prerotated to the widest side of the field or to the strength of the offensive alignment.

Rule blocking—A fixed, written rule committed to memory by an offensive blocker. Example, reach rule: Take the man in your frontside gap, on you, over you, or seal inside in that order.

Run-action pass—Also called play-action pass, it involves a hit-out style of line blocking to mislead the defenders and faking a run to bring the linebackers to read and react to "run."

Running back—The ball carrier other than the FB.

Rush—The people, by number and approach, who pressure the play aggressively, attacking across the scrimmage line. A defensive term.

"Safe" defense — This refers to a "base" or reasonably familiar and sound defense to which a team can always revert if an uncommon offensive threat is shown. Example: Single wing, short punt, spread formations.

Scouting—The preliminary search for younger athletes who are students. Also the knowledge of another team gathered by watching it play a different opponent prior to your own game.

Scramble hook—An offensive blocking technique designed to reach out wider than your alignment and hook in, or position a defensive man from the outside in.

Scrape—Another term for "wipe off."

Screen—A momentary blocking by offensive linemen, designed to induce the defenders into rushing the passer. The bypassed blockers string out a protective wall for a screen receiver to follow and be led upfield—if the QB survives the rushers.

Seal—Similar to reach except the direction of this rule block works to the "back side" rather than play side.

Seams—That point equidistant between two zoning defenders and in complete vision of the QB.

Sequence—Plays that start out the same but attack different areas with the idea of "baiting" the defense into false recognition. The defense can also sequence defensive looks or stunts.

Series—Plays that are strung together to be used in sequence either by pre-calling them in the huddle, or having access to them from a QB audible at the line.

Set step—The offensive pass blocker's original move from the stance when pass protecting for a pocket pass. Twofold goal: (1) To keep from firing out too much and losing balance, and (2) to be able to see stunts and veers or games on the part of the rushers.

Shadow—An offensive blocking term telling the blocker not to go after a rusher who does not penetrate his pass rush. The blocker merely keeps his body between the defensive man and the QB and "shadows him."

Shake pattern — A receiver route which starts out as a straight up-the-field sprint for the deep bomb with a minimum of faking; used either to clear an area or outrun a defender.

Shed — A general term meaning to

315

ward off a blocker or a tackle by delivering a forearm blow and keeping legs free.

Short-yardage defense — Very similar to goal-line defense and many teams employ them as one. Others have distinctly different goal-line and midfield short-yardage defenses.

Shut off—A term loosely used to explain an adjustment or a different alignment which can give defensive *stress* to an area where the attack is hurting the defense.

Single wing—A formation rarely used today by colleges. Allows for a QB to the right or left of center, a tailback immediately behind center about four yards deep, a fullback to the same side as the QB and a wider wingback, all to the same side.

Slam—A blocking technique in which a player influences a defensive man by contact and then releasing for another block. The slam block to a man's outside helps influence him to react there, thus allowing another blocker from the inside an easier task.

Slow block — An offensive blocking technique in which a full block is faked but is held about one half of

the normal interval after which the blocker slips out into a pass pattern or another blocking phase.

Spear technique — A defensive lineman maneuver to avert a double team or "post and drive." To "spear" is to drop a leg to the ground and try to split the seam of the double team while not yielding ground.

Split ends—A break from the normal two tight end balanced line accomplished by splitting the end any distance at all; hence, split end, lonesome end, wide receiver, etc.

Splits—The distance or area between offensive blockers on the line. (Often a key to the area the play will attack.) Wide splits open inside lanes. Tight ones allow quicker leverage outside.

Spin-out — A defensive maneuver in which a player reacts to pressure and allows that pressure to spin him out against a man blocking down on him. Offensively: a ball carrier feels the pressure and allows it to work for his own momentum.

Sprint-out — Very similar to a roll-out except it is usually an opening up to the playside by the QB and running to pass. In roll-out there may be a reverse pivot. (No ball-faking action.)

Square up—A defensive term meaning shoulders parallel to the scrimmage line. As an offensive term, it means the same with respect to a blocker or ball carrier.

Squirm—A defensive technique that is almost a looping maneuver done by one or more defensive men to insure contain or outside leverage.

Stack—A defensive term; a stack is two men aligned vertically either in a gap area or "head up" on a lineman.

Stance—A general term for the basic position of *start* for any position played. It must always be the same or at least not allow a key or tip.

Staring it down—The receiver waiting for the ball and not coming back to it to give him an edge over the defender; also, a QB "stares down" a receiver.

Strength — The number of possible blockers exceeding the defenders as a result of a formation alignment.

Stress areas—Defensive term meaning the area that is given top priority because the attack is hurting a specific alignment. Adjustment to an area is laying stress there.

Strong side—Refers to the alignment of a tight end and flanker to the same side as opposed to the alignment of a split end and regular HB to the same side which constitutes the weak side. Defensively, a strong-side safety is normally to the TE side.

Stunts — Defensive linemen or linebackers' coordinated game to confuse the offensive blockers, the angle of approach being hidden by an alignment adjustment.

Sustaining—The art of going "full go" produced by great effort of maintaining a block, tackle, pursuit, or any action until the play is dead.

Sweep—The sweep area is anything outside of the offensive ends' alignment. Like the inside and off tackle, the sweep area is left and right.

Switch—Defensively, a switch is trading assignments between two people. Offensively, it means two receivers trading routes.

Technique — The employment of a physical method best calculated to

317

perform the duty required according to the pattern of "coaching" philosophy regarding blocking, tackling, running, passing, catching, kicking. "The coached way."

Telegraphing—Staring down, deliberating, cocking, and repeatedly throwing to exactly the same spot is "telegraphing" the receiver and also all defenders around him.

The great interval—The period of live play time—about four sec. A total game roughly estimated to be about six solid minutes offensively and against a similar type team about the same on defense.

Through or around—A simple either/or blocking rule for a lineman assigned to a deep-stacked man or a LB. He takes him if he dogs, but steps around for him if the LB wipes off to play flow. The blocker has his choice based on the defender's reaction.

Throwbacks—A pass pattern that normally employs a roll or sprint-out one way with a long or short throw, at an angle, to the opposite side.

Timing—Usually in reference to the discipline of footwork and action of the offensive backfield, the QB, and receivers.

Trail — The second receiver trailing into an area or zone recently cleared by a *drive-off* man.

Trajectory—The flight or path of a ball over near defenders and short of deeper defenders when passing.

Trap—An inside-out block on a defensive lineman by a removed offensive lineman. In some instances it can be done from the outside-in. This is usually a "fold" block.

Turnover—Any time you turn the ball over to the opponent as a result of a muffed play, i.e., fumble, interception, blocked kick, etc.

Two-back I—The QB, FB and tailback aligned behind the center, the third back "broken" or set apart to bring another quick receiver nearer the scrimmage line.

Underneath coverage—The entire lateral or horizontal area about 12 to 15 yards in depth behind the defensive line of scrimmage; *also,* the means of deployment to cover this area actively versus pass patterns.

Unflanked — The widest man in an alignment with no one positioned wider; a normal end and no one in motion if "unflanked."

Up pattern—A receiver route that is usually tacked on after a quick pattern of *in* or *out* has been run to no avail. The QB *flags* or pumps the ball and the receiver goes deeper on the "up."

Veer—A clearly defined angle of approach with respect to running, blocking, or tackling which is predetermined in that it is not straight forward from one's original lineup.

Waggle—A term which means that two guards pull the opposite way from the direction of the backfield flow. The two letter G's in waggle ignite this move.

Wait block—Similar to a draw block except the blocker waits for the reaction of the defender and takes him in the direction he wants to go merely by adding his own force.

Walk-away position — The defensive term designating the middle area between a wide-split man and the next offensive blocker.

Weak side—The opposite of strong side; there are no TE and no quick receivers. The number of blockers is depleted by the splitting out of the end; hence, weak *side*.

Wipe off—A defensive term regarding linebackers who react laterally and forward immediately to meet the flow of a backfield run action.

Wishbone—Also called the "Y" formation with a fullback moved up and two more deeply aligned halfbacks in a full-house set. Popularized by U. of Texas and referred to as the "wishbone" T.

X—An X game is a defensive term meaning the crossing or X-ing of two members of the alignment. They can be stacked one behind the other, adjacent, or staggered.

Zone—Defensively, covering for the pass and protecting an area, not a man. Any number of people designated can be employed. The larger the number, the smaller the area to cover.

Zone cut — A prescribed pattern or route to be run against a zone defense. Executed on the move or predetermined by the alignment.